Microeconomics
Basic Principles and Applications

N. Y. S. Mdoe, D. W. Ndyetabula and A. A. Temu

Adonis & Abbey Publishers Ltd
24 Old Queen Street, London SW1H 9HP United Kingdom
Website: http://www.adonis-abbey.com
E-mail Address: editor@adonis-abbey.com

Website: http://www.adonis-abbey.com
E-mail Address: editor@adonis-abbey.com

Nigeria:
No. 39 Jimmy Carter Street, Suites C3 – C6 J-Plus Plaza Asokoro, Abuja, Nigeria
Tel: +234 (0) 7058078841/08052035034

British Library Cataloguing-in-Publication Data
A catalogue record for this book is available from the British Library

ISBN: 9781913976200

Microeconomics
Basic Principles and Applications

N. Y. S. Mdoe, D. W. Ndyetabula and A. A. Temu

ADONIS & ABBEY
PUBLISHERS LTD

Table of Contents

Foreword

With the increasing competition of firms emanating from the need to keep pace with the ever-changing world economic atmosphere, development and enhancement of microeconomic analysis is becoming more important. This book is therefore a modest contribution to meeting the many new challenges of microeconomic analyses today.

The scope of materials in this book is wide ranging and reflects compilers' extensive experience in teaching microeconomics at different levels over the years. The ten chapters of this book provide a useful sequential framework for analyzing key issues at the firm level. In tackling these issues contributors have adopted a contemporary decision-oriented approach drawing on relevant microeconomic theory. While the analysis and exposition is primarily from the agricultural perspective, use is made of a wide range of sources.

Learners should find this book invaluable asset to improving their understanding of economic theory.

Dr. Senkondo E. M. M
Professor of Agricultural Economics
Department of Agricultural Economics and Agribusiness
Sokoine University of Agriculture

Preface

This text examines the analytical approach to microeconomics at the undergraduate level.

Our aim of compiling this book is to present analytical methods of microeconomics that would allow students to apply the methods on their own not just to passively absorb the pre-digested cases in the texts.

In this book we have compiled materials that are emphasizing on the fundamental conceptual foundations of microeconomics. While theoretical framework is provided to give an essential underpinning to sensible micro-economic decisions, the book concentrates on contemporary analytical techniques that can be exercised by attempting study questions provided at the end of every chapter.

This text is written to satisfy the needs of a wide market including undergraduate students majoring in Economics and its strongest branch Agricultural Economics. Graduate students with inadequate foundation in economics can find the materials compiled herein valuable.

Although some prior knowledge of Economic theory, and calculus would assist the reader of the materials in this book, much of the content has been designed to be comprehensible to the beginners and non-specialists. Many undergraduate, graduate, and professional majors in Economics are students who should know calculus but don't – at least, not very well. For this reason, we have avoided complex calculus and mathematics in the main body of the text. Graphical methods are heavily applied in most cases instead. However, quantitative/mathematical techniques have been incorporated whenever they are valuable to the microeconomic analysis.

The compilation and organization of materials in this book is modest and innovative in the way that chapters are coherent and short so that readers can read a topic at one sitting. We are optimistic that this book will be of help to learners in their various stages of learning economic theory.

Mdoe, N. S. Y. Ndyetabula, D. W. Temu, A. A.

Acknowledgement

Several people contributed to the production of this book. We would like to thank the many people who participated in different ways in the production of this book. Special thanks go to the late Prof. Ashimogo, G. C. who provided a lot of materials during the early preparation of this book.

We are thankful to Dr. Elibariki Msuya, Mr. Haji Msangi and Mr. Eward Mushi for the valuable editorial and technical assistance. Their comments and suggestions on the early drafts of the text have made a significant contribution to the coherence of the final product. We are thankful to the anonymous reviewers who read the manuscript for this book and provided suggestions for improvement of the manuscript.

Thanks, are also due to Mr. Elias Rwekaza and Mr. Eward Mushi who did the internal proofreading and consistency check during the final stages. Any remaining errors and omissions are entirely the responsibility of the authors.

We would like to especially thank the BSU III Programme at the Sokoine University of Agriculture (SUA) for funding the production costs of this project.

About The Authors

Ntengua Y. S. Mdoe (PhD) is a professor of Agricultural Economics in the Department of Agricultural Economics and Agribusiness at the Sokoine University of Agriculture (SUA), Morogoro, Tanzania. He has more than twenty-eight years of teaching in Agricultural Economics and Management. His research interests are in livelihood and poverty, small business management, agro-processing and agricultural value chain analysis. He has advised over 100 students on various aspects of Agricultural Economics and Business Management. Ntengua has authored and co-authored numerous articles in refereed journals and developed compendia for undergraduate students and training manuals for short courses. He is currently the Chief Editor of Journal of Agricultural Economics and Development. He is also co-researcher of several ongoing research projects at the University. Over the past 15 years, he has held several management positions including Executive Coordinator of the Bureau of Agricultural Consultancy and Advisory Services at SUA, Coordinator of the SUA Corporate Strategic Plan, and Chairman of Board of Directors of a private agricultural company and more recently the Dean of the Faculty of Agriculture at SUA.

Daniel Wilson Ndyetabula (PhD) is a Senior Lecturer and Head of the Department of Agricultural Economics and Agribusiness at the Sokoine University of Agriculture (SUA), Tanzania specializing in agricultural finance and investment appraisal. He is also a visiting lecturer at the Department of Agricultural Economics, Extension and Rural Development at the University of Pretoria, South Africa where he has been teaching finance and investment appraisal related courses under the UP-AERC collaborative master program. He serves as a member of the Academic Advisory Board (AAB) of the African Economic Research Consortium (AERC) and member of the accreditation subcommittee of the AERC. Currently, Daniel's research interests are in the interplay between international development and its role in guiding investment for sustainable agricultural intensification. Therefore, he writes widely on agricultural value chains, livelihood strategies, input subsidies, agricultural development outcomes and, agricultural credit. Daniel is a co-author of a book in Agribusiness Investment Appraisal. He has authored and co-authored several journal articles in refereed journals, technical reports and international conference papers. Daniel is currently the Chief Editor of the proceedings of the Agricultural Economics Society of Tanzania (AGREST) and Technical Editor of the Journal of Agricultural Economics and Development.

Anna A. Temu has a PhD in Agricultural Economics specialized in Marketing and Agribusiness Management from the University of Illinois Urbana-Champaign (USA) and an MSc. in Agricultural Economics from University of Guelph, Ontario (Canada). She has a BSc. Agriculture specialized in Rural Economics from Sokoine University of Agriculture, Morogoro, Tanzania. She is currently a Senior Lecturer in the Department of Agricultural Economics and Agribusiness at the Sokoine University of Agriculture (SUA), Morogoro-Tanzania where she teaches courses in Institutional Economics, and International Trade to Bachelor and Master Students. She is grounded in issues concerning Agribusiness development for Agricultural commodity value chains. She has conducted several studies on Agricultural markets analyzing the international trade effect of market liberalization on Tanzanian coffee market; market organizations and institutions, transaction costs, price analysis; and Input use in coffee production after liberalization and farmers' production responses. She has published in referee journals and she was the country coordinator (PI) for market assessment studies for the bean/cowpea project between Purdue University, USA and Universities in Malawi, Mozambique, and Tanzania. She has worked with various international organizations including FAO, IFAD, IFPRI, and ASARECA, in short term assignments. Currently she is a Chair of Sokoine University Graduate Entrepreneurs' Cooperative (SUGECO).

List of Tables

List of Figures

CHAPTER ONE

Why Economics Matters?

Introduction

What is economics and why is it important to study it? As a student with only the rudimentary knowledge of the subject or one just beginning to study economics, you may already be aware that economics has something to do with money, wealth, income, employment, markets, and prices. And, indeed, it does. But, nevertheless, you are unlikely to have much conception of what is in store during this introduction of the study of economics. As you progress, however, the systematic study of the subject will foster a growing perception of economic events and the ability to comprehend much of what is now incomprehensible.

Economic touches all of our lives in many ways. Yet the systematic study of economics as we know it is barely 200 years old. The study of economics, as we will pursue it, is basically that which has been developed by scholars in the price and market economies of the so-called 'western' world.

At this point, the student may well say, "Wait a minute! Is the subject of economics as is developed and practiced in the western world applicable to the emerging and developing nations of Africa?" The answer is a qualified "Yes". Markets and prices behave in a strikingly similar way under competitive conditions, whether these markets are in a village in rural Tanzania, on a plaza in a Mexican pueblo, or on the floor of the New York Stock Exchange. Various principles are universal and predictable consequence flow from various actions. For example, all else being equal, an increase in the relative price of a commodity is expected to lead to greater production – whether of coffee in Brazil, of maize in Tanzania, or of wheat in the United States. In this sense, the so-called 'western style economics' has a universality which makes it applicable across cultures and societies.

The qualification in the 'Yes' answer has to do with differing social settings, differing institutional set-ups and factors to do with a nation's relative size, income, and stage of development.

While people the world over are found to respond to incentives, such incentives may be *perceived* differently based on their respective risk tolerance. The classic example in economics is that of a subsistence farmer not adopting higher yielding varieties of a food crop. Is the farmer acting irrationally or perversely? If the farmer perceives risk in adopting the new variety, he may well stay with the proven variety to be assured of a crop for the family's food supply, which would be a perfectly natural choice. Thus, while economists have derived universal economic principles, care must be taken in their application.

Even with these qualifications, however, a basic understanding of economics will open new vistas of understanding to the student. And, in so far as the developing nations are striving to increase production of goods and services, and the general level of well-being of their people, an understanding of basic economic concepts is essential.

Let us remember that the Tanzanian college graduate will function in an increasingly complex economic world, *and an increasingly economically interdependent world.* Tanzania is becoming increasingly linked with the rest of the economic world. For better or worse, the welfare of its citizens is dependent in some measure upon economic conditions in the rest of the world. An example is the relationship between coffee prices in Tanzania and supplies of that commodity in the rest of the world. Other examples include the level of foreign tourists visiting Tanzania and the level of world oil prices. Thus, responsible leaders in both the public and private sectors of the economy need to understand economics and the consequences of various economic policies.

The centrally planned economies such as that of North Korea were also faced with such decisions. The debate may differ in a less open society, but decisions on the use of limited resources must nevertheless be made, and it would be naïve to believe that agreement is unanimous, even though debate is less open.

Although economic problems are not unique to Tanzania and the developing nations, they certainly arise out of greater concern. The economic decisions made by those who have the task of improving the welfare of the people of the developing nations touch the lives of every one of the citizens of these countries. Economists everywhere agree that the foremost economic problem is the improvement of the welfare of the large number of poor people in the world. Although the problem of scarcity and choice is not unique to Tanzania and the developing world, the consequences of unwise choices and ill-suited economic policies are more traumatic. The special situation of developing countries compels singular care and wisdom in the exercise of economic choice and economic policy.

With this background, let us now define economics, and develop a more systematic approach to this field of study.

Economics Defined

We have already seen that economics deals with scarcity and choice. Perhaps the best short definition of economics is "the social science which is concerned with the allocation of scarce resources".

A social science is a discipline, which deals with some aspect of the behaviour of people. Other social sciences include psychology, sociology, anthropology, philosophy and political science. Economics is the social science, which deals with the behaviour of people in the production, exchange, distribution and consumption of goods and services. Economics is sometimes said to be a study of the logic of choice, since, as we have already seen, choices must be made in the allocation of scarce resources. What do we mean by 'resources'? For convenience, the scarce resources used in production are generally divided into four categories. These are land, labour, capital and entrepreneurship.

1. Land

Land is a category of resources encompassing far more than what we generally think of as agricultural or grazing land. Land includes natural resources such as water, minerals, forests and wildlife. Perhaps 'natural resources' would be a better term, but 'land' is the term, which economists have historically applied to this category of resources.

2. Labour

Labour refers to human services in general. This includes that of salaried employees and professionals, as well as the services of those who work for hourly, daily of weekly wages.

3. Capital

Capital refers to man-made or cultural resources such as buildings, tools, machinery and equipment. These resources are created by people not for direct consumption but as a means of more efficiently creating other goods and services for final consumption. That is, capital goods are not an end in themselves but a means to an end.

4. Entrepreneurship

Entrepreneurship refers to those human resources, which combine the other factors of production, provide capital, assume risks, innovate new and better methods of production, and generally facilitate the production, distribution and exchange of goods and services. Sometimes these entrepreneurship functions are in the guise of a single individual or family, as in the case of the small farm or an individual business enterprise such as a small restaurant or tailor's shop. In the case of larger enterprises, entrepreneurial functions are usually divided among many people. The people who furnish the capital for an enterprise are often not the same people as those who make the day-to-day decisions on managing the enterprise.

The distinction between resources is not always clear-cut. For example, land, which is improved by leveling or drainage, contains elements of capital. A common dilemma in the field of agricultural economics, for example, is to distinguish between returns to labour and to entrepreneurship, or management, when the farm is family-owned and operated. Nevertheless, even with occasional complications, this classification of resources is widely used, and is extremely helpful for analysing and understanding economic problems.

It is worth stressing, once again, that these resources are scarce or limited in supply. All economic problems have in common the element of scarcity. There is not enough of a scarce resource to do everything that people would like to do with it – otherwise it would not be scarce.

Are There Free Resources?

A resource which is not scarce is known as a free resource, sometimes referred to as a non-economic resource. You should not confuse lack of a price tag with a resource being free. A free resource would be available in such abundance that there is no conflict among its alternative uses. That is, there is no necessity for a choice to be made. It is difficult to think of examples which would qualify under all circumstances. Water is sometimes thought to be a 'free' resource. But again, caution is required. Water used for waste disposal competes with its use for drinking, fishing and recreation. Hence, a choice must be made, we have the basic elements of an economic problem. Along the same lines, it should be obvious that wildlife is not a free resource. Rhinos and elephants are valued for their tusks and hides. Yet, such uses are competitive with their use for viewing and aesthetic enjoyment. Again, the need for choice is readily apparent.

Perhaps the closest we can come to identifying a free resource is gifts of nature such as solar energy, air, winds and tides. However, even with resources such as air and sunshine, excessive air pollution in large cities renders air unhealthy and competes with ordinary breathing. Thus, even with a supposedly free resource such as air, closer examination once again demonstrates the need for choice. To what extent do we compel people to take account of their actions and to reduce the level of air pollution? Clearly this is a policy choice.

At this point, it should be clear that economic problems in society are pervasive. Where there are competing uses for resources, there is, by definition, an economic problem. Choices must be made among competing uses. This is, again, at the heart and soul of economics – be it in Tanzania or anywhere else in the world!

The Basic Economic Questions

If a choice among competing uses or ends is the heart and soul of economics, *incentives* are the prime movers of economic decisions. In the study of economics, particularly in the analysis of economic policy, an attempt is made to assess the consequences of specific policies, and such consequences are analyzed from the perspective of incentives. If the price of maize, for example, rises relative to prices of alternative crops such as potatoes and wheat, economists suggest that more maize will be produced because farmers want the higher incomes associated with the higher price of maize. That is, farmers respond to incentives, as they perceive them.

The number of economic decisions made by decision-making units in the economy is virtually countless. Individuals make some of these decisions, large business firms make others. And still others are made collectively, through government. Decisions are made regardless of the type of economic system or ideology, or the stage of its development, and incentives in some form will affect the results. While the number of specific decisions is countless, there are three basic categories of economic questions faced by every society. Let us examine these questions.

1. What to produce

Are a nation's limited resources to be used to produce coffee, tea, maize, tobacco, farm machinery, schools, or health facilities, and in what combination? The choice obviously depends partly on the resources, which a nation has. Tanzania, being rich in resources suitable for coffee production, will most likely produce more coffee than it will produce products requiring a colder climate. Countries in the temperate zone would be ill advised even to attempt to produce coffee, even though much coffee is consumed in those countries. Apart from such an obvious example, all economies have some flexibility in the use of their resources. Tanzania can either increase its emphasis on *cash* crops such as coffee, tea, and tobacco, only at the cost of producing less *food* crops. Or it could produce more food crops at the expense of less cash crops. The essential point is that each economy must choose.

2. How to produce

Maize can be grown by using a lot of labour and not much in the way of capital or machinery. However, it can also be grown by using more machinery and chemicals, and less labour, which system is 'best'? It depends! Depends on what? It depends on the state of technology, the resources available to the individuals making the decision and, very importantly, on the prices of the available resources. Once again, alternatives are available.

3. How to distribute output

Which members of society receive the fruits of a nation's production, and in what amounts? In a society of hunters and gatherers where each individual or family depends upon itself, this problem is relatively simple. But in any society in which there is even a rudimentary division of labour, decisions must be made on distributing the fruits of production. Perhaps the decisions are made on the basis of custom and tradition, but nevertheless decisions are made.

In today's world, the problem is more complex. When you buy a loaf of bread, what portion of the price goes to the retailer, the baker, the miller, and the farmer? There are many stages and many participants in the production of most products. In what proportion should each participant be rewarded, and how should these decisions be made?

The answers to these questions depend on such things as income, which in turn depends on the amount of resources owned (such as land

and labour) and the return on these resources. In addition, the role of government as it affects income distribution through taxes and various transfers, and a whole range of government policies, including policy toward labour unions, foreign trade and price controls and subsidies, also help determine the answer to these questions.

The three basic economic questions are universal. What differs in different countries is their resource endowments, and the way in which these questions are answered.

The study of economics, in all its complexities, ultimately refers to one or more of these basic questions of the behaviour and welfare of people. The decisions made in answering these basic questions affect all of us.

Micro- and Macroeconomics

The study of economics is generally divided into micro-economics and macroeconomics. This is partly for the sake of convenience, and partly for the sake of logic. Many economic issues involve both micro- and macro-aspects, and it is not impossible to study everything at once.

Microeconomics involves the study of the economic behaviour of the *individual economic unit*, whether that unit is an individual, a household, or a firm. As we will see during our course of study, concepts of marginal analysis play a dominant role. Topics of microeconomics include the economics of production, price determination and consumer behaviour.

Macroeconomics, on the other hand, involves the study of aspects of economic systems, or *aggregate economic unit*. Unemployment, inflation and the role of fiscal and monetary policies are studied in macroeconomics, as well as concept of national income and growth.

Many questions of economic policy, such as agricultural policy, foreign trade, taxation and economic growth, rely on both micro- and macro-concepts. Some knowledge of both is usually necessary to understand issues of economic policy.

Normative and Positive Economics

As economics touches our personal lives and profoundly affects our welfare, it is difficult to remain remote and aloof from questions raised in the subject. Certainly, the student is expected to have opinions on such matters as taxes, wage rates, and government expenditures. Such a question as "should farmers be taxed on the amount of land they own, as opposed to being taxed on the income it generates?" would be expected to elicit a response – especially if you were among those directly affected. But this is a different kind of question from "What will be the expected effect on government revenue if taxes are based on land as opposed to income?" The question of "Should taxes be based on land?" is in the realm of *normative economics*. It involves values, ethics, opinions and judgments. The question of "What are the expected effects on revenue?" is one of facts and relationships which can be determined, or at least estimated, and which are subject to test or verification by techniques which are replicable. Such a question is in the realm of *positive economics*.

A similar comparison can be made regarding the mid-1980s deregulation by the government of retail cereal prices in Tanzania. A normative question is, "Should the government have deregulated retail cereal prices?" A question in positive economics is, "What have been some of the effects (on price received by farmers, for example) of deregulated cereal prices?"

From the latter example, we can easily see that two people who might disagree on whether cereal prices *should* have been deregulated may well agree on some of the actual effects (although not necessarily on the desirability of those effects). To push the example further, suppose that two people *agree* that deregulated cereal prices may result in higher prices at both the producer and retail level in the short term. Our two individuals may *disagree* on the desirability of this, depending on whether they are taking the short-term view of the producer or the consumer.

The point of this illustration is that much of what economists, and other people for that matter, argue over are *questions of personal values* rather than questions of fact. And since matters of economic policy affect our personal lives, as well as national progress, the disagreement of economists is well publicized. There are many things on which the general run of economists agree, but these make rather uninteresting news.

It is useful to remind ourselves that physicists, biologists and other scientists, who agree on mundane facts, often disagree on matters of public policy such as whether a certain pesticide *should* be banned or whether nuclear power is desirable.

The basic lesson here is that it is useful to distinguish matters of value from matters of fact. The distinction between positive and normative economics is useful in this regard.

This course deals mainly with positive economics, emphasizing established principles. We can identify in Tanzania many examples of problems into which micro-economic analysis can offer insights. For example: What are the likely effects of maize flour on the wafere of urban consumers? What are the likely economic effects of fertilizer importation? What are the expected effects of the deregulation of prices of products such as beef, maize and beer? However, the answers to questions such as "*Should* cereal prices be deregulated?" fall into the normative realm. Positive economics provides information and insights. Final solutions involve judgment based on facts and personal values.

Questions for Thought and Discussion

1. Explain in your own words what the study of economics is about.
2. Is time a resource? What qualities does time have in common with resources such as land and capital? What decisions do you make with respect to time?
3. Can you think of any 'free' resources? What makes them 'free?' Can you think of circumstances under which they may not be 'free' in the future?
4. Think of an economic issue such as taxes or subsidies on fertilizer importation. Try to make both positive and normative statements about the issue. Try to be clear whether you are stating something which is subject to test as opposed to something which expresses your values. What values or goals are you expressing in your normative statements?
5. Why is it important for an economist to be aware of both facts and values? Why is it especially important to be able to distinguish between facts and values?
6. In what respects do developing nations such as Tanzania face similar economic questions and problems as more developed nations?
7. In what sense might the emphasis of economic analysis and priorities of developing nations be different?
8. Can you think of examples of the economic experience and history of the more developed countries which might be useful to developing countries?

9. Are there examples which might have little application to developing countries?

CHAPTER TWO

Theory of Consumer Behavior and Demand

Introduction

There are basically three approaches to the theory of consumer behavior namely The Cardinal, The Indifference Curve and The Revealed Preference approaches. Each approach makes certain assumptions that distinguish one approach from another. Of the three approaches, the Indifference Curve approach is the most established and used. However, we shall briefly examine each approach.

The central concept in this chapter is that of *utility*. Utility is basically the quality of a good or services which satisfies wants. Goods and services such as food, clothing, jewelry, books, medical care and so on, all have the power to satisfy wants. They bring utility to the owner. This, along with the ability to put forth money with which to pay for these goods and services, is the basic element underlying the demand curve. Consumers are willing to pay for these goods and services because they bring utility. The *ability* to pay for the goods and services gives expression to the demand curves.

The basic assumption in consumer theory is that the consumer is rational and aims to maximize utility subject to his/her budget constraint. This assumption is translated into choosing commodities that give the consumer a higher level of satisfaction first.

A basic problem with the concept of utility is its subjective nature. It is not possible to measure objectively the amount of utility brought by an additional unit of the product. It is only possible to *compare* preferences of utility brought about by one product or groups of products relative to another product or group of products, including money. In other words, what would a person prefer – a watch, another pair of shoes or a specified amount of money?

Cardinal Utility Approach

Assertions of the cardinal utility

a) *Cardinal utility:*
One of the assumptions in cardinal utility theory is that utility is measurable or can be measured in terms of specific numbers which can be verified. For example, the temperature is 30° Celsius, you have Tsh 100, or the building is 20 metres high. These are cardinal measures. In the cardinal theory utility is said to be measured by the monetary units that a consumer is prepared to pay for an additional unit of the commodity he/she consumes.

b) *Constant marginal utility of money:*
If money is a measure of utility, then its marginal utility has to remain constant. If marginal utility of money declines then the measure of utility would be flexible.

c) *Diminishing marginal utility*
The marginal utility of commodities would be diminishing as more is consumed. The concept of marginal utility is important in our analysis. Let us illustrate this concept with an example. Suppose that you have been working very hard on the farm in the hot sun and you are extremely thirsty – thirsty enough that you could drink four glasses of lime juice. You desperately need *some* lime juice. But you are thirsty enough that you surely would prefer more, rather than less.

Marginal utility refers to the extra, or *additional*, utility you derive from consuming an *additional* unit of the product. The marginal utility from the first glass of lime juice is the utility or enjoyment from that first glass. The marginal utility from the second glass is the additional enjoyment, or how much better off you feel with the second glass compared to the first.

The key question here is: "How much additional utility do you get from the second glass relative to the first? And from the third glass relative to the second? And from the fourth glass relative to the third?"

Clearly, there must have been some extra utility derived from the second, or else you would not have drunk it. But ask yourself, "How much extra utility did I receive from the second glass relative to the first?" From the third relative to the second, and from the fourth relative to the third? Chances are that your extra enjoyment, your marginal utility, of the second was less than from the first, the third was less than from the second, and the fourth was less than from the third. Your *marginal* utility was declining. This is the essence of the law of diminishing marginal utility. *Marginal utility decreases as more of a product is consumed* during a given time period.

Let us illustrate another example, utility derived from additional pairs of shoes, through use of graphs, as shown in Figure 1. As we consume more, our total utility rises, though at a declining rate, as shown in the down panel. Now, ask yourself to what extent you would be willing to pay for extra pairs of shoes. After you already owned three of four pairs of shoes, would you desire another pair? Perhaps you would. But would you be willing to pay as much for the fifth pair as you would for the first? And if the price were the same, would you buy the fifth pair, or would you be likely to buy something else? Because money is limited, and you have other important items on which to spend your money, chances are you would not spend all your money on shoes. The fifth pair of shoes would yield little marginal utility relative to its price. Note in Figure 1 that, as total utility rises at a decreasing rate, marginal utility is falling as consumption increases.

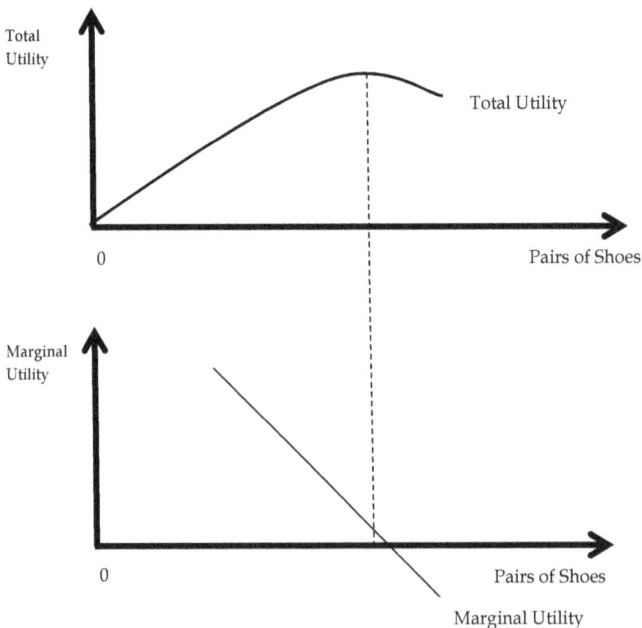

Figure 1: The Relationship between Total and Marginal Utility

33

Maximizing Utility

Given limited income and more than one commodity or good to consume, a consumer would want to purchase a combination of those commodities so as to maximize utility or level of satisfaction. This entails making choices.

The question of choice becomes redundant if:

(i)   There is only one Commodity to Consume
(ii) Commodities are not Competitive
(iii) One has Unlimited Income

Early in our study of economics we emphasized scarcity, and the fact that people's wants exceed the production available from limited resources. This implies that consumers must use the income they have *efficiently*, doing the best they can with the income at their disposal.

How does the consumer do this and what are the implications for demand?

We have seen from the law of diminishing marginal utility, that consumers, in a given time period, attach diminishing value to additional units of a product. Imagine that the consumer, with a limited amount of spendable income, is deciding between beef and chicken, both subject to diminishing marginal utility.

What criteria will the consumer use to maximize utility for a given amount of income?

The student may be tempted to answer that the consumer will purchase that product yielding the greatest marginal utility.

However, what if the product yielding greater marginal utility has a higher price?

The point is that different products have different prices, and the consumer desires to maximize utility *within the constraint of a limited income* and, hence must consider marginal utility *per shilling*.

Suppose that we *could* measure utility in cardinal terms, and that an additional unit of chicken afforded 16 units of utility and cost TShs 2.00, and an additional unit of beef afforded 18 units of utility and cost TShs 3.00. We then have:

$$\frac{MU\,Chicken}{Price\ of\ Chicken} = \frac{16}{2} > \frac{MU\,beef}{Price\ of\ beef} = \frac{18}{3} \quad \dots\dots\dots\dots\dots\dots\dots\dots\dots\dots(1)$$

If efficient use of income is 'doing the best with what one has,' what would the utility-maximizing consumer do in this situation? Buy more beef or more chicken? Clearly, the marginal utility of chicken *per TSh* is greater than the marginal utility of beef *per TSh*. Thus, the next Tsh is more logically spent on chicken. Obviously, the consumer does not go around performing these esoteric calculations. But this illustrates how the consumer acts. The consumer maximizes utility by spending money on those goods affording maximum utility per monetary unit. Saving also affords utility, and if a TShs saved affords higher marginal utility than the TShs spent for a unit of beef or a unit of chicken, it will be saved and not spent. To pursue this example further, suppose that this consumer buys more chicken.

What happens to the marginal utility of chicken, and the ratio of marginal utility of chicken to its price?

The law of diminishing marginal utility tells us that it will decline as more chicken is consumed. Suppose the purchase of more chicken yields the following situation:

$$\frac{MU\,chicken}{Price\ of\ chicken} = \frac{8}{2} < \frac{MU\,beef}{Price\ of\ beef} = \frac{18}{3} \quad \dots\dots\dots\dots\dots\dots\dots\dots(2)$$

Now, the marginal utility per TSh of beef is higher than for chicken. The consumer is thus motivated to purchase more beef (or less chicken). Based on this example, you can see how the consumer would allocate a given budget to chicken and beef. By spending money on that product with the highest marginal utility per TSh, the consumer, in effect, equates the ratios of marginal utility for each product to its price. Extending the two product example to many products, we have:

$$\frac{MUa}{Pa} = \frac{MUb}{Pb} = ... = \frac{MUn}{Pn} \dots\dots\dots\dots\dots\dots\dots\dots\dots\dots\dots\dots\dots\dots\dots \text{(3)}$$

Let us carry the previous example one step further. Starting again with:

$$\frac{MU\ chicken}{P\ chicken} = \frac{16}{2} < \frac{MU\ beef}{P\ beef} = \frac{18}{3} \dots\dots\dots\dots\dots\dots\dots\dots\dots\dots\dots\text{(4)}$$

If the price of chicken _rises_ to 4, and the price of beef stays the same. We now have:

$$\frac{MU\ chicken}{P\ chicken} = \frac{16}{4} < \frac{MU\ beef}{P\ beef} = \frac{18}{3} \dots\dots\dots\dots\dots\dots\dots\dots\dots\dots\text{(5)}$$

The consumer would allocate the next TSh to beef instead of chicken because of the effect of price. This is wholly consistent with our downward-sloping demand curve. The price of chicken rises, inducing a smaller quantity purchased. Consumers now buy more beef, _at a given price_, thereby increasing the demand for beef.

Mathematically,

Suppose a consumer has utility function

$$U = f (q_b, q_c)$$

Subject to an income constraint

$$Y^0 = p_b\ q_b + p_c\ q_c$$

Where, U is total utility, q_b is quantity of beef, q_c is quantity of chicken, Y^0 is fixed income, p_b is price of beef and p_c is price of chicken

Form the lagrangian function

$$L = f(q_b, q_c) + \lambda\ (Y^0 - p_b\ q_b - p_c\ q_c) \dots\dots\dots\dots\dots\dots\dots\dots\dots\text{(6)}$$

The maximization of this function will ensure that:

(i) The Utility Function is Maximized
(ii) The Constraint is not Violated

Differentiating the function with respect to qb, qc and λ

$\delta L/\delta q_b = \delta (f(q_b, q_c)/\delta q_b) - \lambda p_b = 0$...(7)
$\delta L/\delta q_c = \delta (f(q_b, q_c)/\delta q_c) - \lambda p_c = 0$...(8)
$\delta L/\delta \lambda = Y^0 - p_b q_b - p_c q_c = 0$...(9)

From the first two equations (equations 7 and 8):

$\delta (f(q_b, q_c)/\delta q_b) = \lambda p_b$ ....(10)
$\delta (f(q_b, q_c)/\delta q_c) = \lambda p_c$ ....(11)
and $\delta (f(q_b, q_c)/\delta q_b)/ \delta (f(q_b, q_c)/\delta q_c) = p_b/p_c$ ....(12)

But $\delta (f (q_b, q_c)/\delta q_b)$ and $\delta (f (q_b, q_c)/\delta q_c)$ are marginal utilities of beef and chicken respectively.

Therefore, $\delta (f (q_b, q_c)/\delta q_b)/ \delta (f (q_b, q_c)/\delta q_c) = p_b/p_c$,...............................(13)
This means that the ratio of the marginal utilities of the commodities consumed must be equal to the price ratio

.

OR

Dividing $\delta (f(q_b, q_c)/\delta q_b) = \lambda p_b$ by p_b gives $\delta (f(q_b,q_c)\delta q_b)p_b$
$= \lambda$...(14)
And $\delta (f(q_b, q_c)/\delta q_c)$ by p_c gives $\delta (f(q_b, q_c)/\delta q_c)/p_c = \lambda$...............................(15)
Therefore $MU_b/p_b = MU_c/p_c$ ....(16)

This means that the ratio of the marginal utility to the prices must be equal for all commodities. The ratio indicates the rate at which utility would increase given an additional shilling and equilibrium will be reached when the utility or satisfaction gained from the last shilling spent is identical for all commodities (compare equation (16) with equation (3) above.
The Lagrangian multiplier λ is interpreted as the marginal utility of money which is positive

Critique of the Cardinal Approach

There are three basic weaknesses of the cardinal approach:

(i)   That Utility is Measured Cardinally is doubtful
(ii) That Money has constant Marginal Utility is also doubtful. As Money increases the Marginal Utility of Money decreases
(iii) The Diminishing Marginal Utility of a Commodity is Established only from Introspection. It cannot be demonstrated

Indifference Curve Approach

The indifference curve approach to the theory of consumer behavior makes less stringent assertions/assumptions.

(i)   that the consumer is rational hence able to rank commodity bundles in an order of preference
(ii) that the preferences of the consumer are transitive i.e. If he prefers A to B, and B to C then he will prefer A to C.
(iii) that utility derived from commodities need no/is not measurable.

The preference need only to be ranked. If the utility from A is 20 and that from B is 60 it only means that the consumer derives a higher utility from B than A. It is not three times more than A. This is what is referred to as ordinal measure of utility.

In ordinal scale we compare one item with another and rank them accordingly. For example, "I would rather have a glass of lime juice than Coca Cola, and I would rather have the Coca Cola than Fanta." In this case, we are not assigning cardinal numbers, but we are making comparisons – comparisons which are logical and consistent. If the consumer would prefer the lime juice over Coca Cola, and the Coca Cola over the Fanta, she should also prefer the lime juice over the Fanta. These are comparisons made on an *ordinal* scale. They are rational, but we cannot meaningfully assign cardinal numbers to them.

A more advanced analysis of utility, which does not require the cardinal measurement of utility, involves *indifference curves*. The derivation of indifference curves is based on assumptions made on the nature of the utility function and assertion on human behavior. The assumptions made in deriving a utility function are:

(i) For two commodity bundles A and B, either A is preferred to B , B is preferred to A or A is just as well liked as b

(ii) If A and B are available to the consumer, one can find a continuous path of available combinations of A and B

(iii) Given a combination of commodities A, one may define a set of combinations of commodities that is just as liked as A, and others not more liked than A. So if an infinite set of commodity combinations is defined, with each set at least as well liked as A, then the limiting set of goods will also be at least well liked as A. This assumption ensures that consumers preference is continuous.

Other assumptions on the utility function are:

- That the utility function is continuous and has first and second partial derivatives
- That it is strictly quasi concave
- That the partial derivatives are positive, strictly implying that the consumer will always desire more of all commodities
- That the utility is defined with a specific time frame in mind. The time frame is not so short that the desire for variety is not satisfied, yet not too long as to change the taste and preferences

The Concept of an Indifference Curve

Let us again assume two goods, beef and chicken. The consumer enjoys each to the extent that she would like to consume some combination. More is preferred to less of each. Let us start with a combination of 8 units of beef and 8 units of chicken, and ask what combinations of product would be preferred, and what combinations would be inferior. In Figure 2, clearly, all combinations of beef and chicken to the upper right of point C would be preferred, because the consumer would have at least 8 units of beef or chicken, plus additional units of the other, depending on the location of the point.

By the same line of reasoning, all points below and to the left of point C are inferior as the consumer is enjoying less of some combination of beef and chicken than at point C.

What about the remaining spaces? Beginning with the lower right, we ask how many units of beef would the consumer require in exchange for an additional unit of chicken and still remain equally as well-off or as satisfied as before. Suppose that she would be willing to surrender 1 unit of beef in exchange of 1 unit of chicken to be equally satisfied, placing us at point D in Figure 2, the segment from C to D then shows the combinations of product for which the consumer would be indifferent. Points to the right of the segment are locations of grater utility; points to the left are locations of inferior utility.

Now suppose we ask the consumer how much beef she would require surrendering to get yet another unit of chicken. Since she is being asked to give up more beef, it is likely that she would require an increasing amount of chicken for that unit of beef, let us say 2 units of chicken. We can plot that point as E. We can continue the exercise, asking how much chicken would be required to surrender more beef. As the consumer surrenders more beef, we would expect that increasing amounts of chicken would be required for the consumer to be equally as well off.

We can work from point C toward the other direction and ask how many units of beef she would require in exchange for a unit of chicken and still be as well off, or indifferent. As the consumer gives up more and more chicken and still be as well-off, or indifferent, she would probably be expected to require increasing amounts of beef in order to be indifferent. If we connect the points, we have what is known as an *indifference* curve. As shown in Figure 2, the indifference curve is convex to the origin, a fact whose significance will become clearer later.

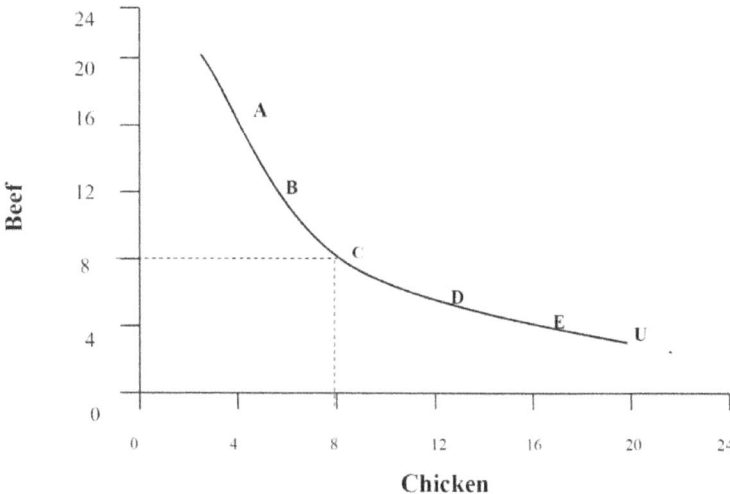

Figure 2: The indifference curve
(All points to the right of the curve are preferred. All points to the left of the curve are inferior. The consumer is indifferent to all points on the curve).

The indifference curve shows the various combinations of goods for which a consumer is indifferent. Any combination of goods on the curve provides equal satisfaction or utility to the consumer. All points to the right (above) of the curve are superior and all points to the left (below) are inferior.

Now, suppose we start out with a different combination of goods, say 12 units of beef and 12 units of chicken. This is a superior combination to 8 and 8 as the consumer has more of each. We could then construct another indifference curve, which would show the combinations of goods for which consumers are indifferent, and label this curve U_2, which indicates a higher level of utility than U_1. Figure 3 shows a set of three indifference curves with the segments between specific combinations smoothed out to form a continuous curve

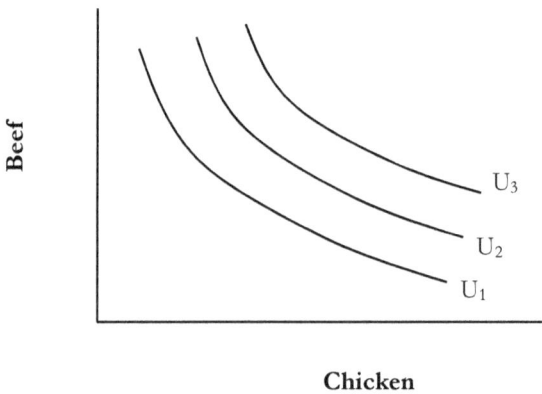

Figure 3: A set of indifference curves
(Each succeeding indifference curve denotes a higher level of utility)

Note that the indifference curves do not intersect. Can you explain why this could not logically happen?

Finally, we can construct an entire family of indifference curves – referred to as an indifference map – for a consumer. As we go to the right or "north-east" we encounter higher and higher levels of utility. The consumer wishes to achieve the highest level of utility within the constraint of her income. It is to this matter we now turn.

In summary, an indifference curve is a locus of all commodity combinations from which the consumer derives the same level of utility or satisfaction. It can also be defined as a curve showing various combinations of goods for which the consumer is indifferent. The following are the main characteristics of indifference curves:

- An indifference curve corresponding to higher level of satisfaction lies to the right or north east of the current/present indifference curve. Moving from U_1 to U_3 in Figure 3 above entails consuming more of both beef and chicken. Hence more satisfaction obtained along U3   compared to U_1 and U_2. This is the result of more is preferred to less.
- Indifference curves do not cross each other. This is the result of transitivity assumption
- An indifference curve is strictly quasi convex. This is the result of the assumption that the utility function is strictly quasi concave

The Budget Constraint

What limits the consumer from attaining higher levels of utility? Obviously, the budget, or income constraint, is the limiting factor as discussed earlier. The objective of this section is to illustrate the concept of the budget line so that we can proceed to analyzing efficient consumer behaviour.

Suppose that a consumer has a budget of TShs 100, denoted by B_1, and that this can be spent on beef and chicken. Assume further, that the price of chicken is TShs 4 per unit, and the price of beef is TShs 5 per unit. The consumer can buy all beef, all chicken or some combination of the two products.

If the consumer spends all Tsh 100 on chicken, she would be able to buy 25 (100/4) units of chicken, or point X, in Figure 4. If she spends all her income on beef, she will be able to buy 20 (100/5) units of beef, or point Y. Of course, she may divide her expenditure in numerous combinations. By spending Tsh 80 on beef and Tsh 20 on chicken, we would be at point Z in the figure. If we connect the points representing the combinations of expenditures possible, we find that we have a straight line, indicating the points attainable by the consumer with a given budget. The straight line, known as *the budget line*, shows that chicken can be substituted for beef (and *vice versa*) in constant ratios, dictated by the price relationship between the two products.

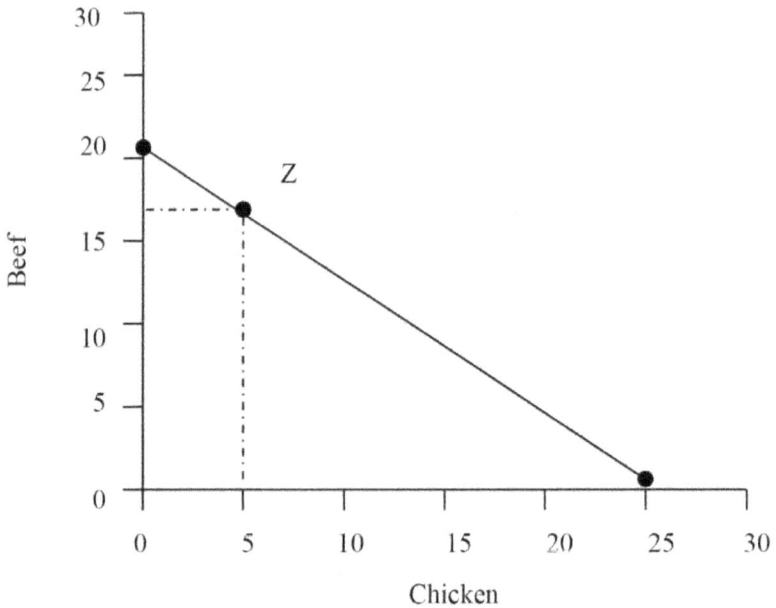

Figure 4: Budget Constraint Showing Combinations of Beef and Chicken Attainable with Income at Given Prices

Suppose that the income to the consumer is increased, say by a factor of two. The consumer would then have new budget possibilities. She could now buy 50 units of chicken, 40 units of beef or some combination thereof. We have a completely new budget line, B_2, as indicated in Figure 5.

Finally, let us ask what would happen if, for example, the price of beef increased to Tsh 10 per unit. The budget line would appear to rotate counter-clockwise, as shown in Figure 6. Assuming our original budget of TSh 100, the consumer could now only purchase a maximum of 10 units of beef, compared to 20 with the old prices. If the price of meat decreases, the budget line rotates in a clockwise direction.

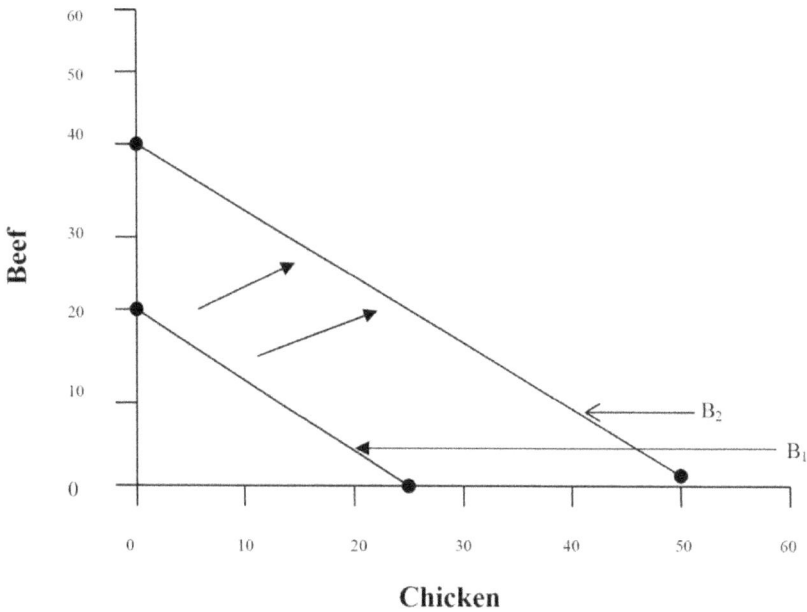

Figure 5: The effect of increase in Income
(If income increases, the attainable combinations of products increase, as shown by B₂).

Test your understanding of this by now asking what would happen if the price of chicken increased relative to beef, if it decreased relative to beef, or if both prices increased (or decreased) by the same factor, with a constant budget.

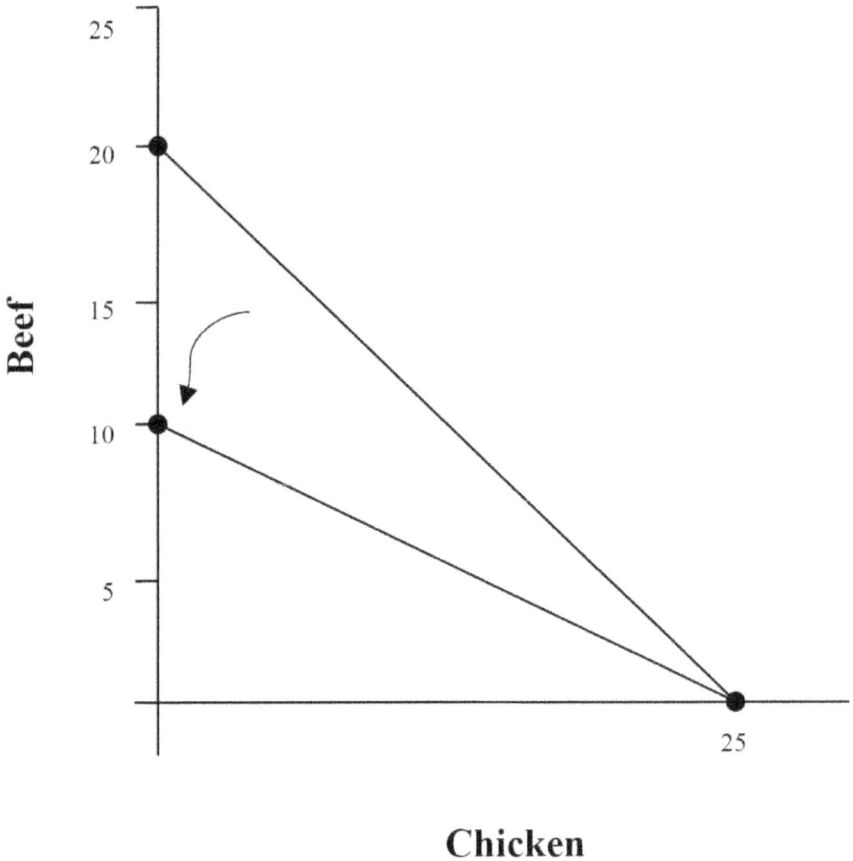

Figure 6: The effect of a price change on the budget line
(The effect of an increase in the price of beef is to rotate the budget line counter-clockwise).

With this background, we can now proceed to the problem of utility maximization using the indifference curve analysis.

You are now familiar with the concept of indifference curves and budget lines. Each consumer can be viewed as having an indifference map, the successive indifference curve representing higher utility as one moves to the 'north-east' on the map. At any given time, the customer has one budget – the constraint under which the consumer operates. The objective of the consumer is to maximize utility, given the budget constraint.

In Figure 7 what would be the highest level of utility which could be reached with the consumer's budget? The consumer could reach U_1, U_2, and U_3. The highest level of utility that can be reached with this budget is obviously U_3. The income is insufficient to reach U_4. Note that the budget line is tangent to the indifference curve at the point E. Thus point E gives the equilibrium market basket of goods, X of chicken and Y of beef, for the rational consumer maximizing utility subject to the budget constraint.

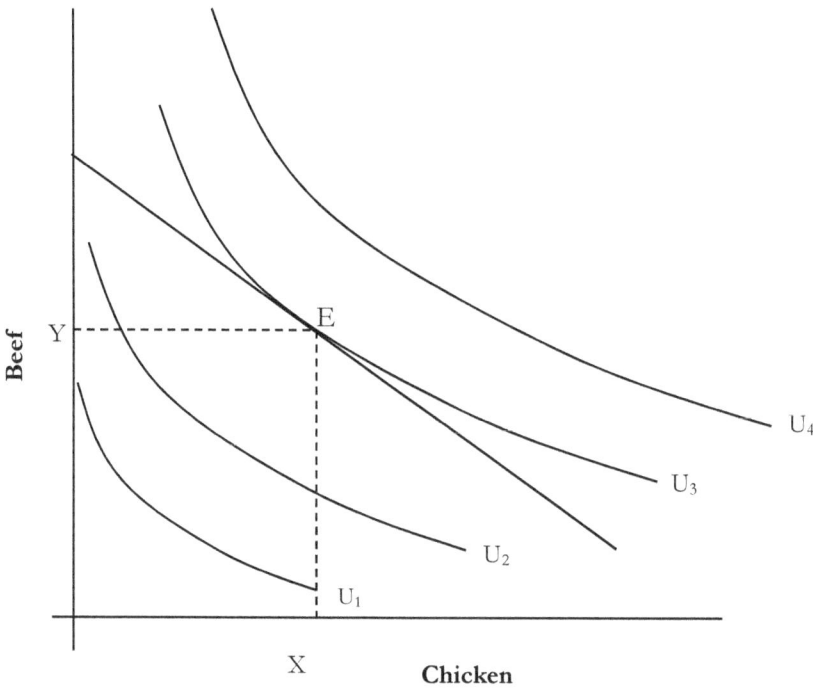

Figure 7: Maximization of utility given the budget constraint
(The highest utility attainable given the budget constraint is U3, indicated at point E)

What happens if the budget increases? If this occurs, the budget line shifts out, as we have already described. This will enable a higher level of utility to be reached, once again, at the point of tangency between the budget line and the indifference curve. By increasing the budget to successively higher levels we can trace out the combinations of goods which would be purchased at successively higher incomes. The line joining the points of equilibrium market baskets, such as E_1 ... E_4 in Figure 8, is known as the income-consumption curve. The curve traces the changes in consumption as the income (budget) increases, given constant price ratios.

Income-consumption curves can be used to derive ENGEL CURVES, which are important for studies of family expenditure patterns. An Engel curve is the relationship between equilibrium quantity purchased of a good and the level of income. The Engel curve can be derive from an income-consumption curve as follows:-

- Considering Figure 8, if the price of good X equals P_x, and that all income is spent on Oc amount of good X, then total income equals $(P_x)(Oc)$ which can then be plotted against Oc quantity of good X.
- With Ob amount of good X, total income equals (P_x) (Ob), which can then be plotted against O_b quantity of good X.
- With Oa amount of good X, total income equals (P_x) (Oa), which can then be plotted against Oa quantity of good X
- These will be three points on the Engel curve for good X for the consumer
- Each of these points show equilibrium amount of good X purchased at certain level of income
- As more points are included, all the points on the Engel curve for good X for the consumer are traced out as shown in Figure 9.

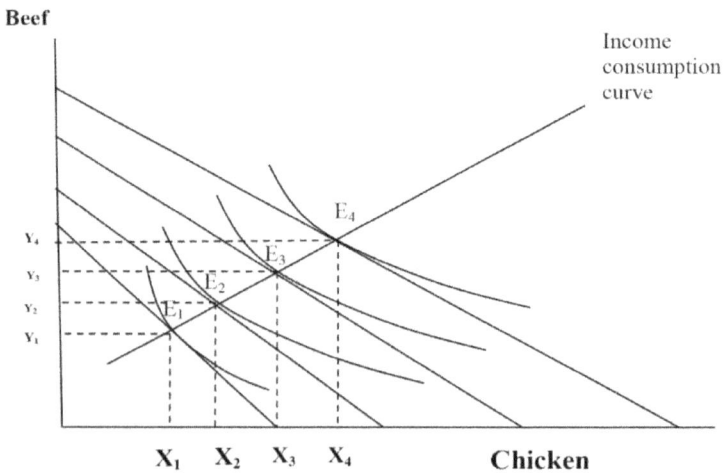

Figure 8: The income-consumption curve
(The curve traces combination of goods which will be consumed with increased in income, given constant prices)

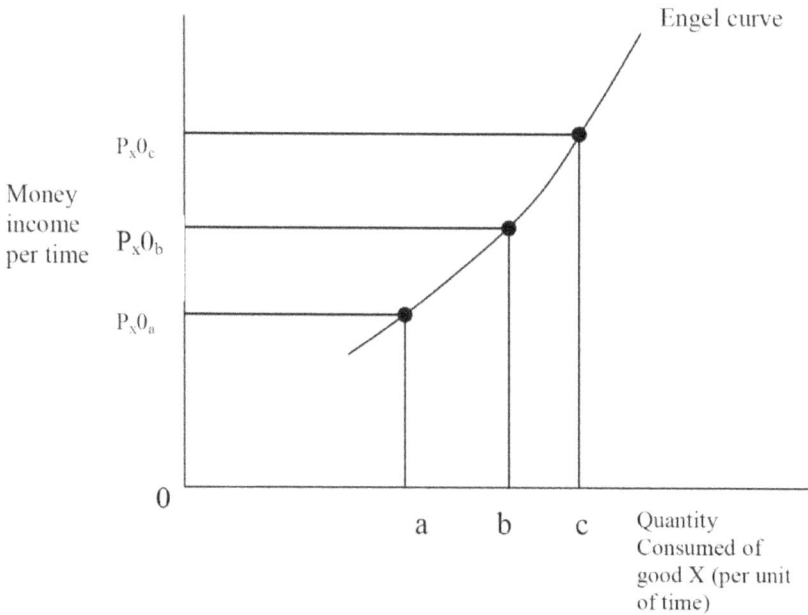

Figure 9: The Angel curve

Effect of Changes in Price

We need to perform one other adjustment to understand more thoroughly our analysis. What happens when the price of one product changes relative to another? The combination of products will change, but this change is not due to a change in utility. It is due instead to the change in products available as indicated by the consumer's new budget line. If the price of chicken falls, more chicken can be purchased than before. If price changes from 4 to 3 per unit, with an income of 12, a maximum of 4 units can be purchased instead of 3. Thus, the budget line appears to rotate in a counter-clockwise direction, as we described earlier. This will enable the consumer to attain a higher indifference curve, or a higher level of utility as shown in Figure 10.

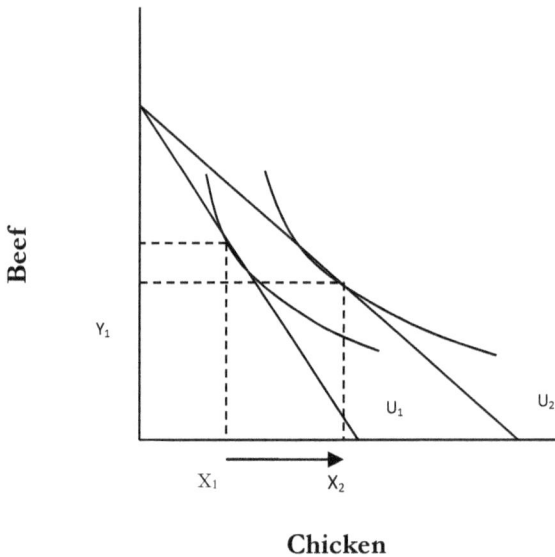

Figure 10: The effect of a change in price on consumption
(As we decrease the price of chicken more chicken is purchased)

As the price of chicken falls, the amount of chicken consumed rises from X_1 to X_2. Again, this is what we would expect. This analysis is simply a way of showing that as price declines, consumers will, all else being equal, tend to purchase more of a given product.

Test your understanding of this concept by lowering the price of beef and then raising the price of beef, relative to chicken, and trace the changes in beef purchased due to these price changes.

Holding income and price of good Y constant, varying the price of good X it is possible to establish PRICE-CONSUMPTION CURVE for good X. Suppose the budget line corresponding to original price of good X is B (Figure 11). Increase in price of good X will lead to less quantity consumed, the new budget line is C, with corresponding new market basket T. Note the increase in price of good X increases the slope of the budget line but does not affect the intercept of the line. The new equilibrium market basket is at the point of tangency between C and U_2 rather than between B and U_3. Similar procedure can generate corresponding equilibrium market basket to each price of good X. The curve connecting various equilibrium points is called PRICE-CONSUMPTION CURVE (Figure 11).

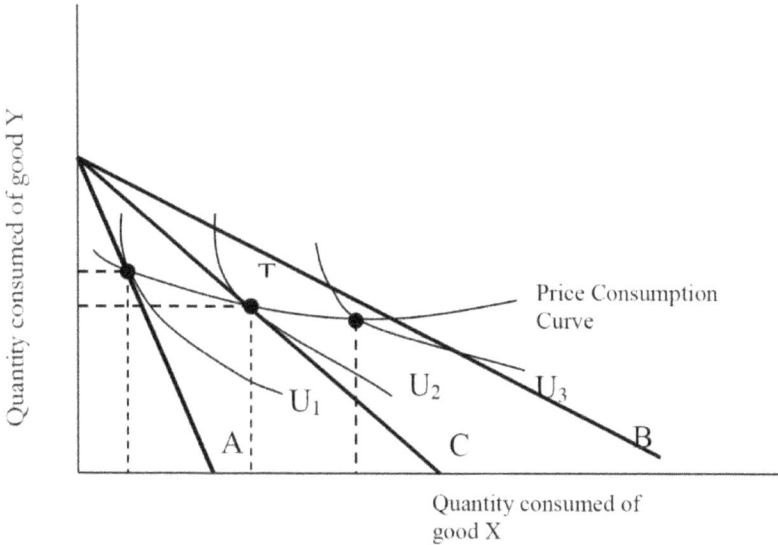

Figure 11: Price Consumption curve

Marginal Rate of Substitution

As we move along a given indifference curve, from point A to point C in Figure 12 for example, we see that a consumer would be willing to give up less and less of good Y to attain another unit of good X, the rate at which a consumer would be willing to give up Y to receive X, and remain indifferent, is known as the *marginal rate of substitution of X for Y, written as MRSxy*

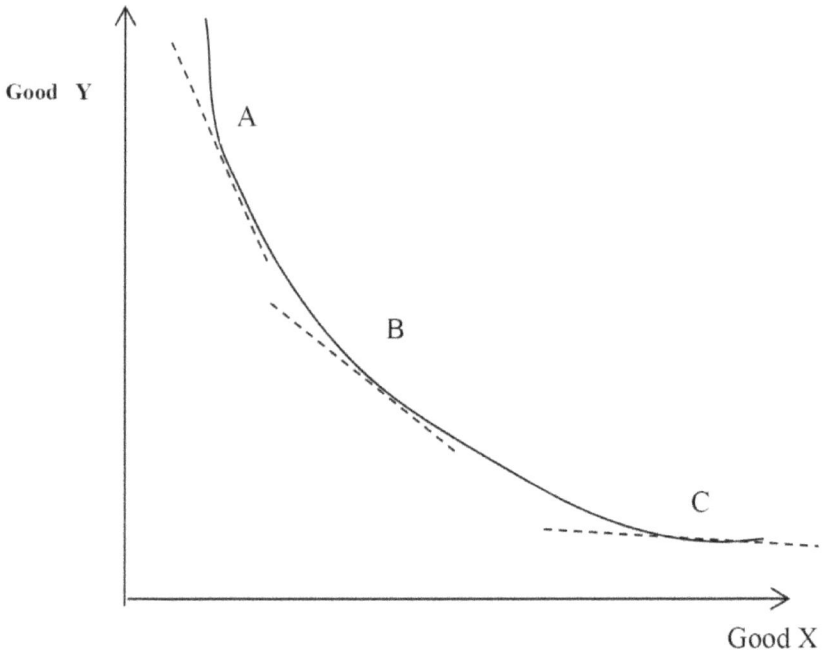

Figure 12: Diminishing Marginal Rate of Substitution of x for Y (MRSxy)
(As we go from point A to B and C, the rate at which the consumer is willing to surrender Y for another unit of X, MRS, decreases as the slope of the indifference curve decreases.)

The marginal rate of substitution is the slope of an indifference curve at any point (remember that slope is measured by a vertical distance divided by a horizontal distance). As we move from A to B to C, we can see that the slopes of tangents to the indifference curve decline, or get less steep. The economic translation is that the marginal rate of substitution is declining – the rate at which the consumer would give up Y for another unit of X declines. This intuitively is what we would expect: because of the law of diminishing marginal utility, as the consumer attains more X and less and less of good Y to attain another unit of good X. The rate at which another unit of X, or alternatively, more of X will be required to substitute one unit of Y.

Now assume that the price of X is 1, and the price of Y is 2. The budget line is pictured as in Figure 13. With an income of 2, the consumer could purchase 2 of X and 1 of Y. With an income of 4, the consumer could purchase 4 of X and 2 of Y. The slope of the budget line, again the vertical distance divided by the horizontal distance, is ½ at all points on the line. This is the same as the price of X divided by the price of Y. Thus, if the slope of the indifference curve and the slope of the budget line are equal where utility is maximized, given the budget constraints, we have:

$$MRS_{xy} = \Delta Y / \Delta X = P_x / P_y$$

The slope at the budget line = Px/Py. Utility is maximized where the slope of the budget line *equals* the slope of the indifference curve, or where $\Delta Y / \Delta X = Px/Py$.

Since $MRS_{xy} = MU_x / MU_y$, this means that at equilibrium $MU_x / MU_y = P_x / P_y$ or $MU_x / P_x = MU_y / P_y$, as was pointed out earlier.

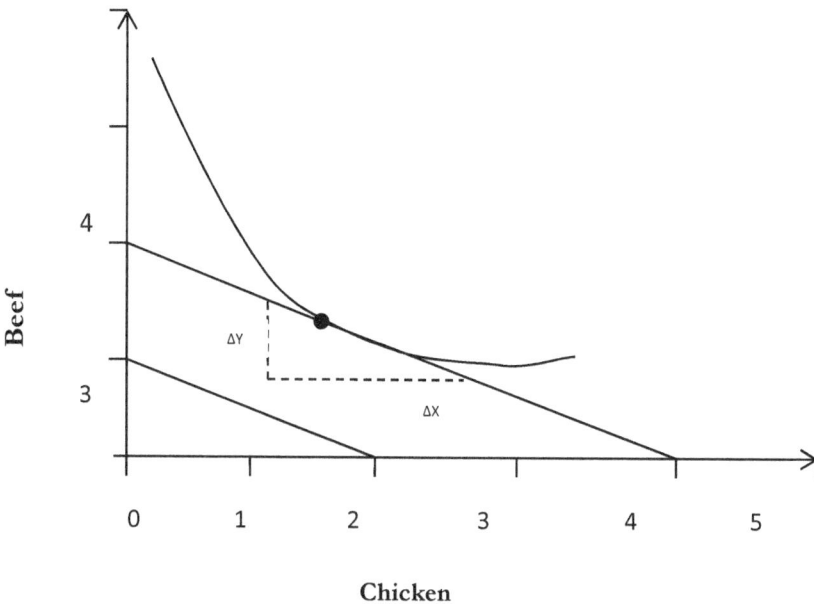

Figure 13: Slope of the indifference curve

Substitution and Income Effects

Changes in price of a good affects a consumer in two ways:

- Consumer attains a different level of satisfaction
- Consumer substitutes cheaper goods for expensive goods

Total effect can be decomposed into substitution and income effects. Figure 14 explains the effects of changing price of good X. Slope of the budget line A gives the original price ratio, and consumer chooses point U on indifference curve 1 and consumes Ox_1. Increased price of good X results in budget line B on indifference curve 2 and consumption of Ox_2. The total effect of price change is a reduction of $Ox_1 - Ox_2$ units. If the consumer is to have the original level of satisfaction following a price increase, one would need to increase consumer's level of income. To do this would mean to have a budget line parallel to B and tangent to indifference curve 1. This gives an equilibrium point W which corresponds to the hypothetical budget line C.

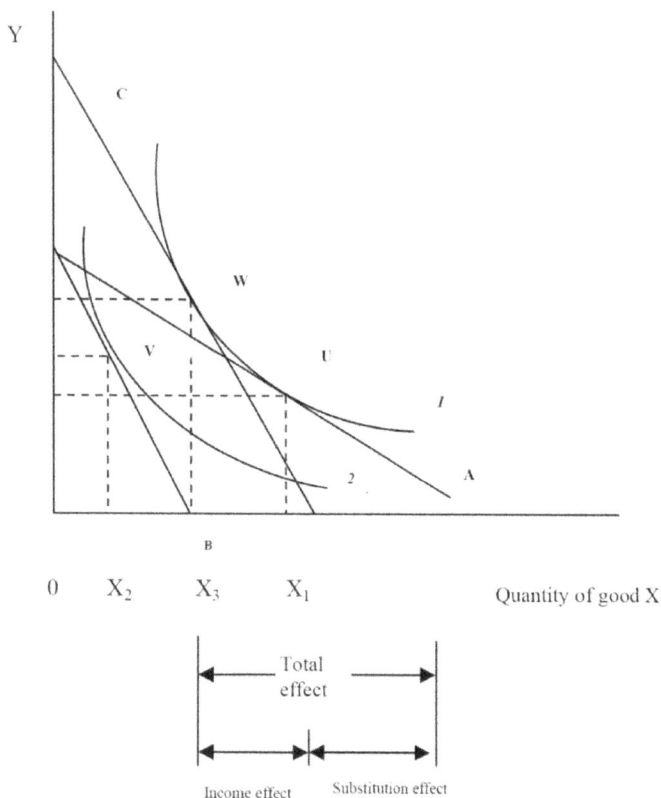

Figure 14: Substitution and income effects

The **substitution effect** is defined to be the movement from the original equilibrium point U to the imaginary equilibrium point W, which corresponds to the hypothetical budget line C. Substitution effect is thus the reduction of the quantity consumed from Ox_1 to Ox_3 units of good X or change in quantity of X demanded due to price change keeping the satisfaction level constant. Movement from the imaginary point W to the actual equilibrium point V is the **income effect**. The movement reflect the change in the level of total satisfaction (from one indifference curve to another) rather than price changes as the price ratio in budget line B is the same as in C. If we define the consumer's real income as his or her level of satisfaction (or utility), the income effect is the change in quantity demanded of good X due entirely to a change in real income, all prices being held constant. In Figure 14, it is the reduction from Ox_3 to Ox_2.

The total *effect is substitution effect* plus *income effect*. Substitution effect is always *negative* and greater than income effect. That is, if the price of good X increases and real income is held constant, there will always be a decrease in the consumption of good X, and if the price of good X decreases and real income held constant, there will always be an increase in the consumption of good X. However, the income effect is not predictable from the theory alone. In most cases one would expect that increases in real income will result in increases in consumption of good X and vice versa. This is the case for so-called normal goods. But not all goods are normal. Some goods are called inferior goods because the income effect is the opposite (of that of a normal good) for them i.e. their consumption decreases with increase in real income.

Revealed Preference Approach

The revealed preference approach is a major development in the theory of consumer behaviour. It was introduced by Samuelson in 1938. It derives a demand function without indifference curve analysis but establishes the existence and the convexity of indifference curves.

Derivation of demand curve for a commodity

Graphical derivation of demand curve

Individual demand curve can be derived from PRICE-CONSUMPTION CURVE, which includes all of the equilibrium market baskets corresponding to various prices of the commodity (Figure 11 above). Individual demand curve shows how much of a given commodity the consumer would purchase (per unit of time) at various prices of the commodity, holding money income, taste, price of other commodities constant.

The individual demand curve of a good can be derived as follows:

- When the price of good X is Oa, consumer buys Ou units of good X
- When the price of good X is Ob, consumer buys Or units of good X
- When the price of good X is Oc, consumer buys Ow units of good X
- When the price of good X is Od, consumer buys Oy units of good X
- These are the four points on the individual demand curve
- By deriving more and more points in this way, one can obtain the entire individual demand curve for good X, resulting to DD" shown in Figure 15.

The demand curve constructed assumes a normal commodity. The demand curve for a normal commodity will have a negative slope.

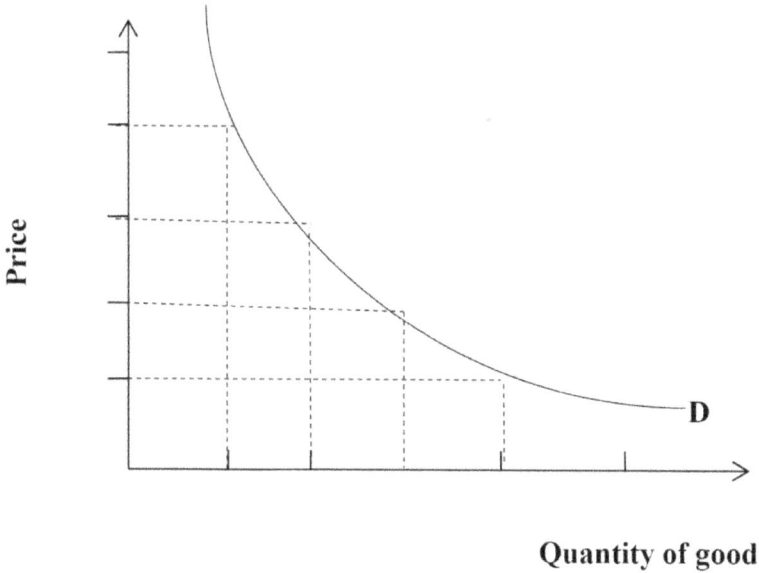

Figure 15: Demand curve for a normal commodity

Mathematical derivation of demand function

Given the utility function

$$U = f(X_1, X_2)$$

and income constraint

$$M = P_1 X_1 + P_2 X_2$$

Where, U is total utility, q_b is quantity of beef, q_c is quantity of chicken, Y^0 is fixed income, p_b is price of beef and p_c is price of chicken

Forming lagrangian function

$$L = f(X_1, X_2) + \lambda (M - P_1 X_1 - P_2 X_2)$$

Differentiating the function with respect to X_1 and X2

$$\delta L/\delta X_1 = X_2 - \lambda P_1 = 0$$
$$\delta L/\delta X_2 = X_1 - \lambda P_2 = 0$$
$$\delta L/\delta \lambda = M - P_1 X_1 - P_2 X_2 = 0$$

Solving for X_1 and X_2 gives the demand functions:

$$X_2 - \lambda P_1 = 0$$
$$X_1 - \lambda P_2 = 0$$

$X_2/X_1 = P_1/P_2$ OR $P_2 X_2 = P1X1$, Meaning that the expenditure on X_1 equals expenditure on X_2.
Constraint:
$$P_1X_1 + P_2 X_2 = M$$
$$P_1X_1 + (P_1 X_{1)} = M$$
$$2P_1X_1 = M$$
$$X_1 = M/2P_1$$

And for X_2

$$(P_2X_2) + P_2 X_2 = M$$
$$2P_2X_2 = M$$
$$X_2 = M/2P_2$$

The demand functions are;

For X1 $= M/2P_1$
$$X_2 = M/2P_2$$

Constant Money:

If we hold money income constant and change only price, a demand curve is obtained.
Example $M = 100$

$$P_2 X_2 = M$$
$$P_2 = 1, 2, 3, 4, 5, 6, 7, 8$$

$P_2 = 1$, $X_2 = 100/1 = 100$ $P_2= 2$, $X_2 = 100/2 = 50$ $P_2 = 3$, $X_2 = 100/3 = 33.3$
$P_2 = 4$, $X_2 = 100/4 = 25$ $P_2 = 5$, $X_2 = 100/5 = 20$ etc
The quantity of X_2 demanded decrease as the price of the commodity

increases

There are two important properties of demand functions:

1. The demand function for any commodity is a single-valued function of prices and income. This follows from the assumption of strict quasi concave utility function. The indifference curve has no straight portion such that given a particular income, a given price leads to a unique value (single) of the commodity demanded. If the indifference curve is not strictly quasi convex (meaning it has a straight portion), the maxima would not be unique. For a particular price, more than one quantity would be demanded.
2. The demand functions are homogenous of degree zero in prices and income i.e. if prices and income increased in the same proportion, the quantity demanded will remain unchanged

Elements of Demand

We derived an individual demand curve graphically using the price consumption curve and mathematically using the assumption of utility maximization subject to income constraint. The demand for a product is basically a relationship between price and quantity purchased during a given time period. All else being equal, the lower the price of a product the more consumers will tend to purchase.

Let us take the example of maize and assume that consumers will purchase various quantities during a given time period, as shown in Figure 16. As the price declines, more is purchased. As the price rises, less in purchased. Why? Because maize can be replaced by other products such as potatoes and rice. As the price becomes more expensive, consumers will have the incentive to purchase less maize and more of something else.

The relationship between price and quantity can be seen clearly when drawn as in Figure 16. By convention, quantity is placed on the horizontal axis and price on the vertical axis.

Also note that we are assuming, for the moment, that everything else is constant. Of course, not all else is constant at any one time in a real- world economy. However, for the purposes of illustration, and to isolate particular important relationships, we need to ask what happens if other things are constant. When we understand the relationships, we may then adjust other factors in the economy.

Factors Affecting Demand

What lies behind the demand curve, or causes is to be located where it is? At a price of 7, why do people buy 400 instead of 300 or 500? Is it possible for changes to occur over time such that, at a price of 7, people would buy 500 instead of 400?

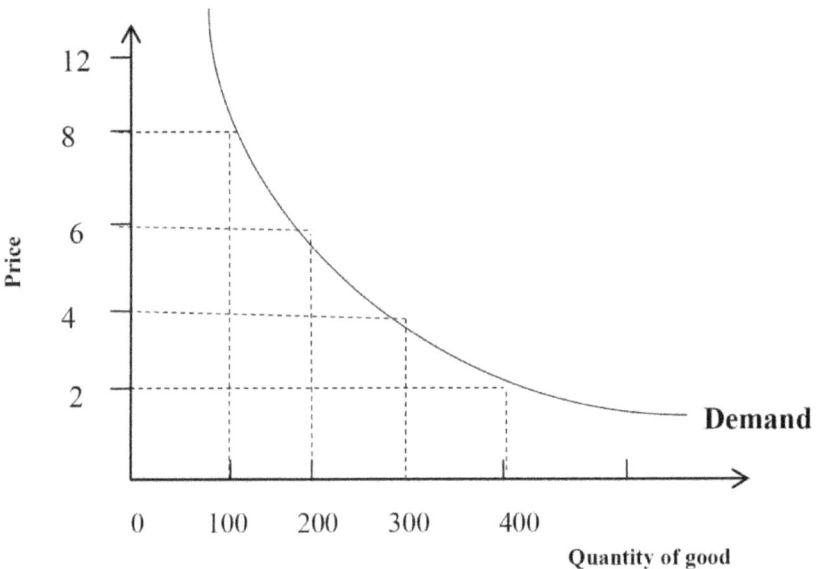

Figure 16: A simple demand curve
(Price and quantity demanded vary inversely. The relationship between price and quantity is inverse. That is, price and quantity vary in opposite directions. As price decreases, quantity increases. Conversely, as price increases, quantity decreases.)

This leads us to the factors affecting demand, which determine the position of the demand curve, and cause *shifts* in demand over time. A shift of the entire curve to the right, as in Figure 17, is known as an *increase* in demand as, at any given price, a greater quantity of product, Q_1 instead of Q_0, will be demanded than before. A shift to the left is known as a *decrease* in demand.

What factors determine the position of the demand curve, and what might cause such changes? There are several factors that affect the demand for a commodity as indicated below.

Tastes and Preferences

People have preferences based on beliefs, cultural values, tastes, habits and a host of other factors which affect what they want and believe to be desirable. We would expect, for example, that in Tanzania the demand for yellow maize would lie considerably to the left of the demand for white maize. The same would be true in Mexico. However, in the United states people prefer yellow maize.

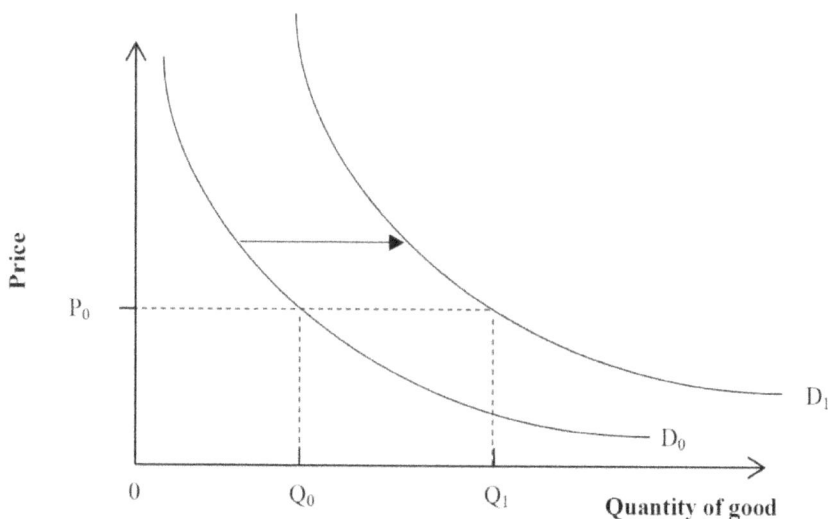

Figure 17: A shift in demand
(An increase in demand from D_0 to D_1 means that at any given price a larger quantity will be demanded.)

Such tastes and preferences need not be apparently rational. Some consumers in Nairobi prefer brown eggs, whereas others prefer white eggs, even though there is no nutritional difference between these two types of eggs.

Tastes and preferences change over time due to such factors as advertising, changing attitude and lifestyles, and a host of other factors; particularly in developing countries such as Tanzania, changing lifestyles and awareness of new products, which are inevitable, will change the pattern of tastes and preference. This can have both negative and positive consequences for a nation, and this complex topic must be deferred until you study economic growth. For now, suffice it to say that tastes and preferences are important factors that affect demand. *Changes in tastes and preferences will lead to increase in the demand for some products while decreasing the demand for other products.*

Level of Income

Demand for a product depends on the amount that people are both *willing* and *able* to purchase. If incomes rise, all else being equal, people would be able to purchase more at any price. Would they be *willing?* That depends on the nature of the specific product. Most goods are referred to as 'normal goods'. As incomes rise, people are both *willing* and able to purchase more at any price. Demand shifts to the right.

There are some goods, however, referred to as *inferior goods*, of which people buy less as incomes rise because they can afford other more desirable goods. For example, a low-income family might derive its primary source of protein from beans. However, with a rising income, they may substitute other more desirable sources of protein such as meat, eggs, and cheese, and buy fewer beans than before. The increased income has *increased* the demand for meat, eggs, and cheese, which are normal goods, and has *decreased* the demand for beans, an inferior good. You should not conclude from this example that beans are an inferior good in Tanzania! Whether a good is inferior or not is a matter that can only be ascertained empirically and obviously depends on tastes and preferences.

Price of Related Goods

What would be expected to happen to the *demand* for beef as the *price* of substitutes such as lamb, pork, or chicken increase? As the price of these products increases, our relationship between price and quantity infers that people would buy less of them, and perhaps substitute more beef, which at a given price has nevertheless fallen *relative* to its substitutes. Thus, for example, more beef would be purchased at a given price when the price of chicken rises from point A to point B, as shown in Figure 18. Now try to figure out what would happen to the *demand* for beef if the price of substitutes for beef falls.

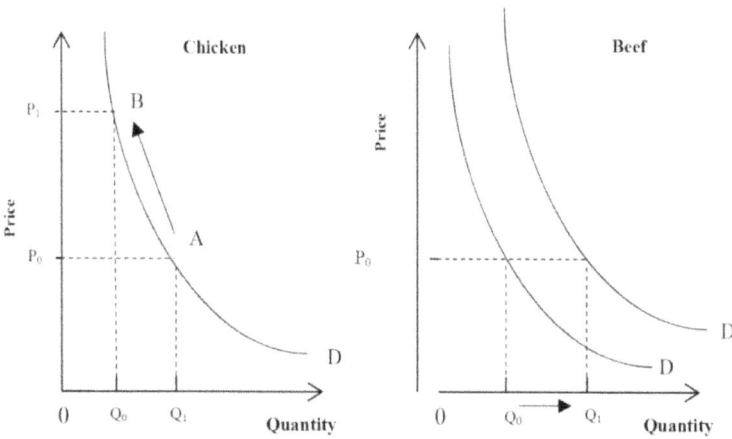

Figure 18: The case of substitute goods
(As the price of a good increases, the demand for its substitute increases).

The opposite case is that for complementary goods. Some goods are used or consumed in combination. An example is roast meat and beer. If the price of beer declined, what might happen to the demand for roast meat? If the two products go together, and the price of beer declines, the quantity of beer consumed would be expected to rise. Therefore, the demand for roast meat, which is complementary to beer, would also be expected to rise.

You should now ask what would happen to the *demand* for roast meat if the *price* of beer rises, and explain this result with the aid of diagrams.

Number of Consumers and Size of Market

In conceptualizing a market demand, it is helpful to think first of an individual downward-sloping demand curve. At a given price, the individual is willing and able to purchase a specific quantity of the product. The market demand can be thought of as the sum of the quantities which all individuals in the market are willing and able to purchase at given prices.

Diagrammatically, the market demand is the horizontal summation of individual demand curves. All else being equal, the larger the number of consumes, the larger the market and the larger the market demand.

Remember, however, that the consumers must have purchasing power with which to express demand. Large numbers of people with no purchasing power do not add to effective demand.

Expectations

Purchases of certain kinds of goods, often referred to as 'durable goods', are deferrable. If people expect prices to increase in the future, they may opt to buy now instead of waiting for prices to rise. This would be expected to raise the demand at the present time. If consumers expect prices to *fall* in the future, what would be expected to happen to *demand* in the present?

Many important goods, such as food, are not durable goods, however, and purchase can neither be significantly deferred nor made in advance if storage facilities are not available, and hence expectations do not play an important role.

Demand Elasticities

Central to the study of demand is the very important concept of *elasticity*. We know that as price decreases (increases), all else being equal, quantity demanded increases (decreases). Elasticity of demand measures the degree of responsiveness of the quantity demanded with respect to price changes. The concept of price elasticity of demand is extremely useful, and has numerous very important policy applications.

Own Price Elasticity of Demand

Own price elasticity of demand is a measure of the responsiveness of changes in quantity demanded to changes in its own price. The measurement is expressed in terms of a coefficient derived by dividing the percentage change in quantity by the percentage change in price, or $\%\Delta Q / \%\Delta P$.

To obtain a percentage change in price, we must take some change in price relative to the original price or $\Delta P/P$. And the same holds true for percentage change in quantity, which is $\Delta Q/Q$. Thus, dividing percentage change in quantity by percentage change in price, we have;

$$[\Delta Q/Q] / [\Delta P/P] = [\Delta Q/Q]. P/\Delta P = [\Delta Q/\Delta P].P/Q$$

Consider the demand schedule in Figure 19. Suppose that we wish to calculate elasticity, or the percentage change in quantity, as we lower the price from 9 to 8 per unit. There is a minor complexity that we get different results if we lower the price from 9 to 8, as compared to raising the price from 8 to 9. We can illustrate this by performing the calculations. If we lower the price form 9 to 8, by plugging into the formula, we have:

$$\frac{1}{1} \bullet \frac{9}{1} = 9$$

(Note that because of the inverse relationship between price and quantity, the formula yields a negative number. As it is understood that the relationship is inverse, the negative sign is often dropped for convenience).

If we raise the price from 8 to 9, by plugging into the formula, we have:

$$\frac{1}{1} \bullet \frac{8}{2} = 4$$

Thus, we have two different elasticity coefficients between these two price-quantity relationships. To resolve this dilemma, we use what is known as the 'mid-points' formula by which we take the middle range of price and quantity. This procedure yields:

$$\frac{Q}{P} \times \frac{\frac{(P_1+P_2)}{2}}{\frac{(Q_1+Q_2)}{2}}$$

$$\frac{1}{I} \bullet \frac{8.5}{1.5} = 5.67$$

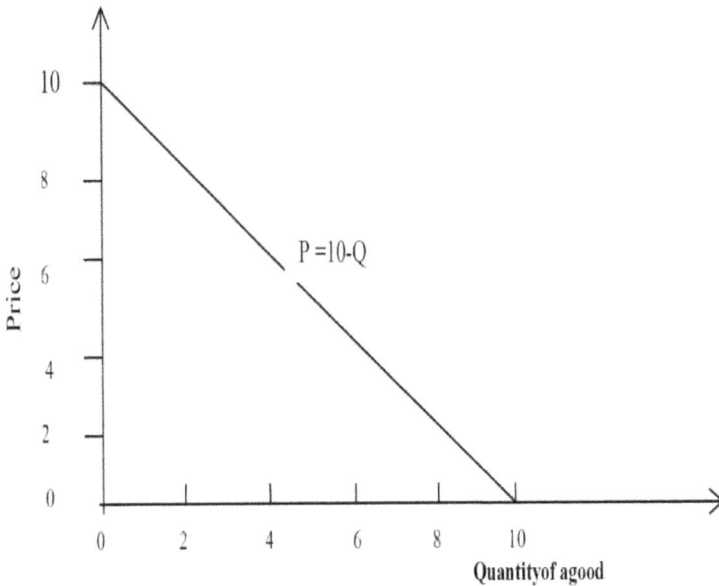

Figure 19: A demand curve P = 10- Q

(Elasticity measures the responsiveness of quantity demanded to a change in price)

Using the mid-points formula yields an elasticity coefficient *between* that yielded by the other two processes. As the points become closer and closer the difference in elasticity as measured from the respective bases becomes closer and closer. Technically, the computation of elasticity between two points is known as 'arc elasticity'. As the points converge to a single point, the elasticity is referred to as 'point elasticity'. Point elasticity of demand E_{iij} is defined as $\delta\,(\ln Q)/\delta\,(\ln P) = \delta Q/\delta P/P/Q$ In the following section, we will confine our analysis to arc elasticity as this represents real-world situations in which, for example, the Strategic Grain Reserve is interested in the response, in terms of quantity demanded, to a specific change in the price of maize.

Let us now calculate the price elasticity of demand for the remainder of the demand curve using the mid-points formula. Note that, as we start with a high price and move to lower prices, the elasticity coefficients become smaller. We say that if the coefficient of elasticity is greater than 1, the demand is elastic. If the coefficient is less than 1, demand is inelastic. An elasticity coefficient of 1.22 is interpreted as: *for a percent change in price, quantity demanded changes by 1.22 percent.*

In summary:

$E_{ii} > 1$ = elastic demand
$E_{ii} < 1$ = inelastic demand
$E_{ii} = 1$ = unitary elasticity

Elasticity and Total Revenue

Associated with each point on a demand curve is *total revenue*, which is obtained by multiplying price by the quantity sold at the prevailing price. Note that as we move 'down' the demand curve, decreasing price and thereby increasing quantity, total revenue increases, reaches a peak and decreases again. Herein lies an extremely important relationship between elasticity and total revenue (Table 1).

In observing the total revenue and elasticity coefficients, note that as price is lowered, and total revenue increases, elasticity is greater than 1. At a price of 5, we note that elasticity is somewhere between 0.82 and 1.22. In fact, if we would use the more precise formula used in more advanced analysis, we would find elasticity at that point *equal to 1*.

Table 2: The Relationship between Total Revenue and Elasticity

Price	Quantity		Total revenue
10	0		0
9	1	19.00	9
8	2	5.67	16
7	3	3.00	21
6	4	1.86	24
5	5	1.22	24
4	6	0.82	24
3	7	0.54	21
2	8	0.33	16
1	9	0.18	9

As we move still further down the demand curve, we find that as we lower price, total revenue decreases and the elasticity coefficient in less than 1. We can summarize this important lesson with a general rule as follows:

If E > 1, as P rises TR falls
If E < 1, as P rises TR rises
If E > 1, as P falls TR rises
IF E < 1, as P falls TR falls

This can be represented graphically. As price decreases from 9 to 8, and quantity increases from 1 to 2, total revenue goes from 9 to 16. Geometrically, total revenue at a price of 9 is shown in Figure 20 as rectangle OBEC (Remember that length times width equals the area of a rectangle.) Since price multiplied by quantity equals total revenue (P.Q = TR), then the relative size of total revenue is indicated geometrically by the size of the rectangle in the diagram.

As we lower price to 8, the size of the rectangle increase to OAFD. We can see from inspection that as price is lowered total revenue increases. Thus we know that elasticity must be greater than 1, a fact verified by our earlier calculations.

We can ask ourselves at what price can we fit the largest possible rectangle into the space delineated by the demand curve. It appears that at a price of 5 and quantity of 5 the largest rectangle can be fitted in. That is, total revenue is maximized at a price of 5, and at this point elasticity equals 1. As we lower price and further down the curve, we see that the possible rectangles, representing total revenue, start to become smaller and smaller, and thus we know that elasticity is less than 1. We can picture these relationships with the diagram in Figure 20.

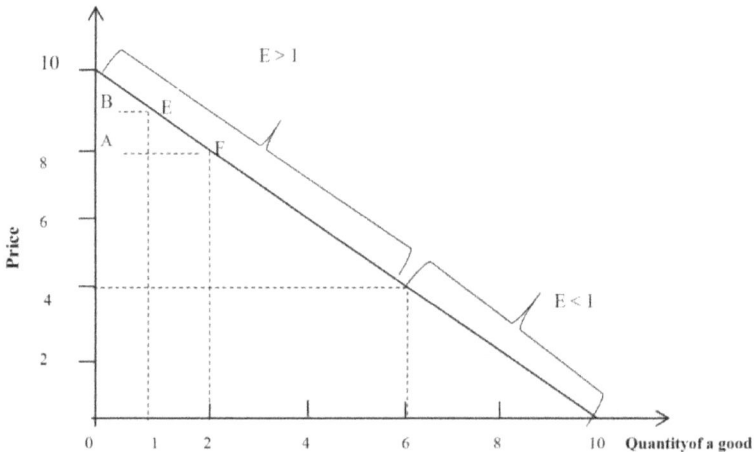

Figure 20: Geometrical representation of total revenue
(*Price multiplied by quantity yields the area of a rectangle, which equals total revenue*)

Let us introduce one more concept before progressing to applications. Total revenue, we know, is obtained by multiplying price by quantity. Marginal revenue, which is another very important concept, is the *additional revenue* obtained from sale of the last (additional) unit of product, or $\Delta TR/Q$.

Looking at Figure 21 again, we see that as long as $E > 1$, sale of another unit of product yields an increase in total revenue. However, these increases in total revenue (marginal revenue) though positive, get smaller, eventually reach zero, and become negative.

Let us now vary price by infinitely small amounts so that we have a smooth curve such as in Figure 22 where we plot total revenue against price.

Recall from your basic mathematics the formula for the slope of a line, which is a vertical distance divided by a horizontal distance. In fact, this would be $\Delta TR/\Delta Q$, which is also the formula for marginal revenue. Thus, if we plot the slope of the total revenue curve, we also have marginal *revenue.*

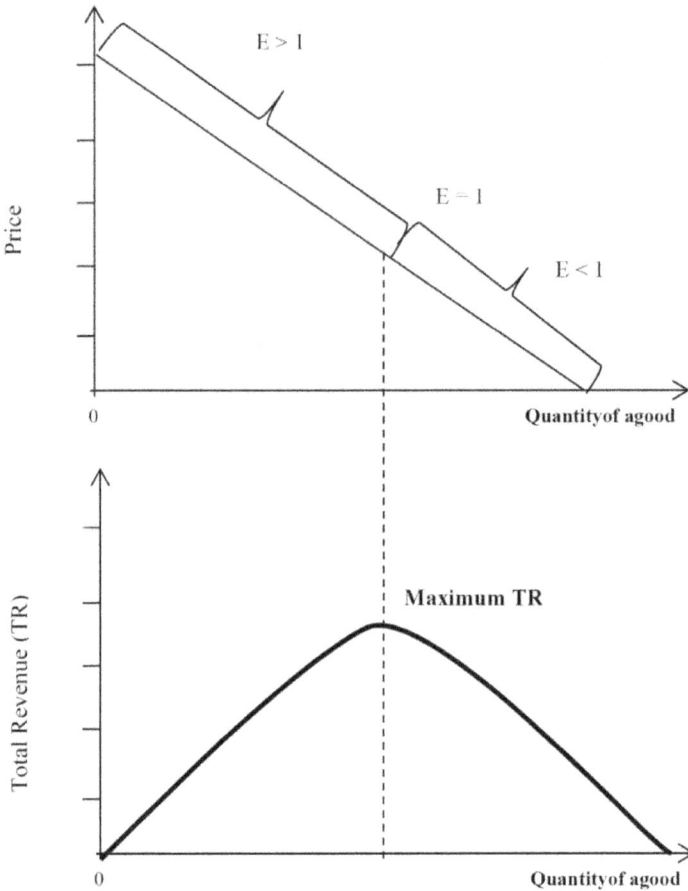

Figure 21: The relationship between elasticity and total revenue
(You should be cautioned at this point that total revenue is not the same as profits. For this, we need to put costs and revenue together, as we will do in latter chapters).

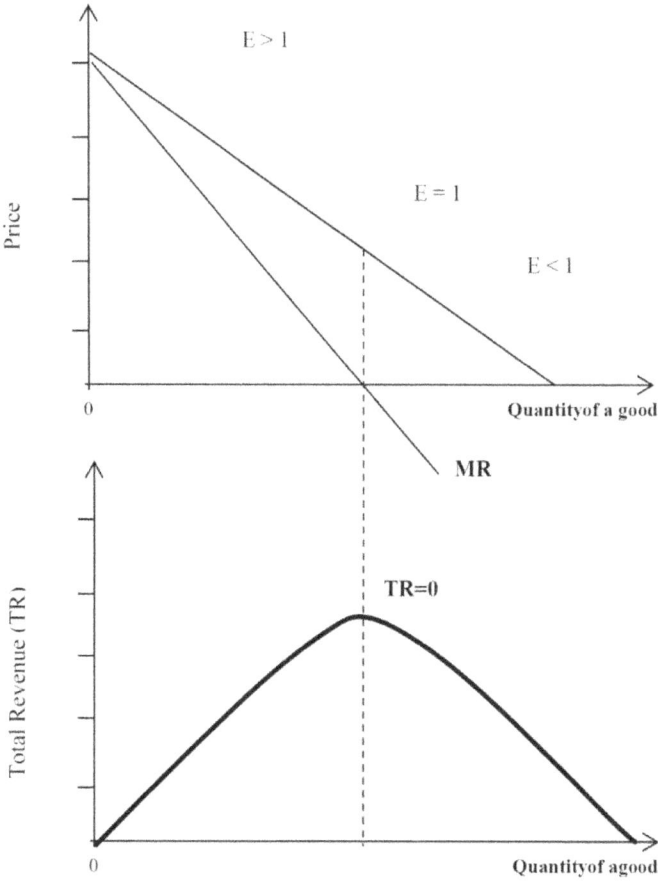

Figure 22: The relationship between demand, total revenue and marginal revenue

Mathematically,

Own price elasticity of demand, $\varepsilon_{11} = \delta\,(\ln Q)/\,\delta\,(\ln P) = (\delta\,Q\delta P)\,(P/Q)$

For the demand function $Q = \alpha - bP$

$\varepsilon_{11} = -b\,P/Q$ Where $-b = \delta\,Q/\delta P$

Price elasticity of demand is negative because the demand curve is negatively sloping

Consumers expenditure on Q = Total Revenue (TR) = QP

and

$\delta(PQ)\delta P = \delta TR/\delta P = Q+P \delta Q/\delta P = Q(1+ (P/Q)(\delta Q/\delta P) = Q(1+ \varepsilon_{11})$

Hence consumers expenditure or producers revenue will:

1. Increase with price p_1 if $\varepsilon 11$ is > -1
2. Remain unchanged if $\varepsilon 11$ is = -1
3. Decrease if $\varepsilon 11$ is <-1

Marginal Revenue and Own Price Elasticity

TR = PQ

$MR = \delta TR/\delta Q = \delta(PQ)/\delta Q = P+ (Q)(\delta P/\delta Q)$

Price elasticity of demand $\varepsilon_{11} = -(\delta Q/\delta P)(P/Q)$

Rearranging $-\varepsilon_{11}(Q/P) = \delta Q/\delta P - P/\varepsilon_{11}Q. = \delta P/\delta Q$

But $MR = P+ (Q)(\delta P/\delta Q)$

Substituting for $\delta P/\delta Q$ gives

$MR = P- Q(P/\varepsilon_{11}Q) = P - P/\varepsilon_{11} = P(1-(1/\varepsilon_{11}))$

What will be the magnitudes of MR if $\varepsilon_{11}= 1$, $\varepsilon_{11}>1$ and $\varepsilon_{11}<1$. What will happen to TR in each case?

Extension of Elasticity

Note that in our illustrations so far we have used a linear demand curve and have found that elasticity varies at different points on the given curve. Hence, we cannot say that the demand curve *per se* is either elastic or inelastic. It depends on where we are on the specific curve.

Yet we often hear references to 'elastic' or 'inelastic' products and demand curves. In popular reference this usually refers to a product for which demand is *relatively* elastic, compared to some other product, even though, technically, elasticity will vary depending on the relative price. This apparent confusion can be explained by viewing the demand for two products, as in Figure 23. If we change price from P_1 to P_2, clearly the change in quantity (and change in percentage quantity) demanded will be greater for the product represented by D_2 ($q_{22} - q_{21}$) as compared to that for D_1 ($q_{12} - q_{11}$). Thus, we say that the demand or D_2 is more elastic than that for D_1, even though the elasticities vary throughout the demand curve.

Several special cases of elasticity need to be briefly discussed. The first is the hypothetical case of a demand curve which is perfectly inelastic. The interpretation of this is that one would pay any price for a given amount of a product. The closest approximation to this would be a situation in which your life depended on a particular drug and therefore you would pay any price for it. Perfect inelasticity is represented by a vertical demand curve.

Note from Figure 22 that as the slope is zero at the top of the total revenue curve, this is also where total revenue is maximum, marginal revenue is zero and elasticity equals 1.

The second case is that of perfect elasticity, represented by a horizontal demand curve. The interpretation of this is that any amount can be sold at the price p. To charge more than p is not feasible for none will be purchased at that price. To charge less than p is not rational because a price of p can be attained. This is a situation faced by a small producer under perfect competition. The individual producer is responsible for such a small portion of total supply that she is unable to affect the market price. By producing more, or less, she affects market supply so little that price remains unchanged. We will use this type of demand curve extensively in our analysis of profit-maximizing behaviour under perfect competition.

Finally, there is the purely academic cases of demand curve of unitary elasticity. Recall that if $E > 1$, and price falls, TR increases. Remember also that TR is maximized where $E = 1$. What would this imply for TR if $E = 1$ throughout the demand curve? The demand curve is shaped in such a way that no matter what the price, total revenue remains constant (Figure 24). Do you suppose this is realistic for many products?

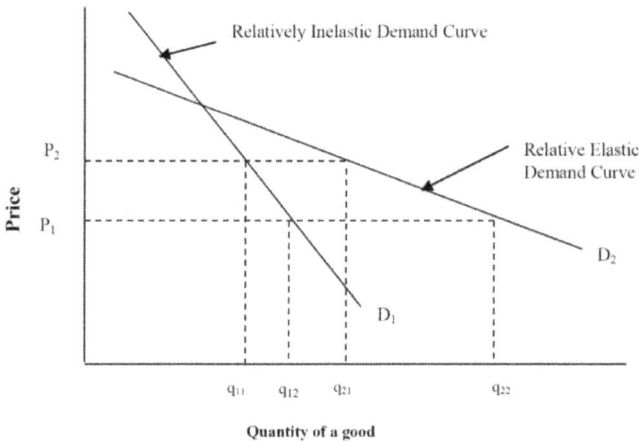

Figure 23: Relatively elastic and relatively inelastic demand curves

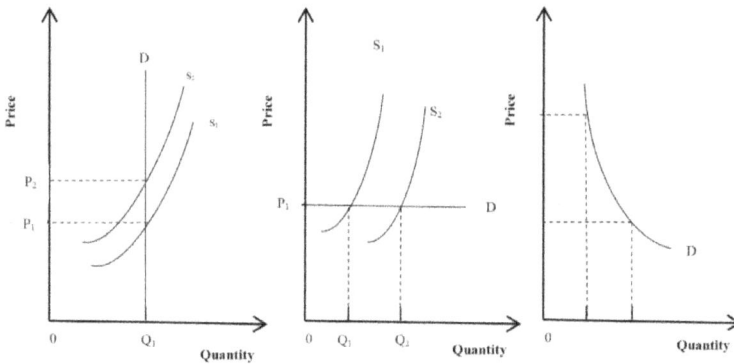

Figure 24: Special cases: Perfect inelasticity, perfect elasticity and unitary elasticity

Determinants of Elasticity

Before we delve into policy implications of elasticity, let us briefly examine some determinants of elasticity. Why is elasticity of demand for some products relatively high and relatively low for others?

A major factor determining elasticity is the degree to which a product is a *necessity as opposed to a luxury*. The greater the degree to which a product is a necessity the more inelastic the demand tends to be, or the less responsive the quantity demanded will be to price changes. We saw in our extreme example of perfect inelasticity that virtually any price would be paid for the lifesaving drug. To say it differently, price had zero effect on quantity demanded. Products such as food, which are necessities, tend to be inelastic, whereas demand for automatic washing machines, which are more of a luxury, tends to be more elastic. In most parts of Tanzania one would find that the demand for maize flour used for making *ugali* is less elastic than the demand for rice. This is because *ugali* is considered a necessity, whereas rice is not yet considered a necessary staple food for many Tanzania families.

A related factors determining elasticity is the degree to which an item has *substitutes*. If there are few substitutes for an item, the quantity demanded would be expected to vary less than that for an item for which many substitutes were available. Which would be more elastic, the demand for food products in general or the demand for beef? Obviously, there is no substitute for food, but there are substitutes for beef, such as fish, chicken, pork and lamb. Thus, the elasticity for a specific food product is greater than for food in general.

A third factor is the durability of the product. The purchase of a product which is durable can be deferred until such time as the price is more favourable. Thus, the quantity demanded might vary considerably with respect to price. In contrast, if a product is not durable, purchase is more difficult to defer, implying greater *inelasticity*.

The proportion of one's income, or expenditure, spent on a product tends to affect elasticity. If an item such as salt, for example, takes only a small portion of one's income, its price may vary considerably without affecting the quantity demanded. However, an item such as housing, which takes up a large portion of one's income is more elastic, particularly if we are talking about housing beyond the bare necessities. This means that, for a particular product, elasticities will differ between two individuals with different incomes depending on the proportions of their expenditures taken by the product. Thus, demand for *kisamvu* may be elastic for an urban labourer but inelastic for a high-income civil servant who likes the vegetable.

Finally, the elasticity of a given product can vary, depending on the time span involved. In the short run, the demand for petrol, for example, may be very inelastic. If you need to drive your car you will purchase petrol regardless of price. Your only option is to drive less, if you can. Your possible response in terms of reducing the quantity demanded is very slight. In the long run, however, you believe that the price of petrol will remain high, you may make other adjustments such as purchasing a more economical, fuel-saving vehicle, or living closer to your work so that you can drive less. Thus, in the long run, demand elasticity of a product tends to be greater than in the short run.

These factors give one an idea of the degree to which products might respond to changes in price. Based on these factors, what might you presume about the relative demand elasticity of cigarettes, designer clothing and ball-point pens?

Cross price elasticity of demand

Cross price elasticity of demand refers to the proportionate change in the quantity of one commodity demanded to the proportionate change in the price of another commodity.

$$\varepsilon_{21} = \delta (\ln Q_2)/\delta (\ln P_1) = (\delta Q_2 \, \delta P_1)(P_1/Q_2)$$

As mentioned above, commodities have been classified as substitutes or complements depending on the sign of cross price elasticity. If ε_{21} is positive, it implies that Q_1 and Q_2 are substitutes. An increase in the price of Q_1 will lead to an increase in the quantity of Q_2 demanded and vice versa.

If ε_{21} is negative, it implies that the two commodities are complements. An increase in the price of Q_1 will lead to a decrease in the quantity of Q_2 demanded and vice versa.

But measuring cross price elasticity on the basis of total effect of a price change without compensating for an income change may lead to incorrect conclusions about the nature of commodities.

If a price changes by a large proportion there will be a substantial change in real income such that the quantities of both commodities consumed may increase.

Two goods are net substitutes if the cross price elasticity is positive after compensating for the change in real income. They are net complements if the cross price elasticity is negative after compensating for the change in real income.

Income elasticity of demand

Income elasticity for ordinary demand function = $\eta_1 = \delta (\ln Q)/\delta (\ln y)$

$$= (\delta Q/\delta y)(y/Q)$$

If η_1 is positive, it implies that the commodity is a normal good.

More of the commodity will be purchased as income increases and vise versa

If η_1 if negative, it implies that the commodity is an inferior good. Consumer purchases decrease as income rises and increases as income falls.

Questions for Thought and Discussion

1. Explain carefully the law of diminishing marginal utility. Of what importance is the time period involved? Cite an example for which you have experienced this law.
2. Explain why indifference curves are convex to the margin. What would be implied by indifference curves represented by a straight line?
3. Explain why indifference curves never cross each other.
4. Why do price affect the amounts of goods consumed even though consumers' utility, or preference, for these goods remains unchanged?
5. Explain how diminishing marginal utility relates to the shape of the conventional demand curve.
6. Compute elasticity coefficients between points on the demand schedule and explain what does each coefficient mean?:

| 60 | 50 | 40 | 30 | 20 |

7. A group of promoters are sponsoring a musical concert but do not anticipate a sell-out. One advisor suggests lowering ticket prices. Another advisor disagree, and says that more money will be taken in by keeping ticket prices high. What must each, perhaps implicitly, feel about elasticities of demand? Explain in some detail why.
8. Are there occasions when a different price might be charged for the same product? Why do airlines often charge higher prices for the same seat to a person taking a short trip than to a person taking a
long trip? What conditions must be present for a seller to charge different prices to different people?
9. Given the demand equation, $Q = 30 - 2P$, where Q is total sales of wheat in kilograms, and P is price in TShs/kg:

   i. Write the equivalent demand equation in a price-dependent form.
   ii. Write the expression for total revenue
   iii. Draw the total revenue curve and show on it the level that maximizes revenues. At that level of sales, what is the price and elasticity of demand?

Mathematical note

The form of the linear demand curve is $P = a - bQ$, where a is the vertical intercept, and b is the slope of the demand curve. Suppose $P = 10 - Q$. Since total revenue is price times quantity:

$$TR = (10 - Q). Q, \text{ or } 10Q - Q^2. \text{ Since } MR = \frac{\partial TR}{\partial Q}$$

in this example, marginal revenue, or MR, $= 10 - 2Q$. TR is maximum where $\frac{\partial TR}{\partial Q} = 0$, or $10 - 2Q = 0$, and $Q = 5$.

Thus, at $Q = 5$, the slope of TR $= 0$. Substituting into the TR function, we find that TR is 25 at that point.

You should verify your understanding of these concepts by considering the demand curve, $P = 20 - \frac{1}{2}Q$. Compute the total revenue function, the marginal revenue function, and find the price and quantity which maximize total revenue, and for which marginal revenue is zero. Plot the functions and compare the geometry with your mathematical analysis. Make sure that you can also explain these concepts verbally.

CHAPTER THREE

Theory of Production

Introduction

We now begin to study the economics of the firm, for which production theory is the foundation. We then analyse the costs of production in the next chapter. Once you have acquired a thorough understanding of the costs of production in their many aspects, we will be able to analyze the decisions of the firms with respect to profit-maximizing behaviour, and to review the incentives of the firm under varying degrees of competition.

The Production Function

The process of production involves the transformation of factors of production (also referred to as resources or inputs) such as labour, land, seed, fertilizer, tools and machinery, into outputs or products, such as maize, beans, coffee, bread and other products. The relationship between inputs and outputs is known as the production function. It is important to emphasize that the production function is a physical or technical relationship. It has important economic implications, but until we attach prices to inputs and outputs, we can draw only limited economic implications from the production functions.

Let us assume that a farmer is producing beans on a given plot of land using his family labour. Land is the fixed input, meaning that it remains constant in the short run. The short run is the farmer's planning horizon, such as one season in the case of beans. Within one season, the farmer will decide to plant beans, for example, on one acre, thus fixing land to the amount. In the short run, the labour input is variable. That is, it can be varied in small increments, as the producer so chooses. Obviously, there will be other variable inputs as well, such as seed and fertilizer, but for now, we keep to the simple case of a single variable input. After harvesting the beans, that is, in the long run, there will be no fixed inputs, as the farmer is then free to vary even the fixed inputs, in this case, the acreage under beans.

As we use more variable inputs with our fixed input, we would expect the amount of output to increase. Again, the specific response to these inputs is a physical, or technical, relationship. Of course, the specific response of output to inputs varies with the product and for a given product over time, as technology changes. However, you may be surprised to learn that diverse production processes have certain elements in common, which can be illustrated by our simple production function.

Mathematically, the simple production function described above can expressed as:

$$Q = f(X_1, X^0_2)$$

Where, Q is the output (beans), X_1 is the variable input (labour) and X^0_2 is the fixed input (land). In this case, X^0_2 is translated as a parameter and Q becomes a function of X_1 alone.

The production function is normally defined for a period of time. This production function is a short run production which is defined subject to three restrictions.

(i)   Sufficiently short so that the producer is unable to change the level of fixed input
(ii) Sufficiently short so that technology is not changed
(iii) Sufficiently long to complete the production process

Graphical presentation of the production function is shown in Figure 25. Note that as we increase inputs, as represented on the horizontal axis, the outputs, represented on the vertical axis, change. Thus, we say that output depends on, or is a function of inputs. It is important to note that this is relative to a given technology. Over time, this technology may change, giving rise to a new production function. For now, however, we assume technology as given. Let us examine the production function in greater detail.

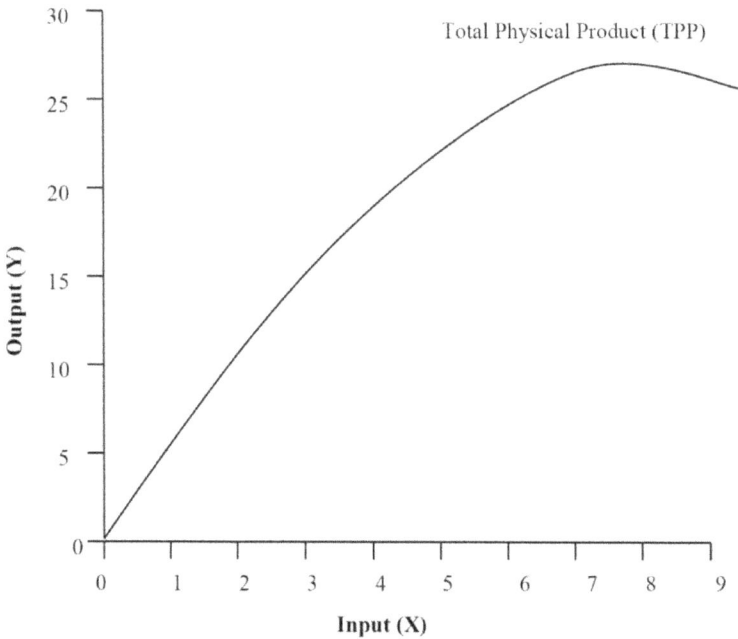

Figure 25: The simple one-variable input production function

Characteristics of the Production Function

- The production function is a continuous function with first and second order partial derivatives
- It is defined only for non negative values
- It keeps track of only technically efficient methods of production
- It is strictly quasi-concave

The law of Diminishing Marginal Return

Let us assume that on our given plot of land we can use varying amounts of labour, X, to produce varying amounts of beans, as shown in Figure 25 and Table 2 again, this basic relationship is our simple production function, the basic physical or technical relationship dictated by the level of technology available to us. Note that as we add varying amounts of the input, the level of output changes. What is extremely important is the manner in which it changes. The production function appears to 'bend down' as more is produced. This phenomenon reflects the 'law of diminishing returns', a very important concept which you must master thoroughly in order to progress in the study of economics. The law of diminishing returns states that as equal increments of a variable resource are added to a fixed resource base, beyond some point, the *increments* to output start to decline. Again, this is a physical relationship, but it has extremely important economic implications. What might seem amazing to you is that this 'law' appears to hold, whether we are talking about production of maize or beans on a Tanzanian shamba, or wheat production on the Great Plains of North America, or even adding additional labour to complex industrial processes. Let us become more familiar with this important concept.

An increment, or addition, to output which we have described is known as *Marginal Physical Product (MPP)*, sometimes referred to simply as marginal product. Marginal product is that amount of product resulting from adding another unit of input. More generally, it is the change in output resulting from a change in input i.e. $\Delta Q/\Delta X$. As ΔQ and ΔX approach zero, marginal product can be expressed as the first partial derivative of the production function i.e.

Marginal product $(MP) = \delta Q/\delta X_1 = f_1(X_1, X^0_2)$

Table 3: Production function relating input to output, including marginal and average physical product

Input X	Output Q	APP	MPP
0	0		
1	5	5.0	5
2	11	5.5	6
3	16	5.3	5
4	20	5.0	4
5	23	4.6	3
6	25	4.2	2
7	26	3.7	1
8	26	3.3	0
9	25	2.8	-1

In Figure 25 and Table 2, the change in input is one, so think of the change in output being divided by one. As we examine the production function, note that as we go from zero to one unit of input, output changes by five. This is the marginal product from the first unit of input. As we add the second unit of input, marginal product is six. As we add the third, marginal product is five. As five is smaller than six, it is thus with the third unit of input that diminishing returns begin. From here, the marginal product continues to get smaller, eventually reaching zero, and becoming negative. Marginal physical product for this production function is shown in Table 2. Graphically the marginal product can be obtained from the total product. The slope at any point on the total product curve gives the marginal product at that particular point (Figure 26). As MPP is the change in total product relative to a change in input, or $\Delta Q/ \Delta X$, this is equivalent to the slope of a tangent drawn to the total physical product curve at any point. A tangent drawn at point A, for example, has a particular slope, or 'steepness', to the curve, as measured by the vertical distance Q, divided by the horizontal distance, X. Thus, the slope of the total product curve, $\Delta Q/\Delta X$ is a measure of marginal physical product. As we move to the right, using more of the variable input X, we at first produce more Y with each unit of X. The slope of TPP, as measured by tangents to the curve, get steeper until point B. That is the point of maximum MPP. From point B the tangents appear to decline, reaching a slope of 0 at point D, implying that MPP is 0.

The addition of another unit of variable input at that point yields no additional physical product. Beyond point D, the slope is 'pointing downhill", or is negative. Can you interpret this? Can you think of a example in which this might occur and explain the reason? Note the similarity of the relationship between total physical product and marginal physical product, with the relationship between total utility and marginal utility as studied in theory of consumer behaviour.

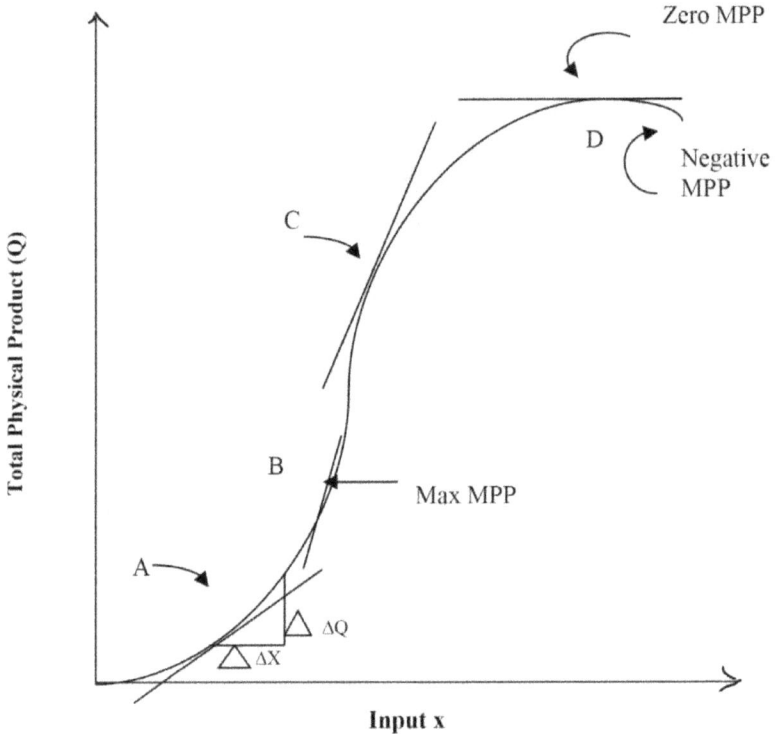

Figure 26: Derivation of marginal product curve from total product curve

Why does marginal product decline, reach zero and even become negative? It is conceivable that by adding more labour to a given plot of land, each labourer would add *less* to total product. Eventually, as more labourers are added, in the extreme case they could get in each other's way adding nothing to the total output, and even detracting from the total output. Obviously, the manger would stop adding labour shot of this point. Thus, from an economic point of view, the relevant area of the production function is where marginal product is still positive. We will examine this later in detail with respect to profit maximization.

Another important concept is *average physical product*. We obtain this by dividing total physical product by the number of variable input used i.e.

Average product $(AP) = Q/X_1 = f_1(X_1, X^0_2)/X_1$

Average physical product for our production function is shown in Table 2. It can be obtained from the total product curve. As average physical product is the output divided by variable input, it is geometrically the slope of a line running from the margin to any point on the TPP curve. This can be seen by the example in Figure 27, TPP = 100 and input is 4. The slope of a line running from 0 to point B is 100/4, that is the vertical distance divided by the horizontal distance.

What happens to the slopes of lines running from point 0 to successive points on the TPP curve? They appear to rise until point C and then fall again. This tells us that maximum APP is at point C, and beyond this point APP is falling. To the left of point C, a tangent to the TPP curve at any point has a slope greater than the slope of a line from the origin to that point. That is, MPP is greater than APP, and APP is rising. Note that APP increases, reaches a peak, and then decreases with increasing input

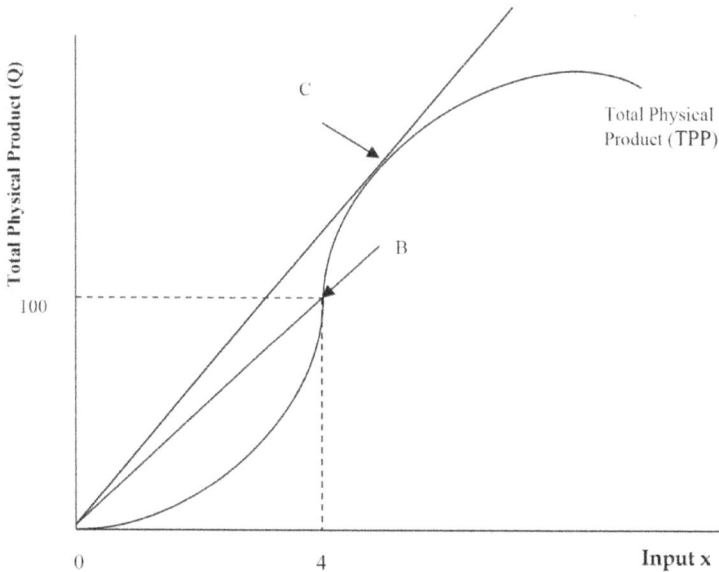

Figure 27: Derivation of the average product from total product

Relationship between total, marginal and average product

It is imperative that the student understands the relationship between total, marginal and average products. This relationship is shown in Figure 28. Note the relative slope of a tangent to TPP at point C, and the slope of a line going from the origin to that point.

The slopes are equal. This tells us that MPP = APP at that point. Beyond point C, both MPP and APP are falling, but MPP is less than APP and becomes zero at point E. When MP is zero TP attains maximum value at point D.

Three stages or regions of production can be distinguished from the relationship between TP, AP and MP. These are stages or regions I, II and III of production or production function. In stage I (From origin to point where APP=MPP), TPP is increasing at an increasing rate, APP and MPP are also increasing with APP reaching its maximum at the end of this stage while MPP attains its maximum before APP. In stage II (From point where APP=MPP to point where MPP = 0 or TPP is maximum), TPP is increasing at a decreasing rate, APP and MPP are both declining but MPP is below APP. In stage III (Beyond maximum TPP), TPP is declining, APP is declining but above MPP and MPP is declining and is negative.

These relationships show that a rational producer will use the variable input in stage I because the TPP, APP which measures efficiency of using the variable input are still increasing. Similarly, a rational producer will not go beyond stage II because in stage III, TPP and MPP are both declining. MPP is not only declining but negative.

If the a rational producer cannot stop in stage I of production because the efficiency of using the variable input measured by APP is increasing and also cannot produce in stage III because APP, MPP and TP are all declining, then the rational stage of production is stage II. However the determination of the exact point in stage II where the rational producer should produce require information on prices of the input and output as will be discussed later.

Output elasticity

This measures the responsiveness of the output Q to changes in the amount of variable input (X_1) used. It is defined as the proportionate change in Q with respect to X_1 i.e.

$$\omega = \delta (\ln Q)/\delta (\ln X_1) = (X_1\delta Q)/ (Q \delta X_1) = MP/AP$$

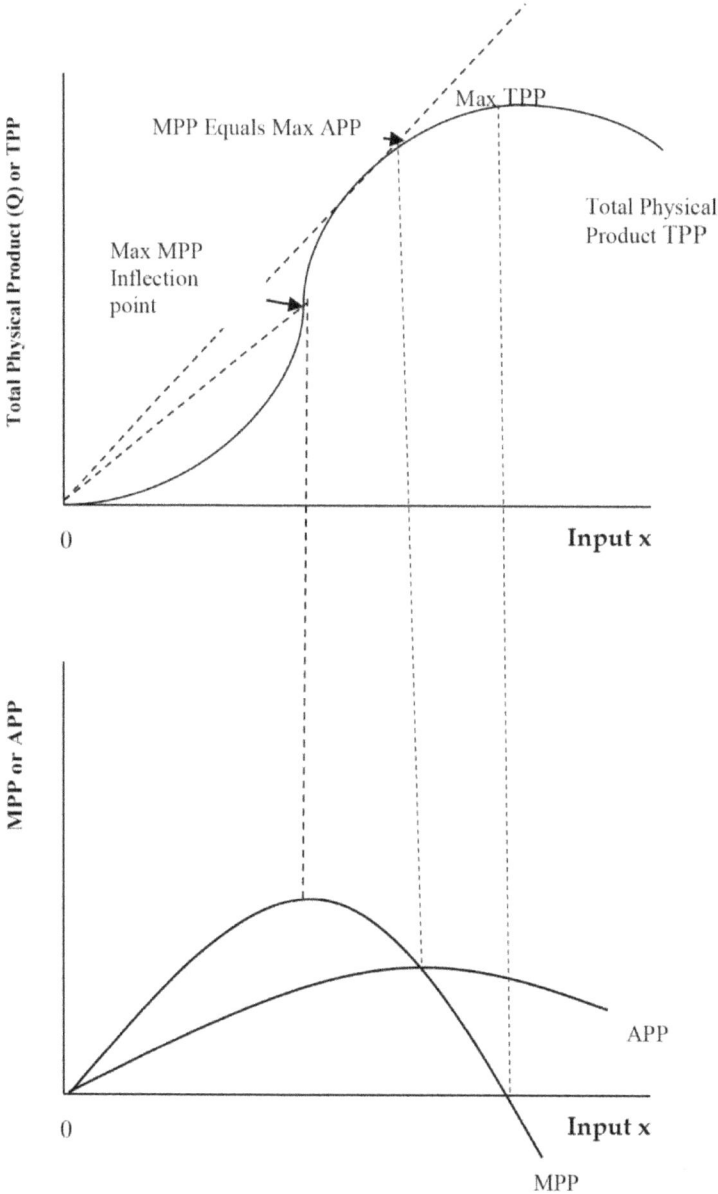

Figure 28: Relationship between total, average and marginal product

Introduction to the Two-Variable Case

Let us continue using the previous example of producing beans by varying amounts of labour input on a fixed plot of land. We introduce capital as a second variable input, while still holding land as a fixed input. Capital can be used in the production of beans in the form of irrigation, ox-ploughs, improved hand tools, tractors and chemicals.

In the case of two variable inputs the graphical representation of the relationship between output and inputs is slightly more complicated in the sense that we get three instead of two dimensions. Hence, instead of a total physical product (TPP) curve as encountered in the one input case, we have a TPP surface as shown in Figure 29. Movements along the TPP surface due to changes in capital and labour use are thus analogous to movement on a hill or an inverted bowl. As more of both capital and labour are used, we move more and more toward point B, or the summit of the hill, meaning that we climb to higher outputs level.

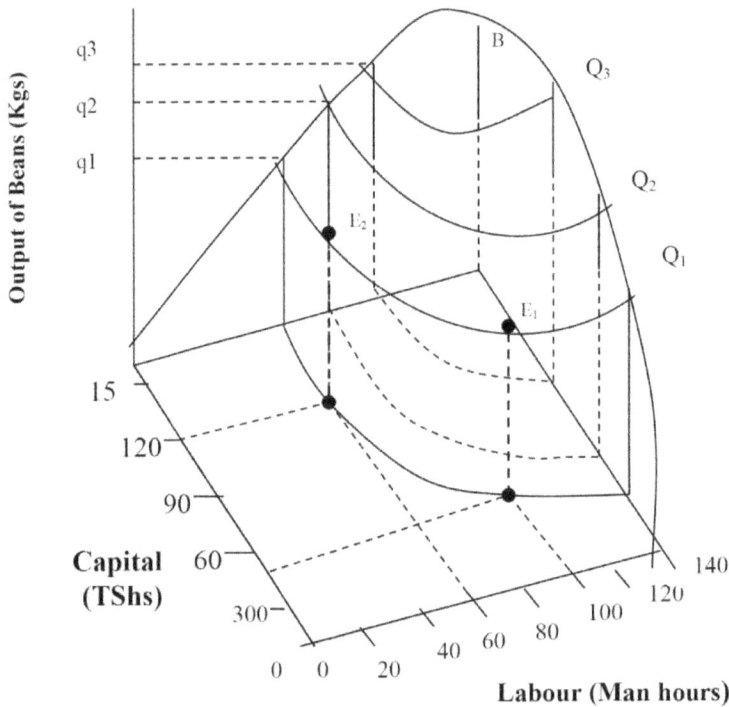

Figure 29: Illustration of the production surface with two variable inputs

We know that some farmers will employ more capital (capital-intensive techniques) than labour, while others, especially most of Tanzania's small-scale farmers, depend on their own labour (labour-intensive techniques). If you are inquisitive, you may already be asking the question; "what is the 'best' combination of capital and labour for producing beans on one acre of land?" And 'best' on the basis of what criteria? These questions will be answered shortly. In the meantime, let us elaborate on some simple concepts and tools to be used in that exercise.

Isoquants

Referring to Figure 29, when we move along the edge marked Q_1 in the direction of capital, it is like walking along a contour on a hill. We know that along a contour the height above a given reference point (e.g. sea level) is constant. In our example, a movement along Q_1 means that we are crossing points such as E_1 and E_2 on which the output of beans is fixed at q_1. Note also that as we move along Q_1 the combinations of labour and capital are constantly changing even though the output is fixed.

Such a contour is known as an *isoquant*, which is defined as a curve showing all combinations of inputs that produce a given quantity of output. It can also be defined as a locus of all combinations of variable inputs that produce same level of output.

As we move straight up the hill, we cross different contours (isoquants) representing different heights (levels of production). In our example, as we move from point 0 directly to point B, we progressively move to higher output levels represented by isoquants such as Q_1 and Q_2, and Q_3. We can, in fact, project the images of the isoquants onto the floor of our three-dimensional diagram and thereby get the same isoquant picture without the difficulty of drawing the total physical product surface. Figure 30 gives the simplification you will encounter in most textbooks.

Isoquant Map

A group of isoquants, as shown in Figure 30, is known as a isoquant map. As you move from left to right in the isoquant map, the output levels progressively increase. Thus Q_1 Q_2 Q_3, where Q_1, Q_2 and Q_3 are the output level of isoquant Q_1, Q_2, and Q_3, respectively. Note that the isoquants do not cross each other on an isoquant map. Can you explain why?

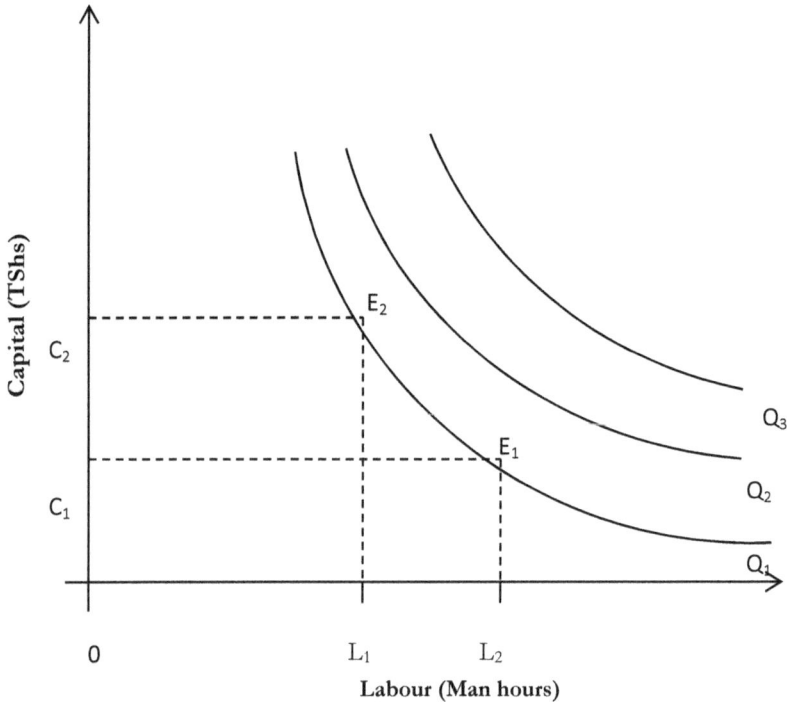

Figure 30: Two-dimensional illustration of the isoquant map

Characteristics of Isoquant

- It is strictly quasi-convex
- An isoquant for a higher output level lies to the right of an existing one
- The slope of the isoquant gives the rate of technical substitution (RTS)

Substitution among Inputs

In the production of beans, a farmer has a wide range of choices of combinations of capital and labor. Let us assume Q1 = 600 kg. This would be equivalent to 5 bags produced on the farmer's fixed land of one acre. If the farmer is not well endowed with capital, he can toil on his shamba for 100 man-hours with limited expenditure of TSh 450 in order to produce the 5 bags of beans. If, on the other hand, he has the financial means, he can spend less labour time (60 man-hours) and more capita (TSh 1,050) to produce the 5 bags of beans. This means that in the production of beans, it is possible to substitute capital for labour, that is, use more of capital and less of labour in order to produce the same output. This is the concept of input substitution which we shall reach shortly.

You should realize that not all production processes allow input substitution. Take the example of a secretary's output. If the secretary is producing 10,000 words per day, the addition of two or three extra typewriters will not change her/his daily output unless, of course, you increase the number of secretaries proportionally. Such a case is known as a 'fixed proportions' production function and its isoquants will be rectangular, as shown in Figure 31.

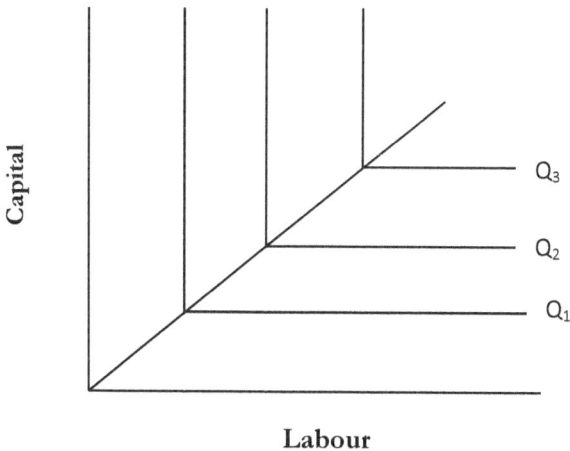

Figure 31: An isoquant map representing fixed proportions in production

Examples can also be found in agriculture. A tractor can only be driven by one worker at a time and a jembe can only be used by one person at a time. You may ask. "How about if the tractor (or jembe) is shared among several workers in the day? Would this still be a fixed proportions production process? The answer is "No", but the production process in this case would not allow *as much* substitution between labour and capital as in the case where the capital is highly divisible. Capital defined in a general form of expenditure on fertilizer, seed, hired oxen or tractor hours and chemical is more divisible than capital defined in units of machines and equipment for which substitution with labour is more restricted. We thus have production processes that allow no substitution among inputs, those that allow only limited substitution, and those which allow a wide variance in substitution. Two inputs can also be perfect substitutes of each other. The student should think of such examples and how the isoquants would appear.

The question may occur to you; "What is the importance of knowing how inputs substitute for each other?" The answer can easily be deduced from the following production scenarios. The developing countries (Tanzania included) have abundant labour but tend to be short of capital in their agricultural sectors. Agriculture is the backbone of many of these countries. It would therefore be necessary to know how much labour is needed to substitute for a unit of capital input without sacrifice in agricultural output.

A related development issue can be put as follows: To what extent can we withdraw labour from agriculture to industry, with the remaining farmers intensifying production through increased use of capital, without lowering the agricultural output? The policy questions of balancing rural employment with intensive use of capital (irrigation, tractorization, imports of fertilizer and agro-chemicals) can also be answered using knowledge of capital-labour substitution. Many more examples could be cited.

The Marginal Rate of Technical Substitution (MRTS)

Now that we know the importance of substitution among inputs, let us go into the mathematics of substitution. We continue with our simplified isoquant map and rename labour as X_1 and capital as X_2. Referring to Figure 32, we note that the output level Q1 represented by isoquant Q_1 can be produced using OX_{21} of capital and OX_{11} of labour, or by OX_{22} of capital and more labour, OX_{12}.

Definition: the marginal rate of technical substitution (MRTS) is defined as the rate at which labour can be substituted for capital (or vice versa) as the change in levels of use get infinitesimally small. In general, it is defined as the degree of substitution between two inputs in production.

Mathematically, MRTS $= \Delta X_2 / \Delta X_1$. As ΔX_2 and ΔX_1 approach zero,

MRST $= d\, X_2 / d\, X_1 = MP_{x1} / MP_{x2}$

Marginal rate of technical substitution is affected by the unit of measure.

Elasticity of Substitution

This is defined as the percentage change in X_2 / X_1 divided by percentage change in MRTS

i.e. Elasticity of substitution $= d \ln (X_2 / X_1) / d \ln (MP_{x1} / MP_{x2})$.

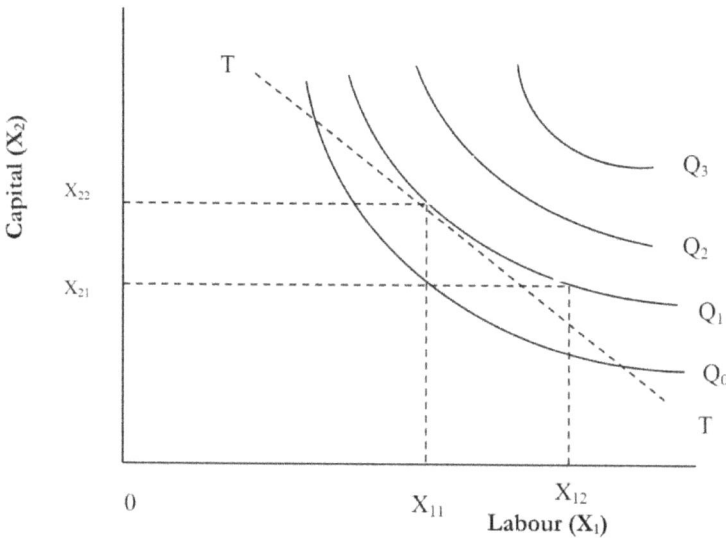

Figure 32: Illustration of marginal rate of technical substitution (MRTS)

Unlike the MRTS, elasticity of substitution is a value free measure of substitution between the two inputs.

The Long-Run

In the long-run all the input $X = X_1 \ldots X_n$ can be varied, assuming we have n quantifiable inputs. Even the land we have been holding constant in the bean production example can be varied. For the sake of discussion, let us assume that $n = 3$, and that the complete list of quantifiable inputs comprises only land, capital, and labour. Let us also assume that we are currently employing 1 ha of land, TSh 1,050 worth of capital, and 60 man-hours of labour. In our earlier example, the gave us 600 kg of beans. If we double the quantity of all inputs, will the output also double? This question brings us to the issue of *returns to scale*. Returns to scale is an economic term referring to the effect on output when all the inputs are increased by the same proportion.

Figure 33 is an Illustration of constant, decreasing and increasing returns to scale. Three outcomes are possible when the quantities of inputs are, for example, multiplied by two (doubled):

- Constant returns to scale describes the case where all inputs are doubled and output also double. In this case, successive isoquants are equally spaced as we move out from the origin on the isoquant map.
- Decreasing returns to scale is when all input are doubled and output increases but is less than double the original quantity. In this case, successive isoquants become closer and closer as one moves out from the origin.
- Increasing returns to scale is when output more than doubles as a result of doubling the quantity of all inputs. In this case, successive isoquants become further and further apart as we move out from the origin on the isoquant map.

Let us illustrate the above by an example. One farmer in Narok district practices mixed farming and has allocated only 10 ha to growing wheat. Another farmer grows only wheat on his 200 ha farm. Ignoring all other inputs other than land, do you think that the second farmer produces 20 times as much wheat as the first one? If he did, we would conclude that wheat farmers experience *constant* return to scale because multiplying land size by 20 results in 20 times as much output.

Since returns to scale have implications for long-run costs, as well shall see in later chapters, we would conclude from this example that small as well as large wheat farmers face the same long-run costs in producing wheat.

The policy implication of such a conclusion would be that subdivision of the large scale wheat farms would not adversely affect total wheat production.

The converse would be true if the 200 ha. farm produces more than 20 times the output of the smaller farm. Per hectare costs of production in this case would be lower in the large farm, thereby giving large farms a preference over small farms, and we would conclude that wheat farming enjoys economies of scale, a concept to be analysed in greater depth in the discussion on costs of production.

We hasten to caution that one cannot on the basis of casual inspection of a process or industry, conclude that it has constant, decreasing or increasing returns to scale. The issue must be empirically settled by analyzing technology, that is, how output is related to inputs. We can, however, speculate that indivisibilities of inputs (sometimes referred to as 'lumpiness' of inputs), ability to use more specialized technologies, as well as improved specialization and division of labour would lead to *increasing* returns as the size of operation increases. Problem of coordinating large scale operations may, however, lead to inefficiency, thereby accounting for *decreasing* returns to scale.

Mathematical Example[*]

We shall briefly describe in this section a production function that has over the years been assumed as underlying many production processes. The production function is known as the Cobb-Douglas production function, and many beginning students of production economics will benefit greatly from knowing something about it.

Given labour (L), capital (K), and land (M), as the variable inputs, the Cobb-Douglas production function takes the general form.

$$Q = AL^a_1 \, K^a_2 \, M^a_3$$

In which Q is the output, A is a constant term (intercept), a_1, a_2, and a_3 are parameters which vary from case to case, but each assumed to be a fraction less than one. Indeed, the problem is usually that of estimating these parameters.

If $a_1 + a_2 + a_3 = 1$, we have the case of *constant* returns to scale, if the sum is greater than one, we have *increasing* returns to scale, while *decreasing* returns to scale would be when the sum of the parameters is

---

[*]This is a slightly more advanced section which can be omitted without loss of continuity.

less than one. These results can be easily proven mathematically, but you need not worry about that now.

There are also other characteristics of the Cobb-Douglas production function which we can summarize as follows:

(a) For each input, the marginal product is equal to the average product multiplied by the corresponding parameter.
(b) The isoquants are convex from the origin, implying a declining rate of substitution between any two inputs.
(c) The total physical product curve for a given input, keeping other inputs constant, increases to a maximum, then starts to decline.
(d) Elasticity of output, defined as the percentage change in output arising from a one percentage change in input, is given by the inputs' parameters. For example, 1% change in capital input (holding land and labour constant) will lead to a 2% change in output.

Perhaps you can see why the Cobb-Douglas function has been so popular and useful: once the parameters are estimated, it is possible to make quick deductions about the firm's technological characteristics. But the real problem is first to acquire information from the firm's managers, or those kept by an agency such as the Central Bureau of Statistics, to enable estimation. That is, you have to estimate the unknowns: A, a_1, a_2 and a_3. We leave this task for graduate studies.

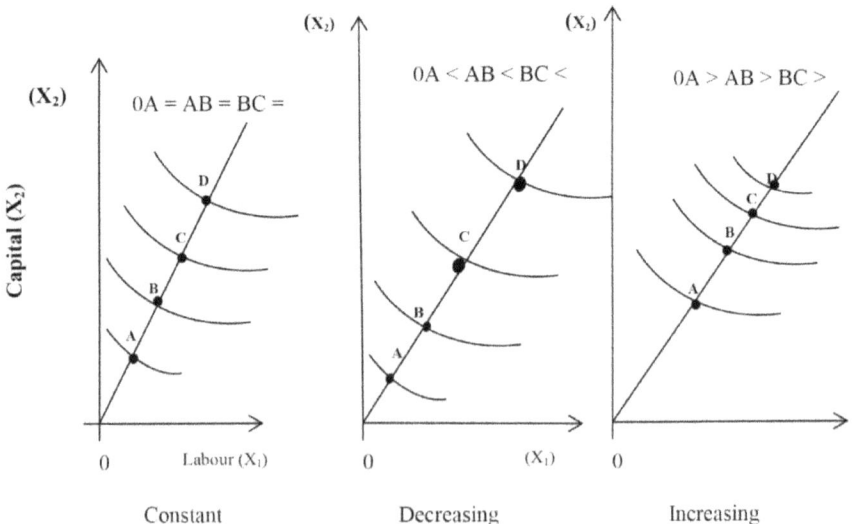

Figure 33: Illustration of constant, decreasing and increasing returns to scale

So far, we know that inputs can be varied to obtain different levels of output and that the relationship can be summarized in what is known as the production function. The production function tells us about the firm's technology. However, in order to know more about the firm and how it makes decisions, we need to know more than just about its technology.

How, for example, does the firm decide on what combination of capital and labour to use in producing a given quantity of beans? That is, given the output level Q, what is the cost-minimizing combination (the combination that does not violate a state budget) of labour and capital? This is the question we now want to look into.

We shall start by making the following assumptions about the firm:

a) The firm faces perfect competition in the input markets. Hence, input prices are taken as given (fixed)

b) Only two variable inputs, for example, labour (X1) and capital (X2) are considered.

c) The total budget is restricted to C.

You should be reminded that when we talk about a firm, we are talking about a profit-making organization such as East Africa Industries (EAI), Tanzania Breweries Limited (TBL), a Daladala owner or an Agribusiness firm. Some of these firms are monopolies, while others, such as daladala owners and farmers, operate under what is close to perfect competition. Under perfect competition, a single firm cannot influence the prices in the market. Thus in the case of a farmer producing beans, we are assuming that the farmer cannot, acting by himself, influence the price of capital (for example the interest rates charged by the lending institutions) or the going rate for hiring labour in his district or location. Budgetary constraints are familiar to everyone – even college students! Think of our allowance ('boom'). Is it always enough for all the things you would like to purchase: clothes, shoes, entertainment, transport and even books for those who are mindful of the future? We are definite that the answer is "No". The same constraint faces firms. And in the case of farmers, wrong choice can lead to family starvation. It is crucial therefore that the choice of inputs is done in a way that minimizes the costs of a given level of output or maximizes the output for a given level of costs. The farmer therefore faces a dull problem of minimizing costs and maximizing output. We shall shortly see how this comes about.

Assume that the price of capital (for example in the form of interest charges or opportunity cost) is P2 and the price of labour (the wage rate) is P1. How much of each input can we get, given a budget of TSh C*? For a start, a turn could go all the way and acquire only labour equivalent to C/P1 units, or only capital, C/P2 units. We know this would not be realistic because a bit of each input is needed in production, unless you are using robots (no labour) or using labourers without a single purchased tool!

In between these extremes, there are many possible combinations of labour and capital that could be purchased by the firm. But in each case, the total expenditure must add up to the total budget, C, as shown in the following equation:

$$P1X1 + P2X2 = C$$

where X1 and X2 are the two inputs and P1 and P2 are the prices. The equation can be reorganized to express capital (C2) as a function of labour (K1):

$$X2 = C/P2 - P1/P2.X1$$

This is the equation for a straight line with the intercept C/P and a negative slope of P1/P2 because C and the input prices are constants. The equation can be put in a graphical form, as shown in Figure 34.

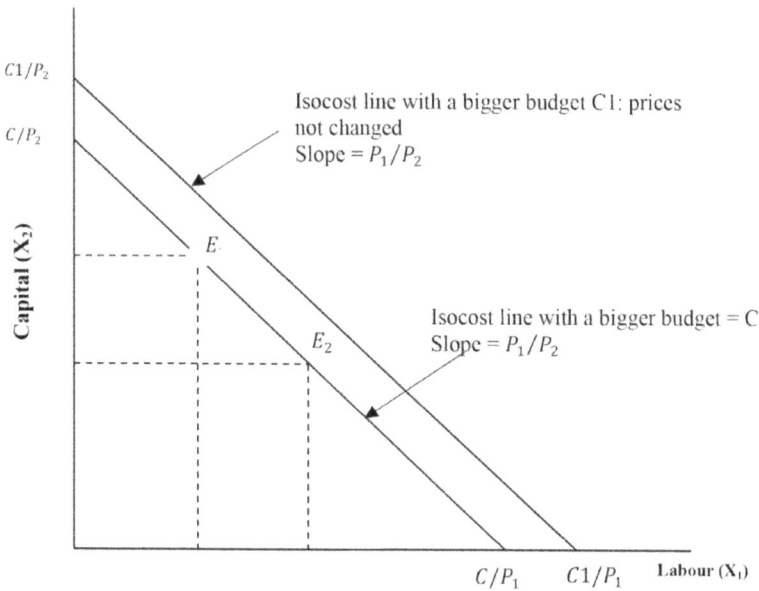

Figure 34: Isocost lines for different budgets
(Different combination of labour and capital, such asE1 and E2 can be obtained at the same cost, C)

The line so constructed is called an *Isocost* line. It is the same as the budget line we met earlier when we were discussing consumer theory. Note that with a bigger budget C_1, the isocost line shifts out to the right.

Definition: The isocost line shows all the possible combinations of inputs X_1 and X_2 that the firm can obtain for the same total cost. For example, the combination E_1 and E_2 can be obtained for the same total cost of C.

We are now ready to answer the question we posed earlier, namely, given a fixed budget, what is the optimal combination of labour and capital that maximizes output? The answer to this question can easily be obtained graphically by superimposing the isocost line on the firm's isoquant map, as shown in Figure 35.

We can identify two distinct regions in the diagram. These are OBC, including its boundaries, and the region beyond the line BC extending through the horizontal and vertical axes. The first region marked F is financially feasible, while the second, marked NF is not feasible because the budget does not allow it.

As we increase output from Q_1 to Q_4 in the direction of the arrowed line, we see that the maximum output we can attain is Q_2 and that the combination of inputs that maximizes output is A and K.

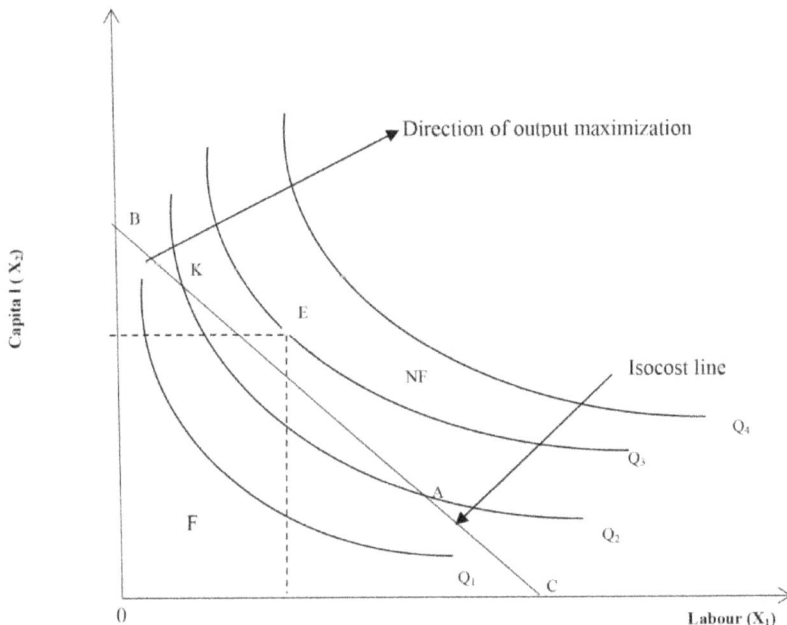

Figure 35: The maximization of output with a budget constraint

Optimization Rule

The point for optimizing input use is found by moving (maximizing) along the isoquant map until we reach a point such as E where the isoquant is tangent to the isocost line. At that point, the slopes of the isocost line and the isoquant are the same. Since the slope of the isoquant is given by MP_1/MP_2 and that of the isocost by P_1/P_2, this means that at point E, $MP_1/MP_2 = P_1/P_2$.

We also know that $\Delta X_2/\Delta X_1$, which we defined earlier as the exchange rate between capital (C_1) and labour (X_2) in production, or the MRST between X_1 and X_2, is equal to the ratio of the marginal products.

This means that at point E, the optimal point of combining X_1 and X_2, the substitution rate in production is equal to the substitutionrate in the input markets or.

$$\frac{\Delta X_2}{\Delta X_2} = \frac{MP_1}{MP_2} = \frac{P_2}{P_2}$$

Let us examine this last relationship more carefully. On the production side, $\Delta X_2 / \Delta X_1$, gives the number of units of capital given up when the use of labour is increased by one unit. That is if labour is increased by one unit, $\Delta X_2 / \Delta X_1$ units of capital must go. And we are saying that at point E, this is the same as P_1 / P_2 in the input markets. This latter ratio can be interpreted as the number or units of capital you could purchase by not purchasing a unit of labour costing P_1. In other words, the ratio gives the opportunity cost of labour.

For example, if capital input is taken to mean only expenditure on fertilizer costing P_2 = TSh 6 per kg, and labour wage is P1 = TSh 3 per hour, then the firm foregoes 3/6 kg or ½ kg of fertilizer for each man-hour of labour. We can put this differently: if the firm did not hire once extra man-hour of labour, it could spend the money saved to acquire ½ kg of fertilizer. Thus the opportunity cost of labour given as P_1 / P_2 is ½ kg of fertilizer. This exchange rate in the market must be equated with the exchange rate in production and that is what gives us the relationship,

$$MP/MP_2 = P_1/P_2 \text{ or } MP/P_1 = MP_2/P_2$$

What happens when the exchange rate in production is not equated with that in the factor markets?

The relationship given above can be interpreted as saying that for optimality in input combination, *the marginal product per shilling spent on labour must be equal to the marginal Product per shilling spent on capital.* Consider the example in Table 3.

Table 4: Substitution between labour and capital in production (hypothetical data)

	Inputs levels		Marginal products	
Steps	Labour (X₁)	Capital (X₂)	MP_1	MP_2
1	5	10	2.5	1.5
2	10	20	3.65	2.0
3	15	40	4.5	6.0
4	20	60	6.0	8.0
5	25	80	5.0	10.0
6	30	100	3.0	8.5
7	35	120	1.0	6.5

For this example, given that wage rate is Tshs. 75 per week, and capital is paid at the rate Tshs. 100 per week, what is the optimal combination of labour and capital?

The price ratio $P_1/P_2 = 75/100 = 3/4$.

Thus, all we have to do is check the marginal product columns for a ratio of $MP_1/MP_2 = 3/4$.

We end up with an interesting result: The ratio of the marginal products is ¾ at two different input combinations, namely $X_1 = 15$, $X_2 = 40$; and $X_1 = 20$ and $X_2 = 60$. So, there is no unique solution to our problem. Can you visualize the shape of the isoquant at the point where it is tangent to our isocost line?

In this example, the two input combinations or any convex combinations* between them) will be optimal because at those point $P_1/P_2 = MP_1/MP_2$, implying that $MP_1/P_1 = MP_2/P_2$. But now look at step 2 where 10 units of labour and 20 units of capital are used. At this step,

$$\frac{MP_1}{MP_2} = \frac{3.6}{2.0} > \frac{P_1}{P_2} = \frac{75}{100}$$

The implication of this is that:

$$\frac{MP_1}{P_1} > \frac{MP}{P2} \text{ or } \frac{3.6}{75} > \frac{2.0}{100}$$

This means that the marginal product per shillings spent on labour is greater than that of a shilling spent on capital, and the wise thing to do is to increase labour use. As we do this, capital use also rises but the latter's MP increases by a large percentage, thus correcting the imbalance. When input use is increased beyond step 5, we realize that:

$$\frac{MP_1}{P_2} = \frac{5}{75} > \frac{10}{100} = \frac{MP_2}{P_2}$$

and, in this case, we correct the imbalance by withdrawing labour. As we withdraw labour, its marginal productivity increases. (Think of the total product curve and how it is related to the MPP and APP curves).

We conclude this discussion by stating that in general, the rule for optimal input combination is that the marginal product per shilling spent on all inputs must be the same, that is:

$$\frac{MP_1}{P_1} = \frac{MP_2}{P_2} = \ldots = \frac{MP_x}{P_k}$$

Where k is the total number of inputs. The student should note that in determining the optimal combination of inputs, we kept the technology constant.

A change in technology would shift point E in figure 34 to a different location, assuming relative input prices do not change. Similarly, a change in relative prices for given technology would alter the input combination. To show your understanding, you should construct diagrams showing these changes.

The optimum situation described above can be arrived at mathematically as follows:

The problem for the producer is the maximization of output subject to a cost constraint. The producer would desire to obtain the greatest possible output for a given cost outlay.

Output $(Q) = f(X_1, X_2)$ and Cost outlay $(C) = P_1 X_1 + P_2 X_2 + b$
Where, P_1 is price of input X_1, P_2 is the price of input X_2 and b is cost of fixed input.

The problem is to Maximize: $Q = f(X_1, X_2)$
Subject to a given cost outlay: $C^0 = P_1 X_1 + P_2 X_2 + b$
Form the function

$$V = f(X_1, X_2) + \mu(C^0 - P_1 X_1 - P_2 X_2 - b)$$

At maximum output, we set the partial derivatives of V with respect to

X_1, X_2, and μ equal to zero.

$$\delta V / \delta X_1 = MP_1 - \mu P_1 = 0$$
$$\delta V / \delta X_2 = MP_2 - \mu P_2 = 0$$
$$\delta V / \delta \mu = C^0 - P_1 X_1 - P_2 X_2 - b = 0$$

Moving the price terms to the right of the first two equations and dividing the first by the second we obtain,

$$\frac{MP_1}{MP_2} = \frac{P_1}{P_2}$$

This equation states that the ratio of the MPs of X_1 and X_2 must be equal with the ratio of their prices.
The optimization conditions may be stated in several equivalent forms. Solving the first two equations for μ,

$$\mu = \frac{MP_1}{P_1} = \frac{MP_2}{P_2}$$

This equation states that the contribution to output of the last shilling spent on each input must equal μ.

Cost Minimization

In the discussions above, we solved the problem of optimal combination of inputs by maximizing output subject to a budget constraint. What would happen if the farmer was a millionaire, and he wants to produce 600kg of beans on one hectare of land using labour and capital? Does this mean that he will just throw money around and not care how much capital would be ideal to combine with a specified amount of labour? These questions fall in domain of cost minimization subject to a production constraint as indicated in Figure 36.
    In this case, it is the budget which is being reduced until we get one such as that represented by isocost line C_2, which is tangent to the

isoquant $Q = 600$kg. Isocost C_3 is not suitable because it entails too much money while C_1 has insufficient funds. The optimal input combination needed by minimizing cost. Alternatively, given a fixed budget, we can proceed as we did earlier by maximizing output. The two problems are interrelated, as you will come to appreciate when you take advanced course-work in linear programming.

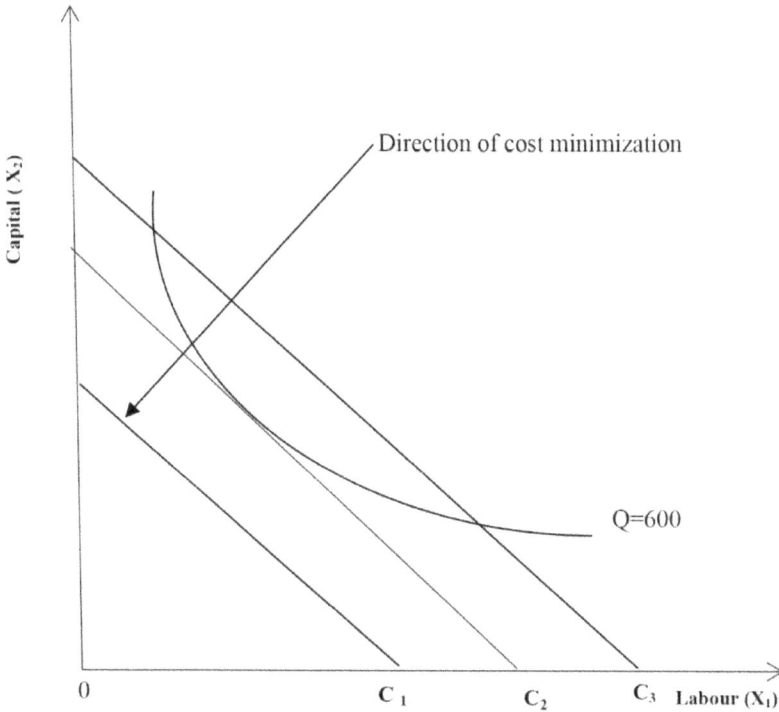

Figure 36: Cost minimization for a given level of output

Mathematically, the optimum condition for constrained cost minimization can be determined as follows:

The problem is to minimize cost of producing a desired level of output i.e.

Minimize $C = P_1 X_1 + P_2 X_2 + b$
Subject to: $Q^0 = f(X_1, X_2)$
Form the function

$Z = P_1 X_1 + P_2 X_2 + b + \lambda(Q^0 - f(X_1, X_2))$ and set the first partial derivative with respect to X_1, X_2 and λ equal to zero.
So

$\delta Z / \delta X_1 = P_1 - \lambda MP_1 = 0$
$\delta Z / \delta X_2 = P_2 - \lambda MP_2 = 0$
$\delta Z / \delta \lambda = Q^0 - f(X_1, X_2) = 0$

Moving the price terms of the first two equations to the right, and dividing the first by the second we obtain,

$$\frac{MP_1}{MP_2} = \frac{P_1}{P_2} \text{ or } \frac{MP_1}{P_1} = \frac{MP_2}{P_2} \qquad \text{or RTS} = \frac{P_1}{P_2}$$

The optimum conditions for the minimization of cost subject to an output constraint are similar to those for the maximization of output subject to a cost constraint. However, the multiplier λ is the reciprocal of the multiplier μ.

Economic Region of Production

In some cases, isoquants may have positively sloped segments, or bend back on themselves as shown in Figure 37. Above OA and below OB, the slopes of the isoquants are positive, which implies that increases in both capital and labour are required to maintain a certain output rate. If this is the case, the marginal product of one or the other input must be negative. Above OA, the marginal product of capital is negative, thus output will increase if less capital is used, while the amount of labour is held constant. The lines OA and OB are called ridge lines. No producer who seeks to maximize profit will operate at a point outside the ridgelines, since he/she can produce the same output with less of both inputs, which must be cheaper. For example operating at point D is more costly than operating at point C in the same isoquant because the producer requires greater amounts of both labour and capital at point D than point C. The area between the ridge lines OA and OB is called the economic region of production. No rational producer will operate outside this region.

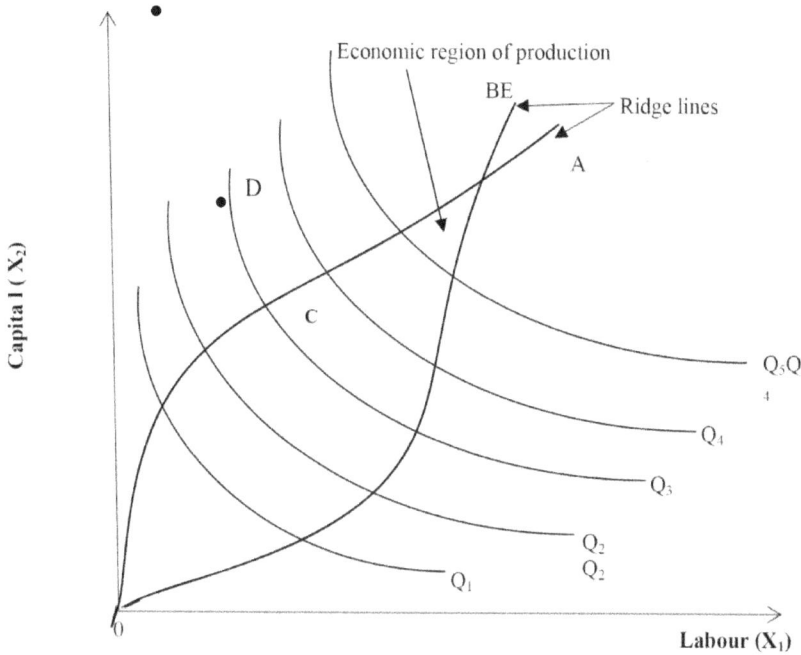

Figure 37: Economic Region of Production

Expansion Path

An expansion path is the locus of all tangency points or points of least costs combination of inputs on the isoquant map. A rational producer will select only input combinations along the expansion path.

Questions for Thought and Discussion

1. Does each isoquant in an isoquant map refer to

   a) A Different Level of Technology,
   b) A Different Output Level, or
   c) A Different Output for the Given Technology?

2. Explain the relationship between the relative prices of a named pair of agricultural inputs and opportunity cost.

3. Describe the factors which influence the shape and location of an isoquant.

4. Give two examples of practical applications of concept of substitution between two inputs?

5. In which possible ways will a change in technology affect a firm's optimal combination of inputs, ceteries paribus (assuming other factors are kept constant)?

6. Show how the law of diminishing marginal returns can be used to demonstrate why MRTS between capital and labour declines as more labour is substituted for capital.

7. The equilibrium market basket (consumer theory) and optimal combination of inputs (production theory) are frequently encountered concepts in microeconomics. Discuss the differences and similarities in the underlying derivation for these two concepts.

CHAPTER FOUR

Costs of Production

Introduction

Our eventual goal is to understand the behaviour of the individual business firm, and insight into how the private sector contributes to the functioning of the overall economy. It is, therefore, essential to understand thoroughly the costs of production and how these affect the decisions of the individual firm, be it the small firm producing maize, coffee, tea or bread, or larger firm, such as Welcome (Tanzania) Limited, producing more specialize products.

As in the previous chapter the basic assumption is that the individual firm wishes to maximize its profits. While there are certainly other goals of a producer, such as providing food for the family in the case of a small farm, or reducing the risk associated with certain business operations, it is nevertheless reasonable to assume that the individual firm will wish to maximize profits in so far as is consistent with these other goals.

In maximizing profits, the firm is concerned with the revenues it receives from its output, as well as with the costs of production. Costs of production are directly related to the production process, which we have just studied in the previous chapter. This chapter will investigate the costs of production as related to the production function, and as a prerequisite toward analysis of production and output decisions of the firm under various market structures.

We will be initially concerned with the 'short-run' as opposed to the 'long-run'. The short run is a period of time such that some factors, e.g. the size of plant or a piece of land, is fixed in supply. Thus, we are dealing with a situation where there are inputs which are fixed in supply.

The Relationship between Production and Variable Costs

The first type of cost, which we will analyze, is known as 'variable costs'. These are costs, which vary directly or depend on the level of production. The easiest and clearest way to illustrate the relationship between production and costs is to use the one variable input production function. We will assume a constant price for the variable input and observe how costs change as we vary the amount of input used.

Let us again begin by observing the same production function, which we have used, in the previous chapter. This is seen in the right-hand portion of Figure 38. On the left-hand side we now plot costs on the horizontal axis against output on the vertical axis.

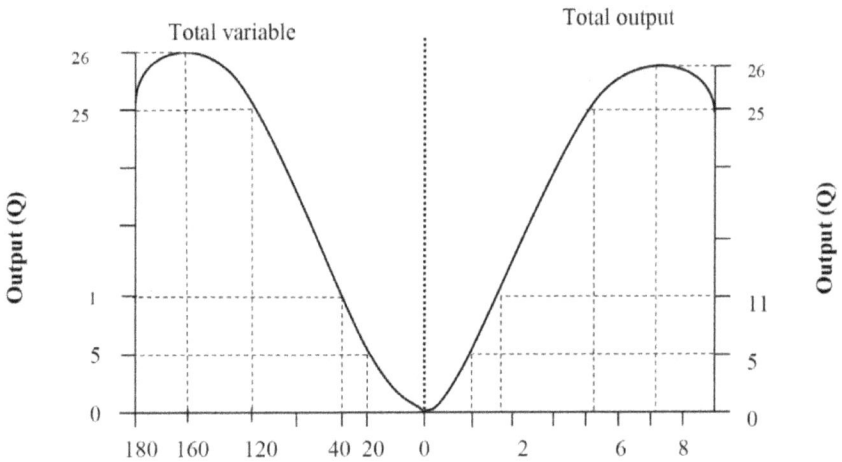

Figure 38: Illustration of total variable costs as related to the production function
(Note that the total variable cost curve is a mirror image of the production function)

As we move out to the right, on the X, or variable input axis, we obviously are increasing our production through the use of more variable inputs. However, these inputs have a cost. Thus, as we increase production, we are obviously incurring more costs. Again, these are variable costs, as they vary with the level of output. Let us assume that each unit of variable input costs TShs 20 per unit. We are now able to plot costs as a direct function of output. With our first unit of input, we produce 5 units of output. We can now plot 20 on the left panel against output of 5 on the vertical axis.

By adding our second unit of variable input, we produce a total of

11. Against this output of 11, we have a total of Tsh 40 in variable costs.

We can continue this process until we have a total variable cost function plotted against output, as shown in the above diagram. Notice how the cost function appears as a mirror image of the production function.

Note that the total variable cost curve 'bends back' beyond an output level of 26. This is analogous to the part of the total physical product curve which starts to decline. It would be irrational to add input to the production process, trying to produce more than 26 units of output if total production would fall. Hence, that portion of the production function is irrelevant. By the same reasoning, that portion of the total variable cost curve which bends backward is irrelevant, as one would not choose to produce an output of 25 by using 9 units of input at a cost of 180, when that same 25 units of output could be produced by using 6 units of input at a cost of 120.

Hence, that portion of the total variable cost curve, which bends backward, can be eliminated from consideration.

You should now analyze what would happen if the production function was raised. That is, suppose a new technique enabled twice the production for every unit of a viable input. What would this do to the cost function? (Remember to read the cost function as variable costs for producing a given level of output). By convention, the costs are normally plotted against output, with output placed on the horizontal axis. Thus, now that we have seen the close relationship between production and costs, we 'lift' the left-hand panel of the above diagram, and place it on its side so that it appears as in Figure 39. We now have our total variable cost function, which resembles an inverted 'S'.

Mathematically, Total Variable Cost (TVC) = f (P_x, Q), Where P_x is price of variable input X and Q is output. Under perfectly competitive market, P_x is constant because an individual producer cannot influence price. Therefore total variable cost is a function of output only i.e. TVC = f(Q)

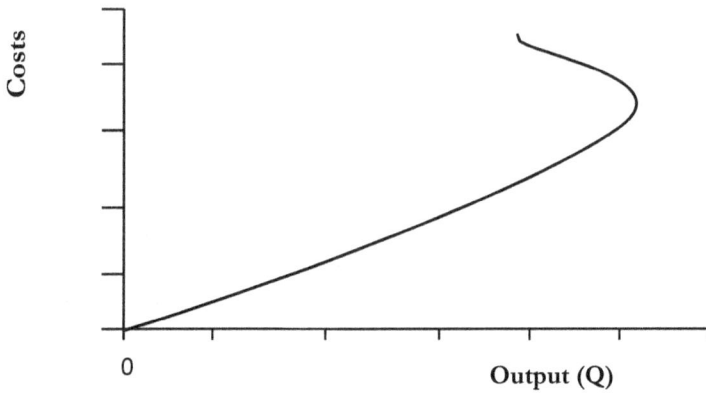

Figure 39: The conventional total variable cost curve

Note that the backward-bending portion in Figure 39, analogous to declining total physical product, is in the irrational stage and can be eliminated from consideration.

What would happen if, through an increase in technology, the production function was raised, i.e. more output could be produced with a given amount of input, as shown in the right-hand section of Figure 40.

As more is produced with a given input (at a given cost), a given amount can be produced with less input (at a lower cost). Recall that the cost function is a mirror image of the production function. When reading the costs against output, note that a given output is produced at a lower cost. Hence, an increase in technology, which raises the production function, lowers the cost function. Is that what you would intuitively expect? While this is early in our study of economics, does this lend insight into the special importance to developing nations such as Tanzania of technology which increases output (i.e. raises the production function) relative to inputs used?

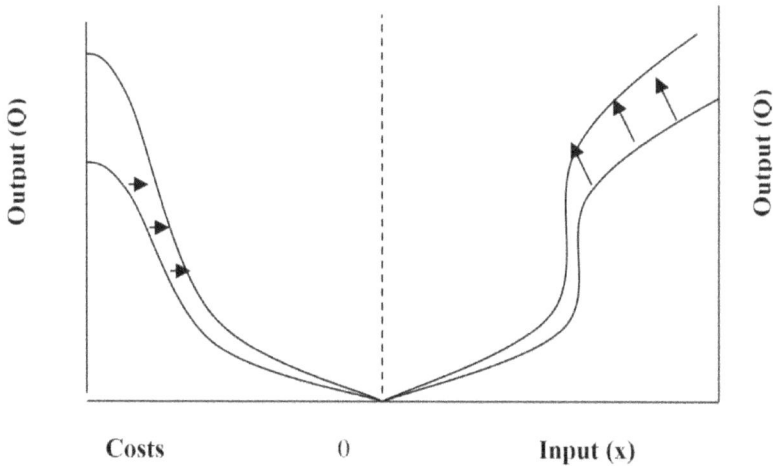

Figure 40: The effect of an increase in technology on the costs of production

Fixed costs

Thus far, our discussion has centred on variable costs, which are costs which vary with the level of output. Another category of costs is *fixed costs,* which are defined as those costs which are *independent of the level of output (Figure 41).* These costs are incurred whether any production occurs or not.

An example of fixed costs is taxes paid on land. These are fixed amounts and must be paid whether or not anything is produced on the land. Other examples would be interest payment on debt, and insurance on productive assets such as building. These charges are incurred whether or not production occurs. Fixed costs are graphed as a straight line, as shown in figure 41 which shows that they are independent of the level of production.

We can add fixed costs and variable costs together to attain total costs as shown in Figure 42. At any given level of output, total costs equal the sum of fixed costs plus variable costs. The vertical distance between variable and total costs is the amount of fixed costs.

Mathematically, Total Cost (TC) = f(Q) + b, where f(Q) is total variable cost and b is fixed cost.

Other important cost concepts are average total costs, average variable cost, average fixed cost, and marginal cost. *Average total cost is* the sum of average fixed and average variable costs. Marginal cost is the addition to total cost resulting from producing another unit of output.

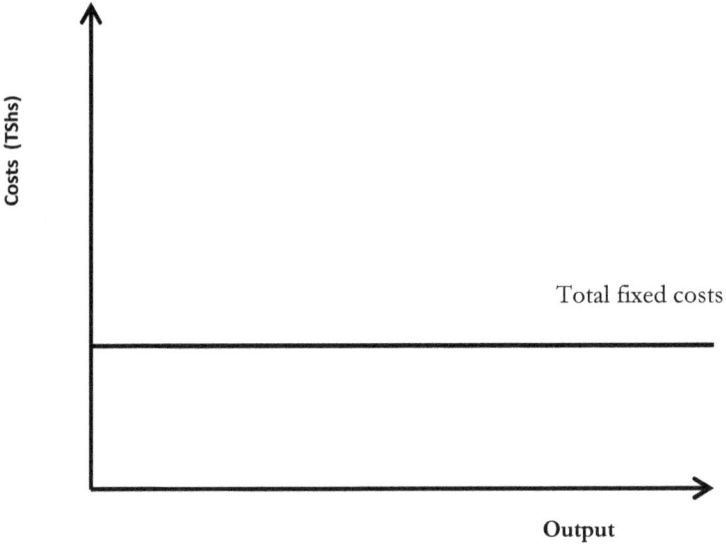

Figure 41: Fixed costs
(These costs are constant regardless of the level of production)

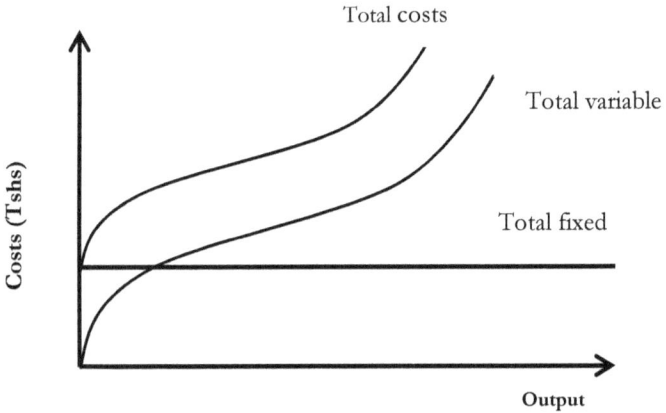

Figure 42: Total costs
(Total fixed costs are added to total variable costs to obtain total costs).

Mathematically,

Average Total Costs (ATC) = $\dfrac{f(Q)+b}{Q}$

Average Variable Cost (AVC) = $\dfrac{f(Q)}{Q}$

Average Fixed Cost (AFC) = $\dfrac{b}{Q}$

Marginal Cost = $\dfrac{df(Q)+b}{dQ}$

where Q is output and b is fixed cost

Let us illustrate these in more detail. Let us assume that we have just derived, from the production function, the variable cost figures, as shown in Table 4. Let us also assume that fixed costs are 100 to which we can add the variable costs to obtain the total costs as shown Table 4.

Table 5: Illustration of costs of production

Output	Total fixed cost	Total variable costs	Total costs	Average fixed costs	Average variable costs	Average total costs	Marginal costs
0	100	0	100				
1	100	50	150	100.0	50.0	150.0	50
2	100	90	190	50.0	45.0	95.0	40
3	100	140	240	33.3	46.7	80.0	56
4	100	196	296	25.0	49.0	74.0	56
5	100	255	355	20.0	51.0	71.0	59
6	100	325	425	16.7	54.1	70.8	70
7	100	400	500	14.3	57.1	71.4	75
8	100	480	580	125	60	72.5	80
9	100	520	620	11.	67.0	74.4	90
10	100	670	770	10.0	67.0	77.0	100
11	100	780	880	9.1	7.9	80.0	110
12	100	1,080	1,180	8.3	90.0	09.3	300

Let us now calculate average costs and marginal costs. We obtain average fixed costs by dividing total fixed cost by output (100/1), (100/2) etc. Similarly, we get average variable costs by output (90/1), (90/2) etc. We obtain average total costs either by dividing the total costs by output, or by adding the average variable cost plus the average fixed costs. The two approaches must give the same answer.

Notice that the average fixed costs decline throughout. This is necessarily so, as a fixed cost is divided by a larger output. The average fixed costs will continue to decline as output increases but will never reach zero.

In contrast, the average variable cost declines, reaches minimum, and then increases as output continues to increase. So, it is with average total cost. It declines, reaches a minimum, and then increases throughout.

Finally, we have the marginal cost, which is the addition to either variable or total cost, as a result of producing another unit of output. The addition (to variable and total costs) must be the same, as addition to fixed cost is, by definition, zero. Marginal cost is seen in this example to decline briefly, then rise.

The relationship between marginal and average costs is very significant. Note in particular, that as long as marginal cost is below average variable cost that average variable cost continues to decline. However, as soon as marginal cost rise above average variable cost, the latter cost rise.

The same relationship holds between marginal cost and average total cost. If marginal cost is lower than average total cost, average total cost falls. When marginal cost is above average total cost, average total cost rises (Figure 43).

Think of the marginal cost as the cost of producing an additional unit. If the cost of producing an additional unit is below the average cost, what must this do to the average cost? If the cost of producing an additional unit is above the average cost, what must this do to the average cost?

Diminishing Returns and increasing Costs

It is useful to consider the reasoning once again behind the shape of the cost curve. The key to the entire structure lies in the concept of diminishing marginal returns in the production function.

Remember how, as we add more inputs in the production process, that the additions to output decline. That is: $\Delta Q/\Delta x$ declines, where Q represents output and X represents input. If $\Delta Q/\Delta X$ declines, this means that $\Delta X/\Delta Q$ increases.

In other words, with diminishing returns, a given amount of input yields less in the way of output. This is the same as saying that it takes more by way of input to obtain a given amount of output. If this, is so, then the costs of attaining a given amount of output must be rising. In other words, marginal costs are rising. Thus, diminishing marginal returns directly imply rising marginal costs.

Recall also that the marginal cost will 'pull' average cost in its own direction. If marginal cost is below average cost, average cost will fall; if marginal cost is above average cost, average cost will rise. Thus, with diminishing marginal physical returns, implying rising marginal costs, this dictates that average costs will also rise if output is increased sufficiently.

You should carefully think through this concept, and thoroughly understand the link between the production function with its diminishing returns and increasing marginal and average cost.

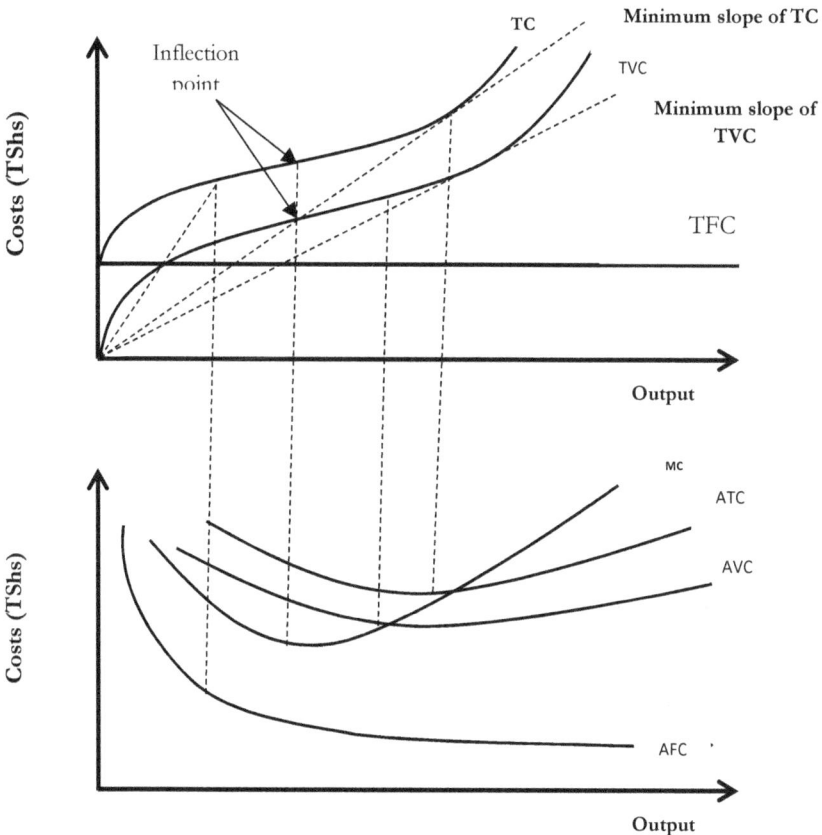

Figure 43: Relationships among cost curves

Long-Run Costs

So far, our analysis of costs has been confined to the short run, a period during which one or more factors of production is fixed in supply. By contrast, in the long-run, all inputs, or factors of production, are variable. Land, buildings, equipment, and other such inputs, which are fixed in the short-run, can be varied, or changed in amount, in the long-run

By changing the amount of such inputs, the firm changes its scale of plant". That is, suppose a farmer would acquire more land and buildings. The farmer would be applying variable inputs to more land and capital, or to a larger scale of operations. Suppose that SRAC, in Figure 44 represents the initial situation facing, the producer. Now, suppose that the producer decides to expand operations, and $SRAC_2$ represents the short-run average cost curve with the larger scale of plant. Note that the entire curve is set lower, and to the right of $SRAC_1$.

Suppose that scale of plant is expanded still further, to $SRAC_3$, giving rise to a still lower average cost curve, as output is increased. Which is the 'best' or most efficient scale of production? If a level of output of q_1 is desired to be produced, it appears that it could be produced at lowest cost with the size of firm indicated by $SRAC_1$. If however, q_3 were to be produced, it is clear that the larger firm, indicated by $SRAC_3$, would be the lowest cost.

Clearly, the minimum average cost associated with $SRAC_3$ is lower than that associated with $SRAC_1$ and $SRAC_2$, giving the large firm the cost advantage in production. This lowering of costs with the larger firm is called economies of scale. This might result from a more efficient use of capital and equipment.

If one is to build facilities for raising baconers, the average cost per baconer may well be less for a facility for 40, than for a facility of 20. If one is going to purchase a small tractor, the average cost of owning the tractor per unit of product may be less for 10 hectares than for 5. These are examples of production processes with economies of scale or increasing returns to scale. With constant returns to scale the minimum points of $SRAC_1$ and $SRAC_2$ would be the same, implying that there are no economies of scale to be gained by having large plant sizes.

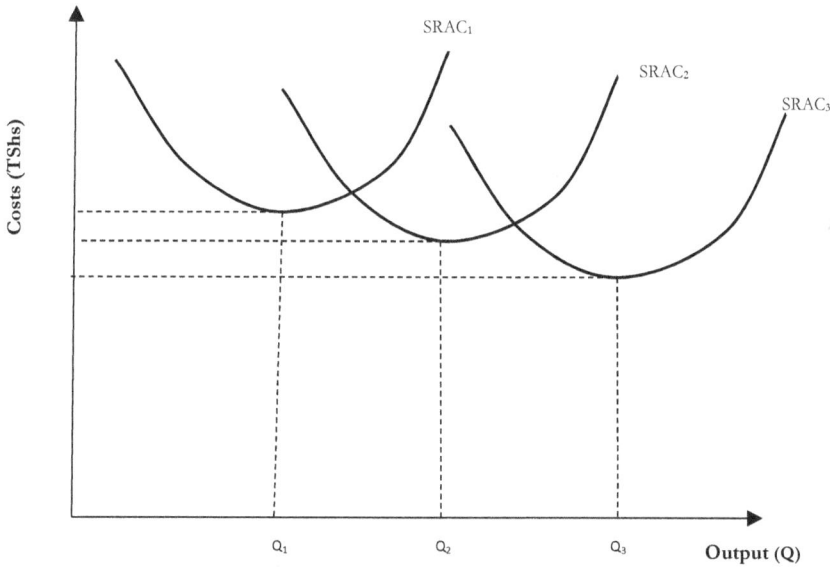

Figure 44: Illustration of three alternative sizes of plant with economies of scale
(As the size of plant increases, the product can be produced at a lower average cost.)

In fact, although we have shown three hypothetical scale of plant, there are an infinite number of possible scales of plant, resembling Figure 45. One can draw an 'envelope curve' tangent to the possible short run average cost curves. This is sometimes called the 'long-run average cost curve', or the firm's planning curve'.

Do 'economies of scale' continue to occur as the firm becomes larger? No, not necessarily. It depends on the nature of the industry. In some cases, economies of scale may be exhausted rapidly, and the long-run average cost curve flattens out. In others, the firm can become quite large before economies of scale are completely realized. For most industries, eventually, 'diseconomies of scale' would be expected beyond some point. These are thought to result from the difficulty and complexity of the management of large operations.

For such activities as growing vegetables, which are labour intensive, and which require many 'on the spot' management decisions, economies of scale may be exhausted fairly rapidly. Activities such as growing wheat, which are amenable to intensive capital use, may not fully realize economies of scale until a large operation is attained. We note, however, that experiences in South-East Asia, are casting doubt on this proposition. Along the same lines, at one time, it was believed that growing coffee and tea required a large firm. However, in Tanzania, it was proven to the surprise of many observers, that small producers, could produce at a cost which is competitive with large producers.

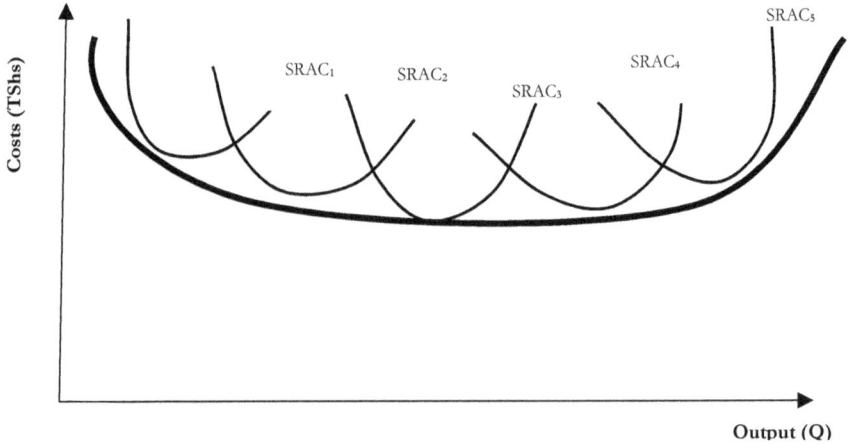

Figure 45: The firm's long-run average cost, or 'planning curve
(There exists an infinite number of possible scales of plant in the long-run.)

The relationship of efficiency to land holdings of various sizes would appear to be an issue of significant importance to Tanzania. What do you suppose the LRAC is like for the enterprise with which you are most familiar? Can you explain why this might be the case? Long run cost curves may vary in shape depending on the long run production function. Figure 46 shows possible long run cost curves.

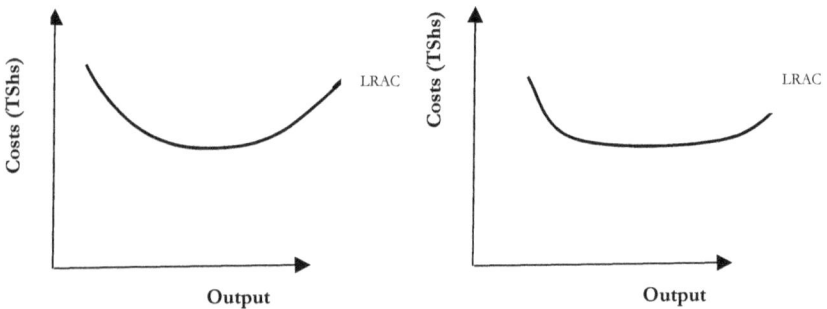

Figure 46: Possible long-run cost curves.

Questions for Thought and Discussion

1. Explain in your own words what is meant by fixed and variable costs. Given examples of each for an enterprise with which you are familiar. Exactly how do marginal and average variable costs relate to total costs?
2. Explain in your own words how diminishing returns relate to increasing marginal costs. What are the implications of rising marginal costs for production on an individual farm?
3. Why must marginal cost cut average variable costs and average total costs at their lowest point?
4. If a train costs TShs 800 and takes 12 hours, and a plane costs Sh. 1,500 and takes 2 hours, why might the businessperson find it less costly to take the plane?
5. With the cost data in Table 5, compute total costs, average fixed costs, average variable average total costs and marginal costs. Plot these on graph paper. Assume fixed costs to be 50.

Table 5: Total variable costs for given level of output

Q	TVC
0	0
1	100
2	190
3	270
4	340
5	420
6	510
7	610
8	720
9	840
10	990
11	1190

6. Draw a total cost curve with a constant marginal cost and show on it the average cost curve.
7. Can you show, without the use of diagrams, how average cost and marginal cost are related to average product and marginal product, respectively?
8. Describe the factors affecting the shapes of the short-run and long-run average cost curves.

9. Using a named example, show how economies of scale and returns to scale are related. Has the law of diminishing returns got anything to do with these two concept?

CHAPTER FIVE

Theory of Supply

Introduction

L ike demand, supply is another relationship between price and quantity. It refers to various quantities produced and made available for sale at various prices during a particular time period. As we have pointed out in the previous chapter, costs of production are directly related to the production process and the cost of production depends on the level of technology and on the relative prices of the factors of production. The supplier has the incentive to use factors of production in such a way as to minimize the costs of production for a given level of output. For example, the supplier of beef will attempt to minimize the costs of production for a given level of beef produced. However, in maximizing profits, the firm is concerned with the revenues it receives from its output, as well as with the costs of production. Since revenue is a function of quantity of product produced and price of the product, the firm maximizes profit by selling a quantity for which marginal cost of its production equals prices. The firm will not supply if the price is less than the abscissa of the intersection of marginal cost and average cost curve. The supply curve is obviously up-sloping. In this instance, price must be equal to minimum average variable cost or greater before any output is supplied.

This chapter discusses elements of supply, different supply functions, factors influencing supply, and elasticity of supply.

Elements of Supply

As stated above, the supply of a product is basically a relationship between price and quantity which a producer is willing and able to produce and make available for sale in the market during some specified time period. All else being equal, there is a direct relationship between price and quantity that producers are willing to make available for sale in the market. As price rises, the corresponding quantity supplied rises; as price falls, the quantity supplied also falls. This particular relationship is called the law of supply. It simply tells us that producers are willing to produce and offer for sale more of their product at a high price than they are at a low price. Why? Like the case of demand, this again is basically a commonsense matter. Unlike the consumer who is on the paying end of the product's price, the supplier or producer is on the receiving end of the product's price. To him, price is an inducement or incentive to produce and sell a product. The higher the price of the product, the greater the incentive to produce and offer in the market.

Just as we did for demand, the relationship between price and quantity supplied can be seen clearly when drawn as in Figure 47. Again by convention, quantity is placed on the horizontal axis and price on the vertical axis. As with demand, the points of the supply schedule can be plotted in a diagram, as depicted in Figure 47. The rationale for the direct relationship between price and quantity is that a farmer, or other producer, will have the incentive to produce greater amounts as the price, which is the *incentive* or reward for increasing production. Again, note that the 'all else being equal' condition holds in the relationship shown in Figure 47. As the other conditions in the economy change, the price-quantity relationship can also be expected to change and will be discussed later.

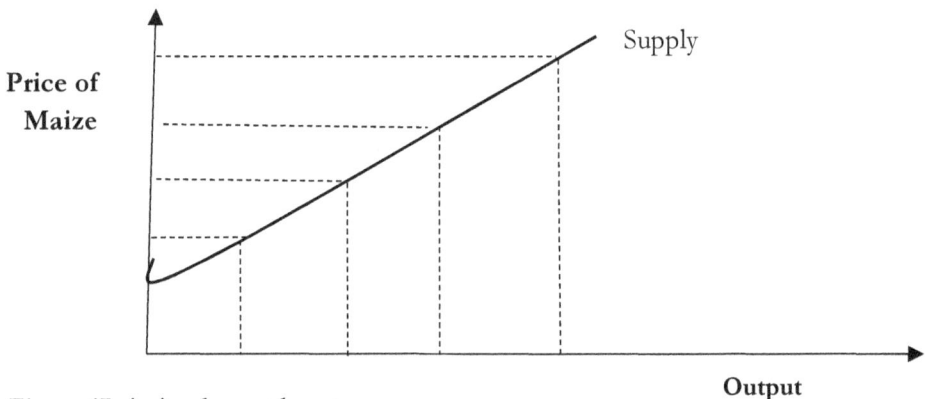

Figure 47: A simple supply curve
(Price and quantity vary directly)

Types of supply functions

Supply functions for an individual firm can be defined for (i) a very short run period during which output level cannot vary, (ii) a short run during which output level can be varied but plant size cannot, and (iii) a long run in which all inputs are variable.

Very short period

This is also called the market period. The supply curve is perfectly inelastic. The supplier will sell his entire output at the prevailing price i.e. assuming no stock carryover.

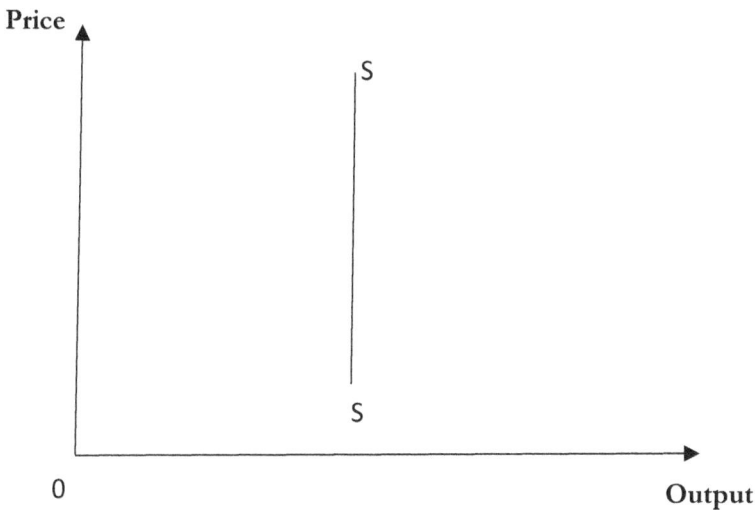

Figure 48: Very short run supply function

Short-run supply

We have seen that the firm will have the incentive to produce as long as it meets its average variable costs. Thus, in Figure 49 the individual firm's short run supply function (curve) is identical with that portion of its short-run MC curve which lies above the minimum point of the AVC curve. Recall that at prices below the minimum AVC, the firm does not produce at all. Hence, quantity supplied would be zero at all prices less than the minimum AVC.

The market supply curve is the sum of the individual firm short-run supply curves, and of course has an upward slope, as do the individual short-run supply curves.

You should once again go through the reasoning as to why the firm will produce to the point of MC = P, and why the marginal cost curve, above the point of minimum average cost, is the firm's short-run supply curve. Above the minimum average cost $S_i = f(P)$. Below the minimum average cost the supply $S_i = 0$.

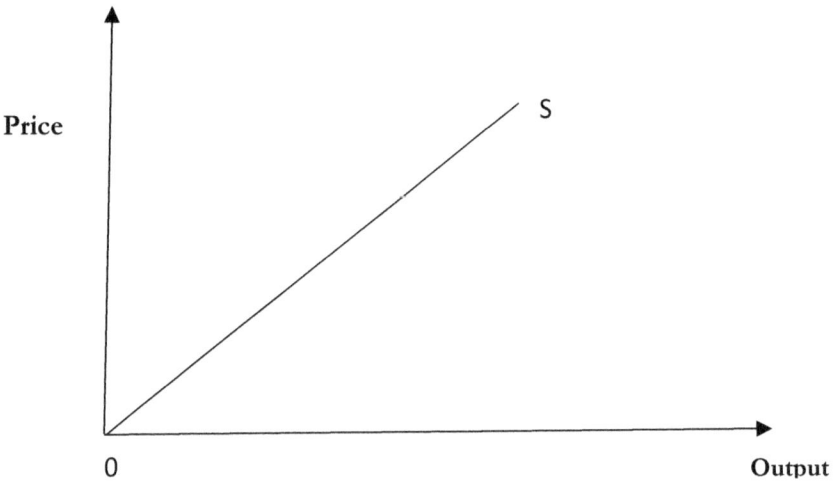

Figure 49: The purely competitive firm's short run supply curve
(As the firm produces to the point when MC= P, the marginal cost curve above minimum average costs represents the firm's supply curve)

Long-run supply functions

We have noted that under pure competition, entry and exit of the firm is relatively easy. What would happen if profits are seen as in Figure 50 with a price of P_o? If this was to occur, additional producers would have the incentive to enter the market. This would have the effect of increasing the industry supply curve to S_1. As this occurs, price would be driven down to P_1, where it reaches minimum average cost. At this point, new firms would no longer have the incentive to enter the industry.

But how can firms survive if they are producing at a point, which just covers their total costs? The answer lies in the distinction between what economists call 'pure' as opposed to 'normal' profits. Normal profits are those which are just sufficient to keep the producer in that particular enterprise or line of production. Were it not for that 'normal' profit are producer would go out of business. The total costs include the imputed, or implicit, costs, the 'payment to himself' which the entrepreneur takes to account for opportunity cost of his time and effort, as well as payment to him as a risk taker. Thus, when the firm is in equilibrium at point q_1. With the marginal revenue just covering the average total costs, account has already been taken of the incentive to stay in that line of business and we say that the firm is making ' normal' profits.

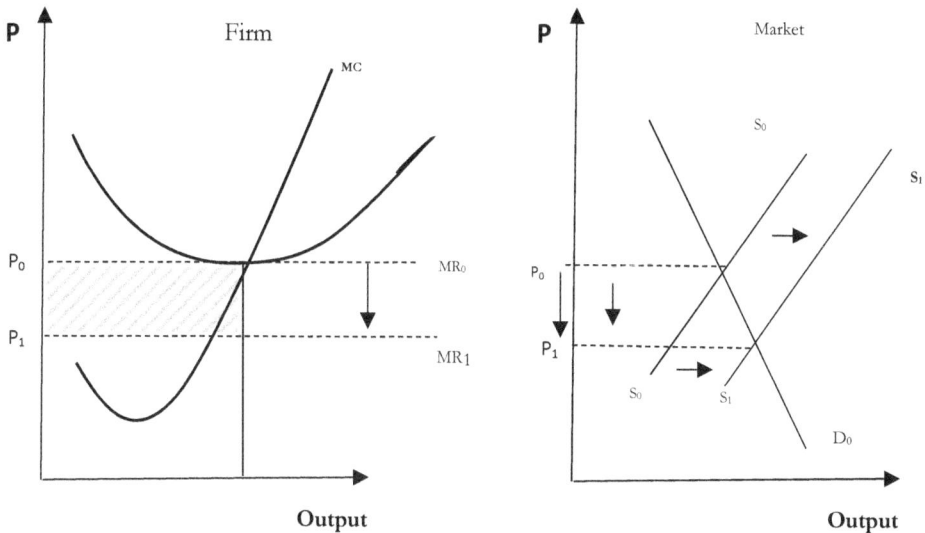

Figure 50: Long-run equilibrium under pure competition
   (In the long-run, pure profits tend to be reduced to zero under pure competition)

In contrast, marginal revenue, such as MR_0, would lead to pure profits equivalent to the shaded area of Figure 50 and would give additional producers the incentive to enter that line of production, thereby increasing market supply and driving down price. It is for these reasons that above-normal profits cannot last for long in purely competitive industry.

Losses have the opposite effect, driving people out of that line of production. This reduces supply, and exerts an upward effect on prices, thereby returning firms toward normal profits. You should attempt tograph the situation with initial losses to firms, and the longer run effect on price changes, restoring the industry toward long-run equilibrium.

The shape of the long run supply curve will depend on the nature of costs of the industry.

1. Constant cost industry

If an industry is in equilibrium and the demand for the commodity increases, output price will increase leading to excess profits. This will in turn attract new firms into the industry. Under the assumption of constant cost industry, new firms will get into the industry and increase output until the initial price has been restored. In this case the long run supply curve will be perfectly elastic at the initial price.

2. Increasing cost industry

Under the assumption of increasing cost (increasing industry supply price) as the industry adjusts through the entry of new firms, input prices increase, thus shifting cost curves upwards. As the industry supply increases, the supply curve shifts to the right but because the cost of production increases, equilibrium is established at a higher price. In this case the supply curve is positively sloped.

3. Decreasing cost industry

In a situation of decreasing cost industry, an increase in demand for the product will lead to an initial increase in price which will attract additional firms because of excess profits. But as more firms get into the industry, scale economies accrue to the industry, thus decreasing the cost of production until a new equilibrium is established at a lower price. Thus long run industry supply curve will have negative slope.

Factors Affecting Supply

What determines the position of the supply curve? Just as with demand, there are forces in the economy which may cause the supply curve to shift, as shown in Figure 51.

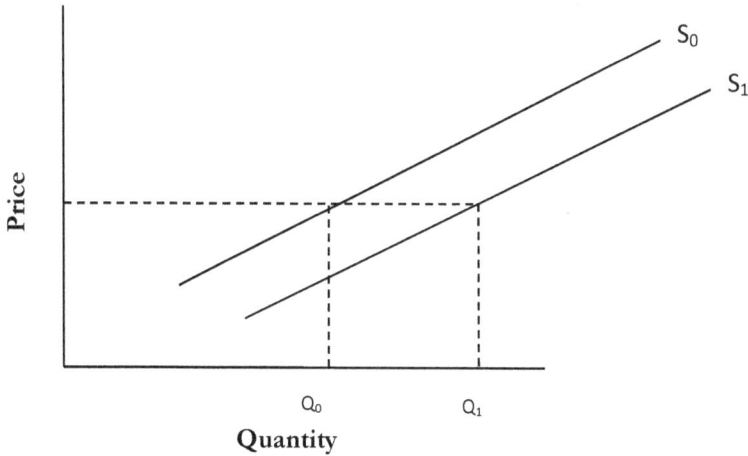

Figure 51: A shift in supply (*With an increase in supply, from S0 to S1, a larger quantity is purchased at any given price*)

A shift of the supply curve to the right is referred to as an *increase* in supply as, at any given price, a greater quantity of product will be produced and made available for sale. A shift to the left is a decrease in supply as, at any given price, a smaller quantity will be produced and made available for sale.

What factors are responsible for the position of the supply curve and for possible changes in supply? Let us review the basic factors affecting supply.

Number of producers

The supply curve for the individual slopes upward (we have seen precisely why when we were discussing elements of supply) and represents the amount the individual will produce at a given price. The market supply is the sum of the individual supply curves, or the total amount which producers would make available for sale at various prices. As more farmers produce maize, the amount made available for sale at any given price will increase, all other factors, such as weather, being equal. If producers should switch from maize to coffee production, however, the market supply of maize would decrease and the supply of coffee would increase, again all else being equal.

Level of technology

The level of technology is an extremely important factor in determining the level of supply, and for increasing supply over time. If, for example, a higher yielding variety of seed is made available, by using the same labour, cultivation and other inputs, the level of maize production, and hence supply, is increased. Thus, improved technology is an important source of increased supply and is a necessary force for driving economic growth in developing countries.

Prices of related goods

As we have noted throughout this analysis, resources have alternative uses. If the price of coffee is expected to rise relative to the price of maize, producers would have an incentive to shift to coffee production. In this event, less maize would be produced, thereby shifting supply to the left.

Prices of inputs

As prices of factors such as labour, fertilizer, chemicals and other inputs of production decrease, all else being equal; producers would tend to use more of them. Thus, with a decrease in the price of inputs, at any given price of the product, more would be produced, which constitutes an increase in supply. Conversely, as the prices of these inputs increase, producers would use them more sparingly. Thus, an *increase* in price of inputs will cause a *decrease* in supply *of the product* for which these inputs are used, all else being equal.

Expectations

If farmers expect the increase in coffee prices to be only temporary, it is unlikely that they will be induced to undertake the capital investment and wait the necessary time for coffee plants to mature and produce. Only if prices are expected to stay high will producers have the incentive to make the necessary investment and incur the necessary costs involved in such an enterprise. If producers expect high and rising prices in the future, this would be expected to increase supply. If producers expect falling prices, this would be expected to decrease supply as farmers would tend to shift production out of unprofitable crops to crops expected to be more profitable.

Other factors

In the case of agriculture, non-economic factors such as weather obviously play a major role in determining supply. In addition, producers have incentives other than those offered by the market-place. The need for home-produced food for the family will require reserving a portion of the *shamba* for the family garden, for example. It is rational to opt for the security of growing that portion of one's food supply, as opposed to devoting those resources to crops and dealing with the uncertainty of the market-place for the family's food.

Other factors, such as the certainty of payment, are also important. A farmer may prefer a lower price with immediate and certain payment upon sale, as opposed to a higher price which may not be received for some time or, indeed, at all.

For this reason, attempts to increase supply by raising prices for commodities such as cotton and pyrethrum may be unsuccessful if farmers anticipate that payments may be made late, or at an uncertain date.

And finally, there are social and cultural factors, such as the desire of the *Maasai* to hold cattle as a form of wealth. Increases in cattle prices may not be effective in inducing sale of cattle due to the importance the *Maasai* place on holding cattle. This is an example of where response to markets and prices may not conform to what are considered 'conventional responses' and it is another example of why culture must be understood when applying economic principles.

Elasticity of Supply

Elasticity of supply is a similar concept to elasticity of demand. It refers to the percentage change in quantity supplied relative to a percentage change in price, or $\%\Delta Q/\%\Delta P$.

The major determinant of elasticity of supply is the length of the time period under analysis. In the short run, supplies of most products are fixed, or can be varied but little. Consider the example of coffee. Over any given time period, only a given amount of coffee exists because of a fixed acreage of the crop. Therefore, the quantity supplied cannot respond to an increase in price. If demand suddenly increases, as occurred for Tanzanian coffee when Brazil experienced bad weather and short supplies, the price increased dramatically because producers were unable to respond in the short run.

Over a season, however, supply is somewhat more elastic as producers can be expected to take good care of their crop through better husbandry methods and thus maximize yield to respond to favourable prices. Over a much longer period, producers can plant more coffee, and nurture the plants to maturity, thereby increasing supply (Figure 52).

The same reasoning can be applied to falling prices. You should test your understanding of this by asking what happens to the supply of coffee and its price is response to falling demand in the short, intermediate and long runs.

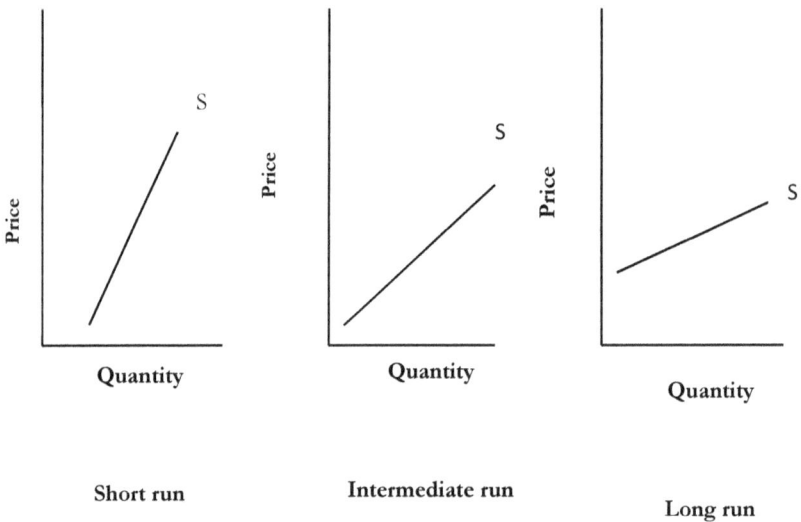

Figure 52: The relationship between time and elasticity of supply *(In longer time spans supply is more elastic because producers are better able to respond to changing prices)*

Questions for Thoughts and Discussion

1. A firm has a cost function given by $c(y) = 10y^2 + 1000$. What is its supply curve?

2. If a firm has the cost function given by $c(y) = 10y^2 + 1000$. At what output is average cost minimized?

3. If the supply curve is given by $S(p) = 100 + 20p$, what is the formula for the inverse supply curve?

4. A firm has a supply function given by $S(p) = 4p$. Its fixed costs are 100. If the price changes from 10 to 20, what is the change in its profit?

5. If the long-run cost function is $c(y) = y^2 + 1$, what is the long run supply curve of the firm

6. Is it ever better for a perfectly competitive market firm to produce output even though it is losing money? If so, when?

7. If average variable costs exceed the market price, what level of output should the firm produce? What if there are no fixed costs?

CHAPTER SIX

Demand – Supply (Market Equilibrium) and Applications

Introduction

The wants of consumers play a major role in driving the market system. This notion is known as 'consumer sovereignty'. What is produced is largely determined by what people are willing and able to pay for. What they are willing and able to pay for helps to determine market demand and prices. If people desire beef, and have the means with which to pay for it, this will offer an incentive, through the price and market mechanism, for its production. Prices vary not only according to how much people desire a product but how readily others are willing and able to supply it. If beef is difficult and costly to produce this will tend to keep prices high. Such factors, as we already seen in the previous chapters, constitute the basic elements of demand and supply.

An understanding of these factors lying behind supply and demand will go far in helping us understand market forces. We now turn to the important matter of price determination.

Determination of Equilibrium Price

When we put together the supply and demand curves, we have the means for determining equilibrium price. Equilibrium price is the price at which the quantity offered for sale equals the quantity demanded by consumers in the market. This is an important price because it 'clears the market', leaving no shortages or surplus. Let us see why there is only one equilibrium, or market clearing price, and how it is determined.

Suppose that in our example, as illustrated in Figure 53, the market price was 8. At that price our demand schedule tells us that consumers would purchase 300 units of that product. At the price of 8, our supply schedule tells us that producers would make available for sale 500 units. Note that a price of 8 would bring forth a greater number of units supplied than demanded, thereby leaving a surplus. If producers wanted to get rid of unsold goods, what would they be forced to do? They would the forced to lower the price, thereby creating downward pressure on the price level.

Continuing our illustration, now suppose that the price is below equilibrium, at 6, for example. At that price our supply schedule tells us that 300 would be made available for sale, whereas our demand schedule tells us that 500 would be demanded. Thus, there would be a shortage of 200 at *a price of 6* . If consumers were willing to pay more than the price of 6 for the amount available, what kind of pressure would be placed on price? It should be obvious that if consumers were willing to pay more, and there is a shortage of goods, that the price can only rise. (The student may now consider what happens to prices in 'parallel markets', that is, in markets outside normal or legal channels, if there is a shortage of goods).

Again, note that given the supply and demand schedules, there is only *one price* at which the quantity demanded equals the quantity supplied, leaving no shortage or surplus. In our diagram this occurs at a price of 7. At this price, there is no shortage or surplus, and we say that the market has cleared. The tendency of prices, determined by the interaction of supply and demand, to clear the market is referred to as the rationing function of prices in the sense that it automatically rations the production to the buyers leaving no shortage or surplus.

Of course, there are no such written or posted schedules of supply and demand in the market-place. Markets existed and functioned long before scholars described this mechanism in such detail. Prices are 'discovered' through the unrestrained interaction of buyers and sellers. The usefulness of this illustration is to assist in identifying and illustrating the relevant forces operating in the market. As these are understood, other factors can be considered, and more complicated questions can be analysed. This powerful tool provides useful and important insights into many real questions of economic policy.

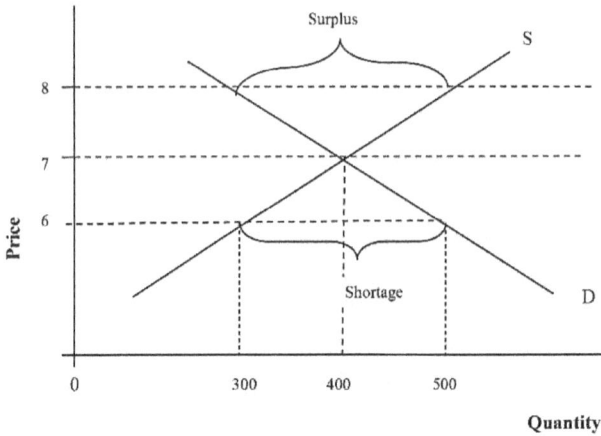

Figure 53: The concept of equilibrium rice (*At the equilibrium price, quantity demanded equals quantity supplied, with no shortages or surpluses*)

Shifts in Supply and Demand

Continuing with perfectly competitive markets, let us recall that demand and supply can shift over time. We arrived at an equilibrium price and quantity of 7 and 400, respectively, in the previous example. Now, suppose that the seasonal rains were shorter than usual, and have resulted in a short supply. That is, the supply curve shifts to the left, as shown in Figure 54.

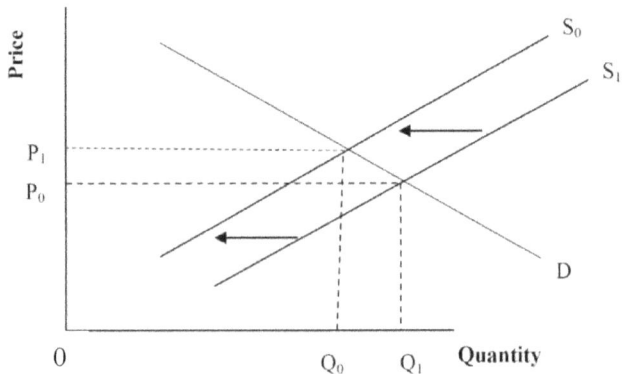

Figure 54: Effect of decrease in supply
(*Note that the supply curve is still upward sloping, but at any given price less will be available for sale than before*).

137

As we can see, the new equilibrium price will be higher, moving from P_0 to P_1, than was the price under the previously large supply. This is what we would intuitively expect, with reduced supplies available due to the lack of sufficient rain. This analysis shows the logic behind what may be intuitively apparent to the student. You should now trace through what happens if supply increases for example through the use of improved technology.

Let us now use the example of an increase in demand because of some factors such as increased income. If the demand for beef, for example, rises from D_0 to D_1, because of an increase in income, as shown in Figure 55, this would tend to drive up the price from P_0 to P_1 and equilibrium quantity from Q_0 to Q_1.

What would happen if, for some reason, the demand decreases?

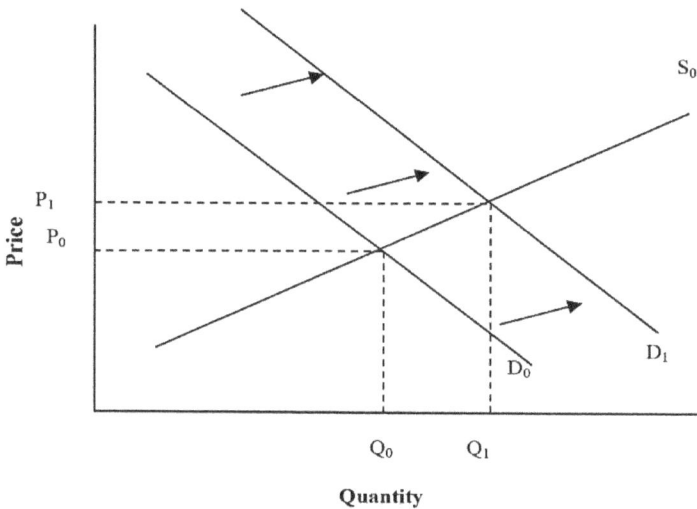

Figure 55: The effect of an increase in demand

At this point, we should note the distinction between a *change in supply* and *a change in quantity supplied*. Remember that a change in supply refers to a change or a *shift* in the entire supply schedule. In Figure 55, has the supply curve shifted? No! Has the demand curve shifted? Yes! Thus, we have in this example an *increase* in quantity supplied which has been brought about by an increase in *demand*. The supply curve itself has not shifted, but the increased demand has resulted in an increase in quantity supplied. A change in quantity supplied refers to a *movement along* a given supply schedule. A change in supply refers to a change or shift in the entire schedule.

Similarly, a change in quantity demanded refers to a movement along a given demand schedule, and a change in demand refers to a movement of the entire schedule. Test your understanding of this concept by keeping demand constant and shifting the supply schedule. What happens to demand and supply? What happens to quantity demanded and quantity supplied?

These examples help us to isolate and examine specific cases. In the real world many things happen at once. Being able to trace through the various steps helps us to understanding what is happening.

What would happen if both the demand and supply of beef increase? The increase in demand would tend to increase price. The increase in supply would tend to decrease price. The net effect on price depends on the relative magnitudes of the changes in demand and supply, and on the slope of the curves. With more detailed knowledge, and careful analysis, economists are able to approximate the effects. You should now analyse what happens if supply increases and demand *decreases*. What happens to price? What happens to quantity? What happens if supply decreases and demand increases; and finally, what happens if both demand and supply decrease? You will find it helpful to use diagrams in arriving at conclusions.

A basic understanding of these simple elements of supply and demand will be extremely useful to students for following certain kinds of economic events in the news and for acquiring a fundamental understanding of basic market forces and their effects. To constructively contribute to questions of economic development it is necessary to be 'literate' in current events both in the national economy and in the increasingly economically inter-dependent world of which Tanzania is a part.

Competition: A Necessary Element

An amazing feature of markets is that equilibrium price is arrived at through the interactions of independent buyers and sellers, each acting in their own self-interest. Through the interaction the market price is determined, or arises, at a level which clears the market.

What ensures that the market price will prevail and that no single participant in the market can take advantage of another? In a word, this depends on 'competition', the existence of a large number of buyers and sellers. If a seller's price is perceived as 'too high', buyers will seek others who are willing to sell at a lower price, thereby forcing the initial seller to lower the price or risk returning home with unsold goods. Similarly, no single buyer can force a seller to sell below market price as long as there are other buyers willing to pay the higher market price.

Thus, the element of competition plays a crucial role in efficiency of markets. We will have much to say about this important matter in latter chapters.

Policy Implications of Elasticity

In studying demand and supply you have already grasped various elasticities of demad and supply as well determinants of these elasticities. Let us examine some of the many applications of elasticity.

A matter of extreme importance to producers and consumers, in addition to the price of food, is *variability* of its price. Prices which fluctuate drastically make it difficult to plan, for both producers and consumers. Consider the diagram in Figure 56. In the left-hand panel, demand and supply are relatively *inelastic*. In the right-hand panel, demand and supply are relatively *elastic*. If demand in each case is shifted to the right by given amount, in which case does price vary the most? Obviously, price changes are more dramatic where demand and supply are relatively inelastic. Check your understanding of the concept by adjusting supply as well.

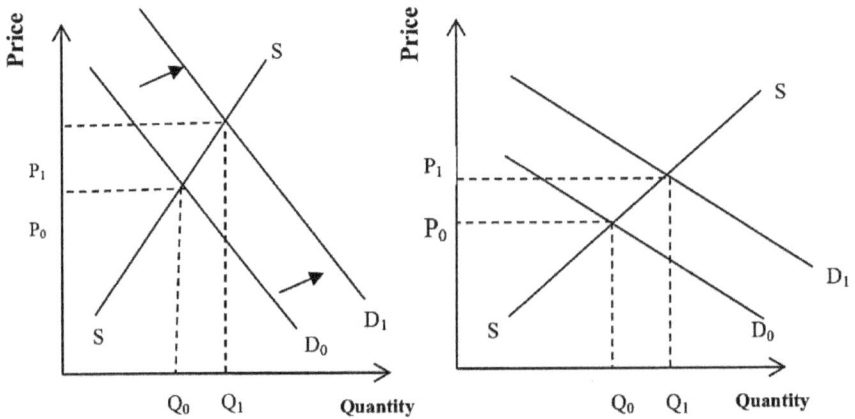

Figure 56: The effect of elasticity on variability of price

The demand for food products tends to be inelastic, as does the supply in the short run. Given short-run supply due to weather and other factors, what does this suggest for price variability for both producers and consumers? Obviously, short supplies can drive up price with potential hardship to consumers, particularly low-income consumers. Sharply increased supplies can drive down prices, to the detriment of producers who depend on stable prices for their incomes. This price variability in the short run partially explains the rationale for governments in both developing and developed countries to try to assure stable prices and supplies of food. The dilemma of policy-makers is to allow prices to fluctuate sufficiently to enable realistic price signals while protecting producers from precipitous price drops and consumers from dramatic price increases. Suffice it to say that this is a dilemma never totally resolved by policy-makers in *either* developing or developed nations. However, an understanding of supply, demand and elasticity is of tremendous assistance in understanding the issues involved.

A related issue of concern to developing nations is that they tend to be exporters of primary goods such as agricultural products which tend to be inelastic in demand. Thus exporters of primary products are, in a sense, 'at the mercy' of world markets. If elasticity of demand is less than 1, what did we conclude would happen to total revenue when price increases? Total revenue also increases, which, of course, is in the interest of producers. Obviously, however, when prices decline total revenue falls and creates hardship for the exporting country. Thus, declining revenue in time of falling prices, as well as price variability, explain the basic rationale for policy measures which attempt to stabilize prices to producers over time. Can you explain the advantages of, as well as anticipated difficulties which might be experienced with, such attempts?

Perhaps you are beginning to see why the application of economic principles to real-world policy issues is fraught with problems. Nevertheless, clear economic thinking can do much to clarify the issues and contribute to national, constructive debate on how to deal with these problems which are of such importance to the livelihood of so many people.

Another example of the effects of elasticity has to do with the oil embargo of the Organization of Petroleum Exporting Countries (OPEC) in the 1970s. The demand for petroleum products tend to be inelastic in the short run. If $E < 1$, and price rises, total revenue rises. Thus, those countries which import petroleum products experience an increased monetary outflow to the petroleum exporting nations.

In the long run, however, demand is more elastic, as nations can take energy-saving measures to make themselves somewhat less vulnerable to price increases.

You should now begin to see the many implications of price elasticity in the day-to-day world of economic activity. For example, in a hypothesized regulated industry such as maize, what considerations would you recommend to be taken into account concerning producers and consumers before raising retail or producer prices?

Questions for Thought and Discussion

1. Sketch hypothetical supply and demand curves for a product such as Tanzanian coffee. Suppose that Brazil has an abundant crop and is able to sell more to its customers. What might this do to the demand for Tanzanian coffee? What institutional agreements have been attempted to limit price fluctuations in commodities such as coffee? Do such arrangements negate the law of supply and demand? How do they accomplish their objective?

2. It is sometimes argued that producers need 'price stability' for economic planning. In what sense might this be so?

3. Explain why only one equilibrium price can exist in a given market at one time. Is it ever possible for two prices to exist at a given time

for a given product? What conditions would be necessary for this to occur?

4. Consider a market demand by American tourists to view wildlife in Tanzanian game parks. Since the recent economic changes, more American tourists have wanted to visit Tanzania. What has this done to the market demand for viewing Africa wildlife, and to the tourist industry which serves such tourists?

4. Although some American tourists to Tanzania visit Zanzibar, it is easier, faster and cheaper for Americans to go to Mexico for this purpose. Therefore, if Tanzania desires to maintain a high level of American tourism, what recommendations would you make to the Government regarding game parks and reserves?

5. (a) Plot the data in Table 6 on graph paper and indicate the equilibrium price:

Table 6: Data for determination of equilibrium price

Price ($£$)	Q_D	Q_S
10	5	25
8	10	20
6	15	15
2	20	10
0	25	5

(b)   What would happen if the maximum price would be held to £2? What would happen if the minimum price were set at £7? Illustrate the results by diagrams and explain these situations verbally.

(c)   What would happen if tastes for this product changed such that at any given price twice as many would be purchased as before? Show this

(d)   change on your diagram and explain the result. What might account for such a change in tastes?

CHAPTER SEVEN

Price and Output under Pure Competition

Introduction

A basic premise of economics is that individual economic units respond to incentives to maximize their own economic well-being. In this chapter we try to understand how the individual purely competitive firm responds to market price, and how this affects production at the level of the firm, and for the market as a whole.

Conditions of Pure Competition

In a pure competitive market, there are enough buyers and enough sellers, each accounting for such a small portion of the total market that no single buyer or seller has any perceptible influence over price. This is sometimes referred to as 'atomistic competition'. In addition:

- There are no barriers to entry to or exit from the market. Buyers and sellers are free to enter and leave the market at will. If a potential seller sees an opportunity to sell goods, she is free to bring goods to the market.
- The output or product produced is homogeneous. Hence no reason for preferences
- Finally, there is readily available information. This means sellers and buyers have complete knowledge of the market conditions. One can easily compare prices of maize, beans, pigeon peas or any other product with those of other sellers. The readily available information renders it difficult for any participant in the market to take unfair advantage of another.

These features of pure competition, many small buyers and sellers, freedom of entry and exit, and readily accessible information, approximate the conditions found in the countless small markets in villages, pueblos, hamlets, and towns the world over. They seem to arise spontaneously, not out of any grand design, but through each individual acting in his own self-interest, yet contributing to socially useful and necessary activity which adds to the welfare of the community. This is the essence of Adam Smith's 'invisible hands' the proposition that through the market mechanism each individual acting in his own self-interest automatically furthers the welfare of society.

As powerful a mechanism as the market, however, it is crucial to stress that as markets become larger, more complex, more specialized, more centralized, or attain a host of other complicating features, the conditions of pure competition often do not prevail. As we shall see as we study other market forms in the next chapter, markets often attain 'imperfections' which cause them to function less efficiently, and often with less equity. This is an extremely important problem in developing economies, as well as in industrial economies where the conditions of pure competition, often, are absent. This does not mean that markets cannot perform necessary and useful functions. It may mean, however, that special attention needs to be devoted to rules for maintaining competition, or for otherwise ensuring efficiency and equity in the marketplace.

Prices and the Purely Competitive Firm

We have been introduced to some basic economics of production and its relation to costs. What remains now is to put together revenues and costs to determine how much will be produced. Obviously, the level of production at both the micro and macro level will certainly be affected by incentives, as seen by the producer. Let us proceed to see why this is so.

Remember that pure competition refers to a market situation in which there are large numbers of buyers and sellers- numbers so large that no single buyer or seller can influence price. We say that an individual who produces in a purely competitive market is a price taker, in that the seller must take the price, which is offered, or nothing at all. By withholding a product from the market, the individual producer, acting individually, cannot affect the price because his/her share of the market is so small.

This situation is shown in Figure 57. The market price, Po, is determined by the interaction of supply and demand. The market price is reflected to the individual firm, or producer. The horizontal line on the left-hand panel is, effectively, the demand for the product as faced by the individual firm. The interpretation of this horizontal demand curve is that the firm can sell all it wants at the given price, but nothing at a higher price. Recall that a horizontal demand curve is referred to as a perfectly elastic demand curve. Of course, you must bear in mind that this can only occur if the firm produces a very small portion of the total market, which, by definition, is atomistic or purely competitive. If market supply increases, as indicated by S_1 in the right-hand panel of Figure 57, price declines to P_1, and is reflected to the firm as lower demand, or market price, as indicated by the downward shift in the left-hand panel.

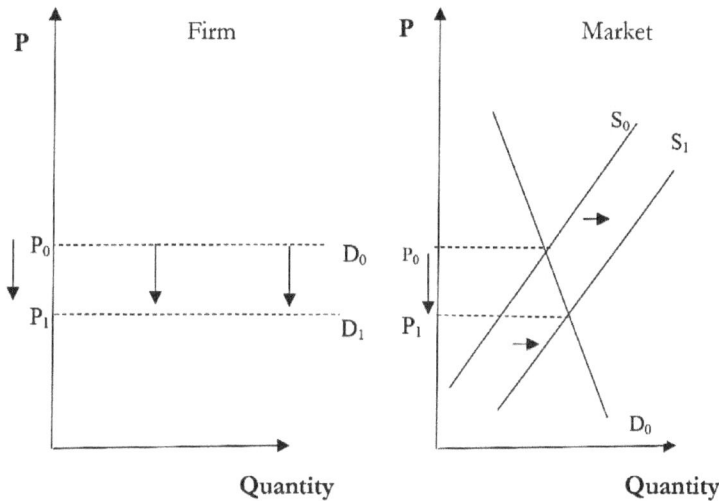

Figure 57: The determination by the market of the demand faced by the individual firm *(The demand faced by the individual firm is perfectly elastic.)*

Recall also that the total revenue is the price of the product multiplied by the quantity sold. As the firm sells more; the price remains constant. Assuming a price of TShs. 5 per unit, we obtain the total revenue as shown in Table 7 and which can be graphed as a straight line, as in Figure 58.

Table 7: Total and marginal revenue for a competitive firm where price is shillings per unit

Q	P	TR	MR
0	5	0	
1	5	5	5
2	5	10	5
3	5	15	5
-P-4	5	20	5
5	5	25	5

Recall also from previous Chapters, that marginal revenue is the change in total revenue resulting from the sale of an additional unit of product. Geometrically, it is the slope of the total revenue curve. Since the slope in Figure 58 is constant, we know that marginal revenue also must be constant. In fact, the marginal revenue from an additional unit sold under pure competition must be the price, since an additional unit sold will add to the total revenue exactly the price of the last unit sold. Thus, under pure competition, marginal revenue is equal to price, which in turn gives the demand curve faced by the individual purely competitive firm. In other words, the individual firm can sell any amount at that price - because the contribution of the individual firm is a very small portion of the total market.

With this, we now have how to put the entire analytical apparatus together.

Profit Maximization

The central assumption made in this analysis is that in its attempt to maximize profits the firm will respond to prices. In general, we can say that the firm will attempt to maximize profits, the difference between total revenues and costs, while taking due account of risk, and with the provision that food security is provided for the family. Thus, while the individual farmer, for example, will act in such a way that his family will be assured a food supply of minimum acceptable risk, he/she will nevertheless respond to prices in attempting maximize profits.

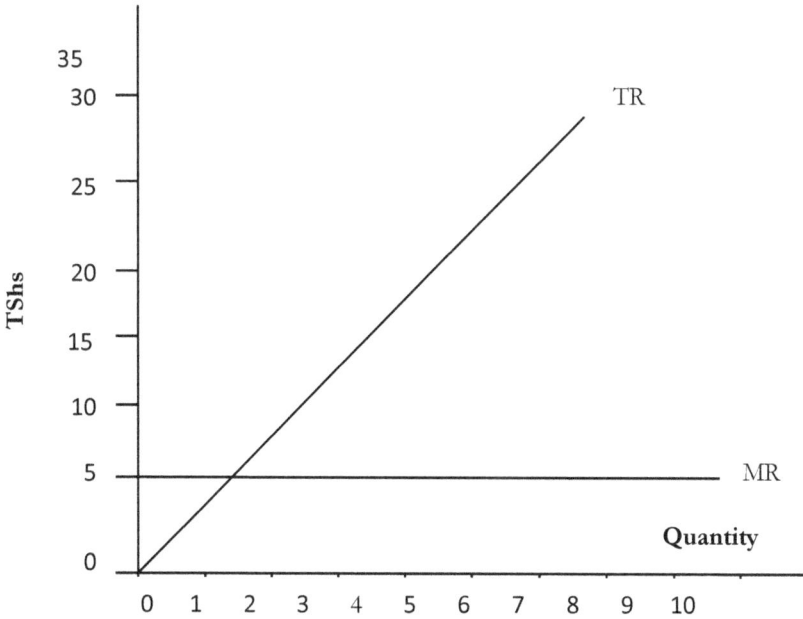

Figure 58: Total and marginal revenue under pure competitive market *(As marginal revenue is constant, and equal to price, total revenue increases at a constant rate with increased sales.)*

Let us use an example to show the way in which the purely competitive firm might respond to changing prices in maximizing profits.

Consider the cost data in Table 8. Note that the costs follow the pattern which we have studied in the previous Chapters. If the firm desires to maximize profits (total revenue minus total costs) at a product price of 60 per unit, profits would be maximized at a production level of 5. At that level of production, total revenue is 300, or (5 x 60), and total cost is 205.

What happens if product price is raised? With a price of 100, total revenue minus total cost is maximized at an output level of 7. Thus, we can see that as product price rises the producer has the incentive to produce more. Note that this is consistent with the upward sloping supply curve, which suggests that producers are more willing to produce and make greater quantities of product available for sale at higher prices.

Table 8: Hypothetical revenue and cost data for a purely competitive firm
P1 = 60   P2 = 100

Q	TFC	TVC	TC	TR	TR-TC	TR	TR-TC	MC	MR	MR
0	50	0	50	0	-50	0	50			
1	50	30	80	60	-20	100	20	30	60	100
2	50	55	105	120	15	200	95	25	60	100
3	50	75	125	180	55	300	175	20	60	100
4	50	105	155	240	85	400	245	30	60	100
5	50	155	205	300	95	500	295	50	60	100
6	50	255	275	360	85	600	325	70	60	100
7	50	315	365	420	50	700	335	90	60	100
8	50	425	475	480	5	800	325	110	60	100
9	50	555	505	540	-65	900	295	130	60	100

The 'Marginal Cost equals Marginal Revenue' Rule

It is very instructive at this point to make use of the marginal concepts which we have learned. Recall that under pure competition, where the price of the product to the firm remains unchanged as more is sold, marginal revenue, the addition to total revenue of another unit sold, is constant and equal to price. Remember also, that marginal cost is the addition to total cost of another unit produced and increases because of diminishing marginal physical productivity. Note that the cost of the fifth unit is 50. Thus, with a price of 60, the marginal revenue from the sixth unit is greater than the marginal cost. However, if we go to the sixth unit of production, the additional cost of 70 exceeds the additional revenue of 60. In other words, it costs us more to produce the sixth unit than the revenue it brings in, and the producer will have no incentive to produce it. Profits are maximized at a level of 5.

Similarly, with a price of 100, the additional revenue of the seventh unit (100), exceeds the additional cost (90). But if we go to the eight unit, the additional revenue (100) is insufficient to cover the additional costs (110). Thus as long as the marginal revenue exceeds the marginal cost, the firm has the incentive to increase production. However, if the marginal revenue is less than the marginal cost of another unit, the firm does not have the incentive to produce that unit. If we could break down the units of product into fractional unit the firm would tend to produce the theoretical limit of where the marginal revenue just equals marginal cost. However, in this example, we restrict ourselves to discret units, and thus the firm stops producing at an output of 5 at a price of

60, and at 7 with a price of 100.

Mathematically, profit is maximized when $\dfrac{d(TR-TC)}{dQ} = 0$

$$\dfrac{d(PQ)}{dQ} - \dfrac{df(Q)+b}{dQ} = 0$$

P - f '(Q) = 0, where P is output price and f '(Q) is marginal cost i.e. MR = MC

A graphical analysis

At this point, it is instructive to illustrate the profit-maximizing behaviour of the firm through the use of graphs and simple geometry. The upper panel of Figure 59 shows the 'total revenue and total cost approach', and the lower panel shows the 'marginal cost equals marginal revenue' approach.

In the upper panel are total revenue and total cost curves. Point A is the point of minimum slope, or minimum marginal costs. Point B is the point of minimum average total cost, and point C is the level of output where the difference between total revenue and total cost is greatest. The difference between total revenue and total cost, once again, is the firm's profit.

We can show the same information in the lower panel. Recall that as the slope of the total revenue curve is constant, this implies that marginal revenue is constant, or a straight line, as shown in the lower panel. The marginal cost and average cost curves follow directly from the total cost curves, as we have learned in Chapter Four. If profits are maximized where marginal cost equals marginal revenue, then production will be at a level of q1. Profits are indicated by the shaded area representing an average profit per unit, multiplied by the number of units sold.

Note also, in the upper panel, that at point C the slope of the total cost curve is equal to the slope of the total revenue curve. Thus, this again shows that marginal revenue is equal to marginal cost at that point since the slopes represent marginal costs and revenues.

You should master thoroughly the concepts depicted in these diagrams and understand the reasoning behind them.

Let us examine once again, what happens as price is raised. In the upper panel of Figure 60, TR1, represents total revenue at the original price. Profits are maximized at the level of q1. The same is shown in the lower panel, as MR1 represents price at the original level. As prices are raised, total revenue rises to TR2. (Can you explain why?) Also, as price rises, this raises the MR curve in the lower panel. (Can you explain why?) We can observe that the difference between TR and TC is greater as TR rises, and that the maximum difference occurs at a higher level of production. Similarly, by viewing the lower panel, as we raise price, or MR, profits rise, and maximum profit occurs at a higher level of output. Try to trace out the new profits realized in the lower panel at the higher price.

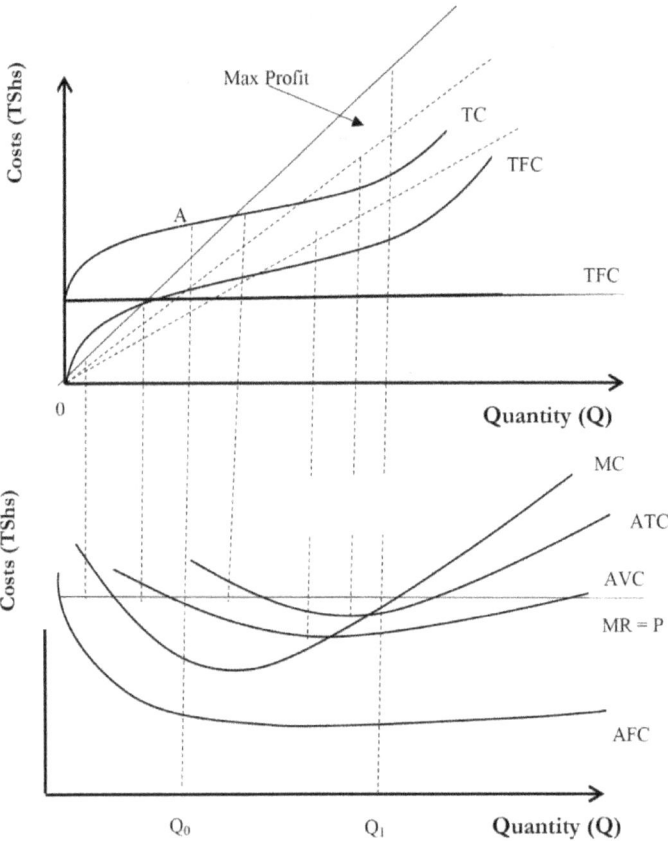

Figure 59: Profit maximizing by the purely competitive firm *(Profit are maximized where marginal costs equal marginal revenue. This is where the slopes of the total cost and total revenue curves are equal on the upper panel)*

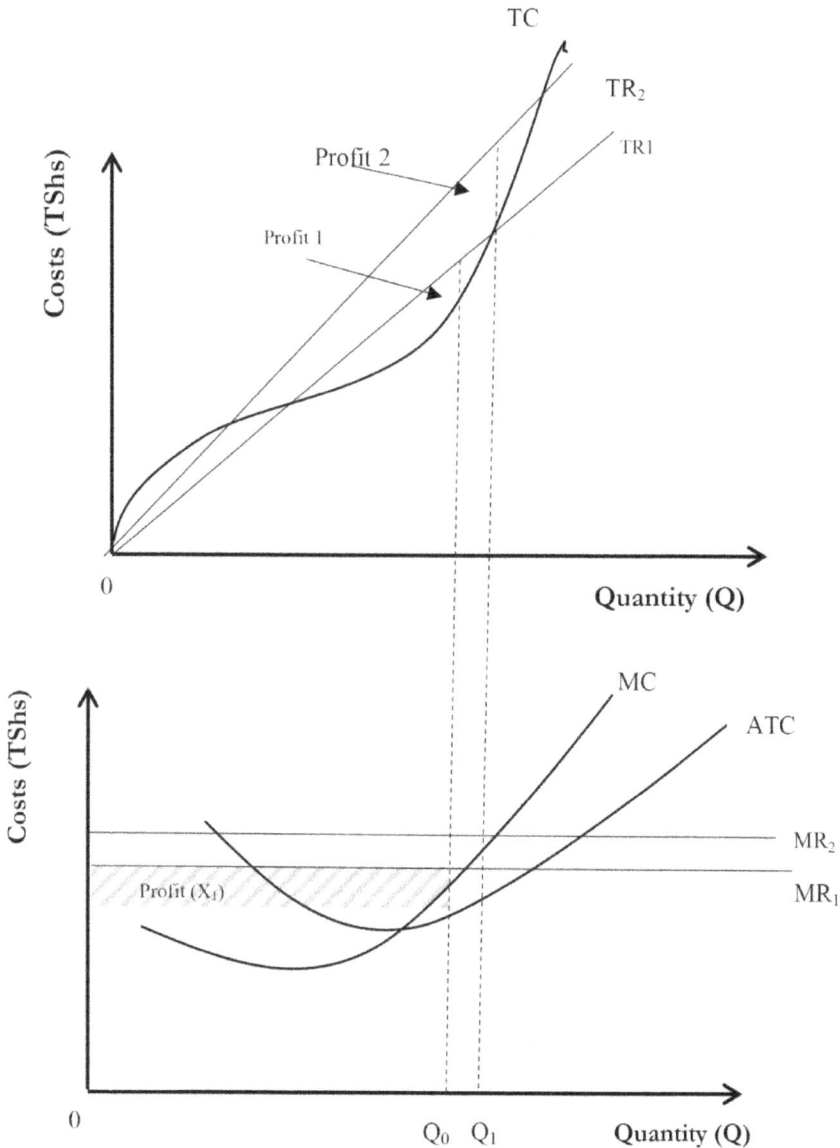

Figure 60: Illustration of rising profits at increasing prices *(As price rises, both the level of output and profits rise)*

Loss minimization

Thus far, we have examined profit-maximizing situations. What happens in case of losses? There are, in fact, situations in which it is rational to produce at a loss. Of course, this can only occur for a short period of time, else the firm will soon be put out of business.

Let us once again examine the cost data in Table 8 above. If we construct a total revenue schedule with a price equal to 35, losses are minimized by producing at a level of 4. Note also that this is consistent with our marginal cost equals marginal revenue rule. Marginal costs of producing the 4th unit are 30 as opposed to marginal revenue of 35. However, marginal costs of the 5th unit are 50 if losses are 15. If the firm would not produce at all, it would still lose its fixed cost of 50. However, if the firm produces 4 units, it covers its variable costs in addition to a portion of its fixed costs. Thus, the firm should go ahead by producing, rather than closing down.

Graphically, we see in the upper panel of Figure 61 that the total revenue curve at an output level of q1 covers the variable costs and some portion of the fixed costs (the distance between TC and TVC), but fails to cover total costs. Similarly, in the lower panel, we see that the firm produces at where MC = MR, but that marginal revenue covers something above average cost, but fails to cover total costs and losses result.

However, these losses are less than if the firm would not produce at all! For example, a farmer with ripe coffee berries should go ahead and harvest as long as the total revenue cover the variable expenses such as weeding, spraying, pruning, harvesting and transport to the factory for sale. In other words, he should harvest and sell his coffee even if the fixed costs of irrigation equipment, land, taxes and insurance are not covered. If he does not harvest his berries, losses will be higher that season than if he harvests. In the long-run, however, the fixed costs too, must be covered.

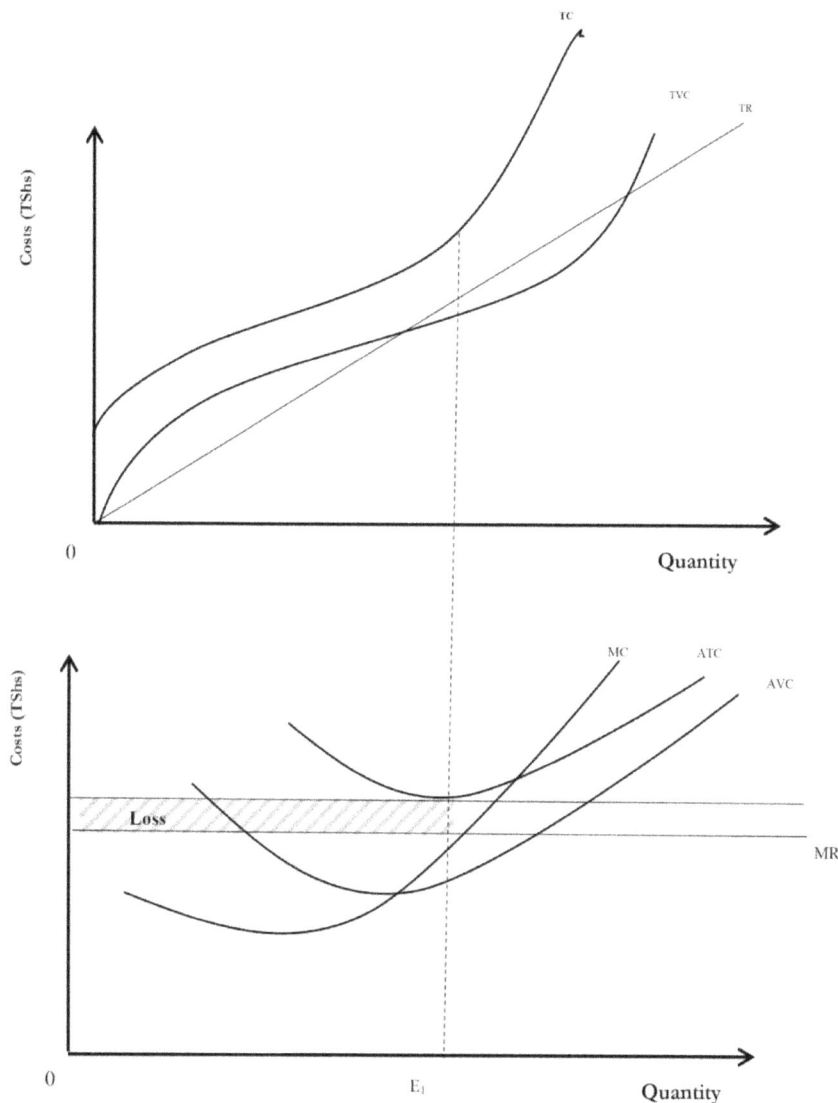

Figure 61: The case of loss minimization (*The firm is better off to produce q1 as revenues cover variable costs plus a portion of its fixed costs*)

A special case of loss minimizing occurs in the 'close-down' case. Let us assume that price is 20, using the cost data in Table 8. You should construct a total revenue schedule and verify that at no point can the firm cover its variable costs. Thus, if the firm produces anything at all, it loses its fixed costs plus additional variable costs of production.

Graphically, the 'close-down' case is shown in Figure 62, where total revenue does not cover total variable cost nor does marginal revenue cover even minimum average variable cost

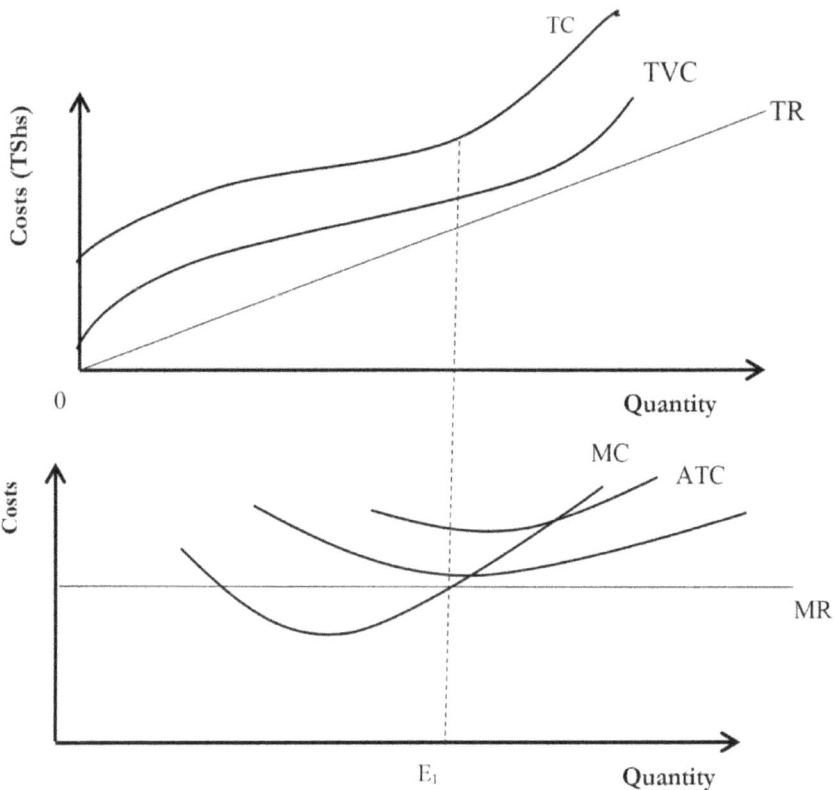

Figure 62: The 'close-down-case (*At no point can the producer cover his variable costs. Thus, the incentive is to not produce at all*)

Other Considerations

In our analysis we have assumed that costs and returns are known with certainty. Obviously, this is seldom the case in the real world. In most agricultural activities, problems with weather, disease and uncertainty with respect to price, as well as the exact response of crops to various inputs give rise to numerous uncertainties.

Nevertheless, experience throughout the world has shown that producers will respond to higher prices with increased production, assuming that they, rather than a landlord, realize the gains from higher prices or adoption of better technology. Even though farmers may not know the exact numbers, or go through the formal procedure which we have done, they have demonstrated knowledge of being able to respond in rational ways to price incentives. Such incentives have proven to be powerful influences on production – against assuming that the gains accrue to those who work on the land and bear the effort of production.

We should also note that factors such as certainty and promptness of payment for commodity sold enter into the farmer's perception of prices and revenues. If a farmer is not paid for the crop until six months after harvest, this is correctly perceived as effectively a lower price, and producers should be expected to act accordingly.

Finally, we must remember once again that farmers, as purely competitive producers, maximize profits subject to other objectives such as maintaining food security for their families, and in essence reducing the risk associated with producing a single crop for cash sale. Even if high cash returns are anticipated, for coffee or tea for example, the producer may well reduce output of these crops in favour of food crops such as maize, beans and potatoes, which can be consumed directly.

With these qualifications, an understanding of the concepts presented in this chapter will aid the student in understanding price and market incentives.

Questions for Thought and Discussion

1. Assume that a perfectly competitive firm has fixed costs of £40 and variable costs as shown in Table 9 below. Compute total costs, average fixed costs, average variable costs, average total costs and marginal costs. Illustrate the results by diagrams on graph paper.

Table 9: Data for graph/plotting the relationship between Total Costs and Average Fixed cost

Total product	Total variable costs
0	0
1	55
2	75
3	75
4	90
5	110
6	135
7	170
8	220
8	290

2. At prices of 30, 40, 22, and 14 per unit of product how much would the firm produce in the short-run? Verify your answers using both the 'total cost minus total revenue' approach and the 'marginal cost equals marginal revenue' approach. Add these results to your diagrams in Question 1.

3. How do your results relate to the firm's short-run supply curve?

4. Explain why normal profits tend towards zero in a perfectly competitive industry

5. The assumption that firms maximize profits does not apply in certain cases. Can you think of two such cases? Explain the examples you give and whether or not profit maximization could still be used as a reasonable proxy.

6. Show diagrammatically and explain how a competitive firm in equilibrium, with output Q and output price P, will react to a government tax, t, charged per unit of output.

CHAPTER EIGHT

Pricing and Output under Imperfect Competition

Introduction

The student of economics is first introduced to the subject of price and output determination through the analysis of pure competition. This is because it is the easiest market form to understand, and because it produces results which are theoretically efficient in the allocation of resources, and hence provides a norm to which other market forms can be compared. In the real world, few economic situations approach pure competition. However, when you understand pure competition you will be prepared to progress to other market forms.

The extreme case is pure monopoly. Between pure competition and pure monopoly, are monopolistic competition and oligopoly. Oligopoly and monopolistic competition are categorized, along with pure monopoly, as 'imperfect competition'. All have in common a downward-sloping demand curve to the individual firm, some degree of control over price, and a differentiated product. Let us begin by examining pure monopoly.

Pure Monopoly

Monopoly is a situation where there is only one seller of a commodity. Monopolies arise for several reasons. A firm might gain control of the entire supply of raw materials with which to manufacture a product. An example is an aluminum manufacturing firm in North America, which, in the 1940s, gained sole control over the supply of bauxite, which is the raw material used in aluminum manufacture. Second, a firm may invent a new product and obtain a patent, or an exclusive legal right, to produce and market a product. Third, a firm may have a cost structure such that profits are attainable only with an output large enough to fill the entire market. In the extreme, this could result in a 'one-firm' industry. These are referred to as natural monopolies. And, finally, a firm may be awarded by the government an exclusive right to a franchise to market a product. In such a case, the firm often is regulated through price controls.

In many developing countries the size of the market is small enough so that the entire market demand can be satisfied by only one firm or a small number of firms.

The monopolist's demand curve

The demand curve of the monopolist is the market demand.

$Q = f(P)$ or $P = f(Q)$, The demand curve has a unique inverse $dP/dQ < 0$, quantity demanded decreases with an increase in price.

In perfect competition

$MR = P$ because $dP/dQ = 0$

In monopoly situation, MR is less than price as shown below.
$R = PQ$

$MR = dR/dQ = P + Q(dP/dQ)$
Since $dP/dQ < 0$, MR is less than P

If demand $\quad P = a-bQ$
$\qquad TR = aQ-bQ^2$
$\qquad MR = a-2bQ$

Profit maximizing under monopoly

A popular perception is that the monopolist is free to charge any price and will therefore charge 'the highest'. A more accurate interpretation is that the monopolist has the incentive to charge the price perceived to be consistent with *maximum profits*. The monopolist can control price, but not *both* price and quantity. The monopolist must consider the consequences with respect to quantity sold and profits when considering price.

Consider the demand schedule shown in Figure 63. Note that with the downward-sloping demand schedule, the total revenue first rises, then falls, as opposed to the straight line under the purely competitive situation in Chapter 7. This also implies that the marginal revenue curve declines rather than being constant, as in pure competition. We can see in Table 10 that at any quantity greater than 1, marginal revenue is less than price. Geometrically, the demand, marginal revenue, and total revenue curve look as depicted in Figurte 63 – similar to those in our study of elasticity.

If we look at Table 10 again, we see that total profits are maximized at an output level of 4. We also see, once again, that if marginal revenue exceeds marginal cost the firm will have incentive to produce. At output of 5, for example, if marginal revenue fails to cover marginal costs, the firm would not produce. If the price could produce divisible units, it would produce somewhere between 4 and 5, as long as the marginal revenue from a fraction of a unit would cover the marginal costs of producing that fractional unit. Thus, the 'marginal cost equals marginal revenue' rule holds for profit maximization under monopoly, just as it does for pure competition.

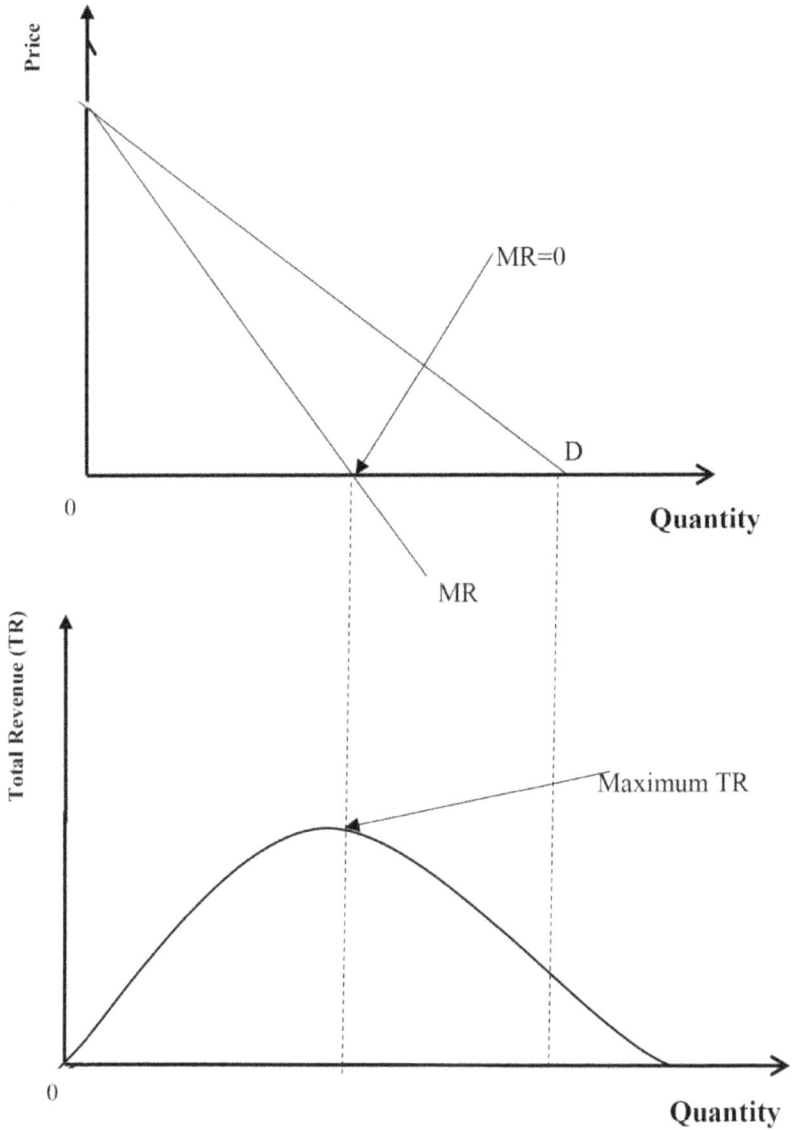

Figure 63: Demand, total revenue, and marginal revenue with a downward-sloping demand curve

Table 10: Hypothetical cost and price data for a monopolist

Q	P	TC	MC	TR	MR	(TR-TC)
0	200	145	-	0	-	-145
1	180	175	30	180	180	5
2	160	200	25	320	140	120
3	140	220	20	420	100	200
4	120	250	30	480	60	230
5	100	300	70	480	-20	200
6	80	370	70	480	-60	110
7	50	460	90	420	-60	-40
8	40	579	110	320	-100	-250

We can illustrate profit maximization by the use of diagrams. In the left-hand panel of Figure 64, we have the usual total cost course, and the dome-shaped total revenue curve. Profits are maximized where the slope of the total cost and total revenue curve as equal, indicating MC = MR.

In the right-hand panel, note that the MR curve lies below the demand curve, i.e. MR < P, reaches zero, and becomes negative.[*] Profits are maximized where MC = MR, at q1. The price is then read off the demand curve, at P_m, and profits are equal to price minus average cost, multiplied by the quantity of output. We read price off the demand curve because at output level q_1, buyers are ready to pay P_m.

You should thoroughly master these concepts, being able to explain them geometrically, and in clear English.

---

[*]Demand is given by P – a-bQ, and total revenue by PxQ-aQ-bQ$_2$ which account for the dome shape of the total revenue curve. The marginal revenue, which is MR = a –2bQ, accounting for the fact that it has the same intercept as the demand curve but differs in slope.

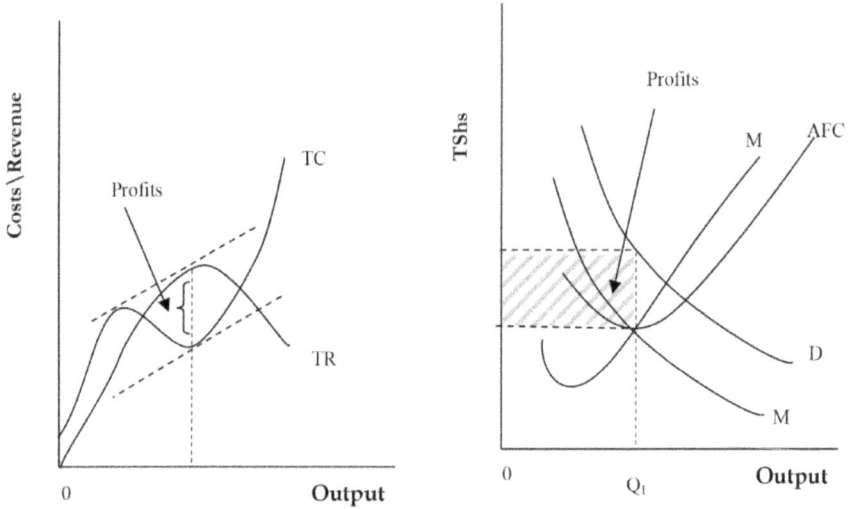

Figure 64: Profit maximization under monopoly

In summary, the monopolist maximizes profit by equating MR with MC. Suppose a monopolist faces a linear demand curve, $P = 100-4Q$ and cost function $C = 50 + 20Q$. Calculate the profit maximizing output, price charged by the monopolist and his profit.

Also calculate the profit maximizing output, price and profit if the producer was in a perfectly competitive market.

Effects on price and output

Recall that under pure competition, the individual firm produces to the point where price (marginal revenue) equals marginal costs. In Figure 65, under monopoly, the firm is producing at qm which is short of where the price equals marginal cost at qc. This has implication for both equity and efficiency.

The equity implications are probably more readily apparent. The monopolist, by restricting output, raises price relative to that which would occur if output would be increased to point qc, where price would equal marginal cost. Thus, under monopoly pricing, the distribution of income is shift from the consumer to the monopolist.

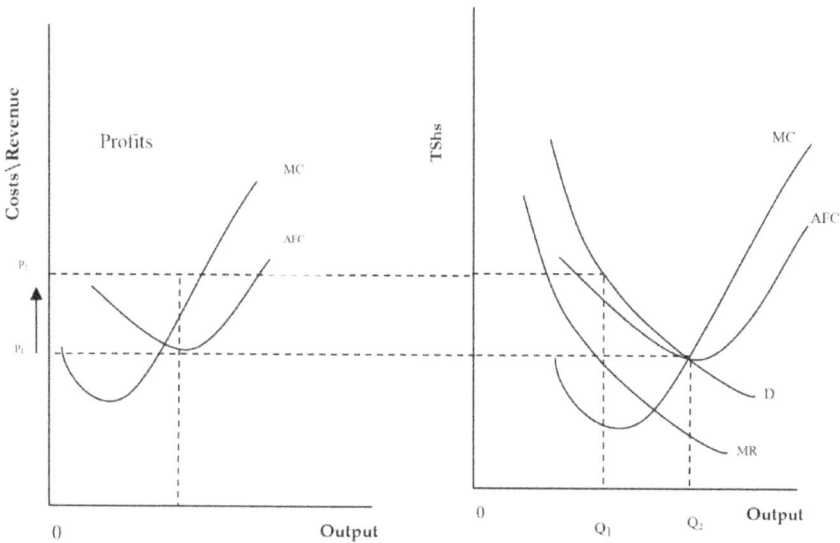

Figure 65: The effect of monopoly pricing (*The monopolist restricts output and raises price*)

The efficiency implication is more subtle. Why do economists say that it is efficient and desirable for price to equal marginal cost? Price is an estimate of the value which consumers place on another unit of a particular product. Marginal cost represents an estimate of the value of resources used in producing another unit of a product. Because resources are limited, they have value in alternative uses, and could be used for producing something else. Thus, if price *equals* marginal cost, consumers value another unit of this product, and hence use of the resources, as much in the production of this product, as in the production of something else. In contrast, if price is *greater* than marginal cost, as in the monopoly pricing situation, consumers value this product more than they value other products for which these resources might be used. Thus, scarce resources used in producing this product would promote a higher level of welfare than current uses of those resources.

By extension of this concept, in accordance with diminishing marginal utility, *increasing the output of the monopoly product would lower price, at the same time if would increase marginal cost, eventually bringing price and marginal cost to equality.* This would allow for an improvement in pricing efficiency.

This is not to say that it would necessarily be desirable to convert monopolies into purely competitive producers. Economics of scale may make it infeasible to produce through many small firms. It may be necessary to produce some items through large-scale production. For example, it may not be feasible to have many small firms supplying electrical power to consumers instead of just the Tanzania Power and Lighting Company. Nevertheless, it is necessary to recognize the efficiency and equity implications of monopoly pricing which would occur in the absence of price regulation.

Average cost pricing

Even though marginal cost pricing is desirable from a social point of view, sometimes such regulation is not feasible. Economies of scale may be such that minimum average cost occurs at an output large enough that average cost at the level cannot be covered by price. Consider the case shown in Figure 66. The monopolist would prefer to charge price P_m. If the firm were regulated by government to marginal cost pricing, the price would be P1. However, at that price, losses would occur, as average cost is higher than price at that level of output. In such cases, if a monopoly is regulated, the solution is often 'average cost pricing', restricting the monopoly to price P2. Note that this precludes a 'pure profit', restricting the firm to the 'normal profit' which is included in the firm's average costs.

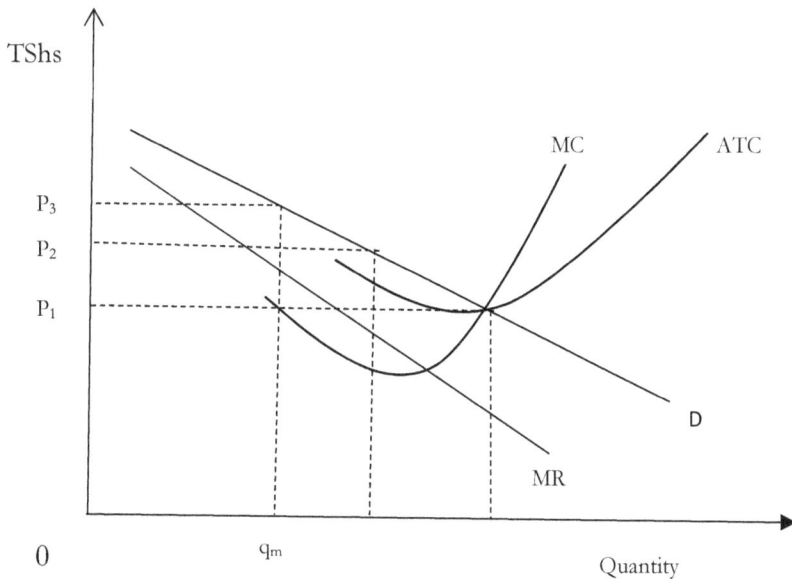

Figure 66: Average cost pricing (*In this case, marginal cost pricing, at P1, would cause the firm to incur losses). Hence, restricting price to average cash at P2 would be a possible solution*).

Price discrimination

A monopolist can discriminate among consumers so as to increase his profit levels. A monopolist can practice price discrimination if :

- The markets can be kept separate so as to prevent the arbitration of prices between the markets
- The elasticity of demand in the two markets are different

The monopolist can sell q_1 in market I at P_1 and q_2 in market II at P_2 To maximize profit, the monopolist has to set MR in each market equal to the MC of the output as a whole. This implies that MR in both markets are equal.

Monopoly and the long run

Remember that in pure competition, in the long run, pure profits are completely removed, leaving firms to only a 'normal profit'. In contrast, under monopoly, the firm has the *incentive* to move toward the most efficient scale of plant, but does not have the same compelling motive as firms in pure profits may continue to exist because entry of competing firms is blocked.

Monopolistic Competition

Monopolistic competition is the market form in which there are many firms, each producing a slightly differentiate product. Examples are restaurants, barber shops, dry cleaners who may vary slightly, for example, through services, or even location. Price-setting ability exists, but is limited, due to the existence of a large number of competitors.

The products are differentiated yet they are close substitutes. Also there is free entry and exit of the firms from the product group as well as factor or input prices and technology are given.

Conceptually, price and output determination is the same as under monopoly. Profits are maximized where MC = MR, as in the left-hand panel of Figure 67. Some profits exists, as indicated by the shaded area. The difference between monopolistic competition and pure monopoly arises over the long-run. Since entry to monopolistically competitive industries is not blocked, the existence of above normal profits will attract competitors to the industry. The increased competition for a limited market will cut into individual firm'smarket share, thus shifting its demand curve to the left. Note in the right hand panel that the profit-maximizing level of output, where MC = MR, enables a price that just covers average costs.

If price would fail to cover average costs, losses would occur, and the firm would be driven out of business. This phenomenon explains the large number of new firms entering, and old firms leaving, industries such as retail trade and restaurants. The readiness of new individuals to enter such businesses is explained by the hope for profits. However, such profits are often elusive, being relatively small, or not realized at all. Many firms survive on only normal profits, which others soon leave the industry.

The firms in monopolistically competitive industries often resort to advertising and attempts at product differentiation, real or contrived, to increase the demand for their particular product.

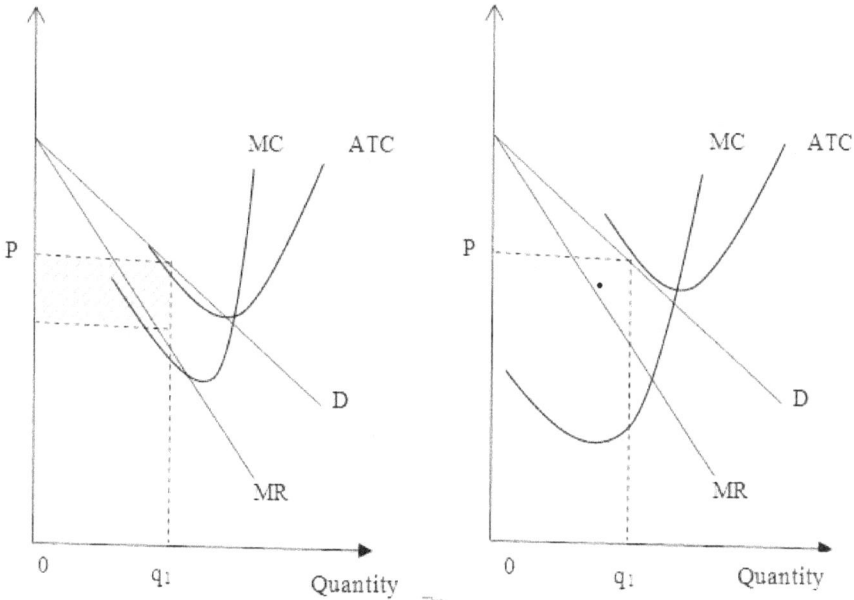

Figure 67: Long-run equilibrium under monopolistic competition (*Short-run profits, indicated in the left-hand panel, attract additional competitors, which cuts into the market share of existing firms. In the long-run equilibrium, the firm attains only normal profits*).

Duopoly and Oligopoly

Duopoly is a market which has two sellers and oligopoly is the name given to industries in which there are a few firms but more than two each of which controls a large share of the market. Thus 'inter-dependency' characterizes oligopolistic firms. Each firm is affected by pricing and output policies of the others. The oil companies, such as Shell, Total, Kobil, BP, etc., constitute an example of oligopoly. Agro-chemical and pharmaceutical industries in Tanzania are also oligopolistic.

Oligopoly may arise because economies of scale may be such that only large firms can produce at low costs. Thus, it is difficult for potential competitors to enter the industry. Further, smaller competitors may merge to form a larger firm by which to increase its market power.

Competition among buyers will lead to a uniform price but each seller is sufficiently large to affect other producers in the industry.

An output change by one producer will affect the prices of other producers as well. These producers will react. Hence the results of any move on an oligopolist or duoploist will depend on the actions of his rivals.

Because of the interdependence of oligopolistic firms, there is a tendency to avoid price competition. They may therefore agree to act together so as to maximize the total profit of the industry. When they act together they will behave like monopolist. They are actually colluding. *Collusion* is the co-operation and agreement between firms in an industry in setting prices, dividing markets or reducing the level of competition. Such collusion may be explicit or more tacit and informal.

In many economies, formal collusion is illegal. Perhaps the best known example of explicit collusion, international in scope, is that of the Organization of Petroleum Exporting countries (OPEC). A producers' association which is formed for the purpose of restraining competition is known as a *cartel*. Again, this is generally illegal at national levels, but OPEC, being an international association of producers, is not subject to such law. OPEC has been successful in its early years during the 1970s in increasing prices of its crude oil. For a cartel to be successful, however, it must control a major share of the market.

An interesting aspect of cartels is that once formed, and decisions made with respect to price and each members' share of output, there is an enormous incentive on the part of each member of 'chisel', or increase its share of output relative to the others. Because one country's oil is an almost perfect substitute for another's, the elasticity of demand for a single nation's oil is grater than the elasticity of oil in total. Hence, by lowering price only slightly, it could greatly increase its quantity and revenues at the expense of the others. During negotiating sessions, a major task is for the cartel to divide and agree on each member's share of output.

In addition to the difficulty of negotiations, another effect of a successful cartel is the incentive arising to consumers and to existing and potential competitors from higher prices. Higher price induce consumers to conserve on the product and to find substitutes. Further, high prices induce other supplies outside the cartel to increase production. The high prices induced by OPEC during the 1970s , encouraged other producers to seek new supplies, such as in the North sea, and induced production from oilfields which were marginal and unprofitable at the old, lower prices. Thus, the high prices brought forth new supplies, which served to dampen the price increases.

Collusive oligopoly leads to essentially the same analytical result as in monopoly, where profits are maximized. However, a special case exists with non-collusive oligopoly, where there is no agreement, formal or tacit, among the producers. In such a case, each firm must be concerned with the actions of its competitors. Consider the firm in Figure 68, with price of P1 and output 11. If the firm raises price, it may suffer a significant decrease in sales, because its competitors may leave prices at the lower level, increasing their sales at the expense of the one which increases prices. However, if it lowers price, it may not gain much in the way of sales because other firms may match the price cut. This gives rise to the 'kinked' demand curve, and the accompanying marginal revenue curve shown in Figure 68. The end result of this is a system of inflexible prices. Each firm is reluctant to change prices because it is unsure of how the others will react.

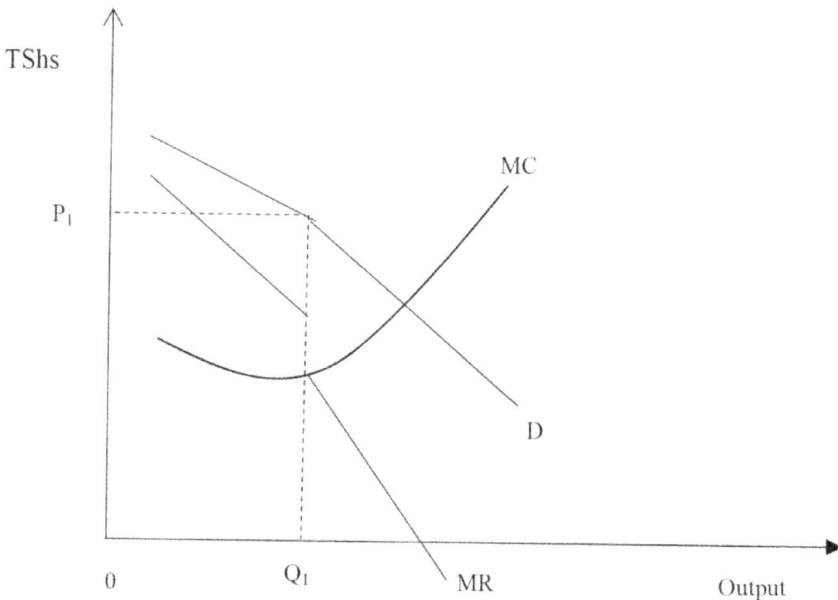

Figure 68: The 'kinked' demand curve as a special case of oligopolistic pricing

While the application of this situation to the real world may be limited, it offers one explanation of 'sticky' prices in some oligopolistic industries. Bear in mind that this requires *no* collusion, tacit or otherwise.

A common form of tacit collusion is *price leadership*. Under price leadership, a dominant firm may raise prices, and other firms soon do the same. While not illegal, it is simply a case where it is tacitly understood that price competition, while generally good for consumers, is not in the best interest of the oligopolistic firms, and each refrains from 'rocking the boat'.

Oligopolistic firms generally engage in vigorous non-price competition, with each firm trying to increase its market share, and differentiating its product in real or psychological terms. This is far more common than vigorous price competition in oligopolistic industries.

Questions for Thought and Discussion

1. Using the data in Table 11 and assuming fixed cost = 100, compute the profit-maximizing level of output for the monopolist. Use both the 'total revenue minus total cost' approach and the 'marginal revenue equals marginal cost' approach. Present the results as diagrams on graph paper.

Table 11: Total product, price and total variable costs data

Total product	Price	Total variable costs
0	201	0
1	191	102
3	181	190
3	171	270
4	161	340
5	151	420
6	141	510
7	131	610
8	121	720
9	111	840

2. Cite examples of oligopolistic and monopolistically competitive industries in East Africa.

3. Explain in detail why the marginal revenue is less than price under imperfect competition.

4. What would you expect the relationship to be between the existence of significant economies of scale in an industry and the type of competition which would emerge? Explain why such a relationship exists.

5. What would you expect to be the relationship between the size of an economy and the level of competition? What are the implications for the

role of government in such a situation?

6. Explain the role of prices in an economy and how this role might be distorted by imperfectly competitive enterprises.

7. Many observers from both within and outside Africa assert that Africa should engage in more intra-African trade, such as forming regional trading areas. How might your answers to Questions 3, 4 and 5 lend credibility to this assertion?

8. Although you have not yet studied international trade, what do you anticipate would be some problems which would have to be overcome to form such common trading areas in Africa?

9. Under what conditions would pure monopoly be recommended in favour of perfect competition? How would you expect the price charged by a monopolist to change when the demand for the product shifts to the right?

10. Cite examples of natural monopolies in Tanzania

11. Under what market structure would you categorize the following:

    (a) A Private Clinic operated by a Medical Doctor
    (b) The Sokoine University of Agriculture
    (c) A Band of Local Musicians
    (d) Tanzania bus Services
    (e) Brooke Bond Tanzania Limited, and
    (f) An Agricultural Economics Consultant.

12. In the above cases, which ones would favour price discrimination (which means charging different prices to different consumers)? What are the common features of the products/services and sellers in the cases you have identified?

CHAPTER NINE

Factor Markets

Introduction

W e have analysed price and output determination from the viewpoint of product markets. We now turn to markets for the factors of production and how they affect the decisions of the individual business firm. Input markets are important not only for how business decisions are affected, but because markets for inputs, particularly labour, affect the level of employment in the economy and the incomes of families and individuals. The most significant factor of production which most individuals have to offer for sale is labour. For this reason, we concentrate initially on labour.

We will introduce the marginal productivity theory of labour inputs. The real world has many deviations which render this theory less than a total explanation of how labour markets actually behave. Nevertheless, an understanding of this theory offers a useful starting point for analysing the market for factors of production.

Derived Demand for an Input

The fundamental proposition of the marginal productivity theory for a factor of production is that demand for the input is a *derived demand*. The demand for the factor is derived from the demand for the product for which the factor is used in production. To illustrate this concept, consider Table 12. In this example, we are assuming pure competition in the sale of the product (we can sell as many units of this product as we choose at a constant price). We are also assuming pure competition in the factor market. That is, we can *purchase* as many units of the input as we choose without affecting its price. The firm is such a small demander for the factors, that by employing more, it does not affect prices.

Note that the production function shows the usual diminishing marginal physical product. Instead of deriving cost of production on the basis of output, however, as we have done in Chapter Four, we calculate the cost directly on the basis of input use.

Table 12: Hypothetical data showing a firm's demand for a single input

Labour	Total physical product (Q)	Marginal physical product (MPP)	Total Revenue (PQ) P = 3	Marginal revenue product (MRP)	Total variable cost $P_X = 10$	Marginal resource Cost (MRC)	Profit (TR–TC)
0	0		0		0		
1	8	8	24	24	10	10	14
2	17	9	51	27	20	10	31
3	25	8	75	24	30	10	45
4	32	7	96	21	40	10	56
5	38	6	114	18	50	10	69
6	43	5	129	15	60	10	71
7	47	4	141	12	70	10	71
8	50	3	150	9	80	10	70
9	52	2	156	6	90	10	66

We calculate profit to the firm by subtracting total costs from total revenue and see that by using seven inputs profits would be maximized. If we worked through this on the basis of output, we would get the same answer.

At this point, we need to introduce two new concepts. Marginal revenue product (MRP) is the addition to *total* revenue as a result of adding another unit of input, or $\Delta TR/\Delta X$.

Marginal resource cost (MRC) or marginal input cost (MIC) is the addition to *total* costs *as a result of adding another unit of* input, or $\Delta TC/\Delta X$ $\Delta TC/\Delta X$. Note that these concepts are similar to marginal revenue and marginal cost, except that we are now viewing additions to costs and revenues as related to inputs, instead of as related to outputs.

Note in Table 12 that marginal resource cost is constant, and *equal to the price* of the input. This is a direct result of the assumption of pure competition in the factor markets. Adding another unit of input adds to costs an amount equal to price of the input. Note also that marginal revenue product, $\Delta TR/\Delta X$, declines even though the *price of the product* remains constant as we sell more. The falling MRP is a direct result of diminishing marginal physical productivity. Each additional unit of input results in a smaller amount of *additional* product. Hence, the *value* of additional output (MPPx Pq) falls, even though the price of the product *per unit* remains constant. In this regard, the marginal physical product of each unit of input (MPP), valued by the price of the product (Pq), yields marginal revenue product, or MPP x Pq = MRP. This will no longer be true if we assume imperfect competition in the product market.

However, with pure competition on the product market, MRP can be calculated either by the addition to total revenue from another unit of input, or by multiplying marginal physical product by the price of the output. The student should verify in Table 12 that this is indeed the case.

Note in the table that the profit-maximizing level of inputs is 7. At this level, the MRP of 12 is greater than the MRC of 10. In other words, adding another unit of input adds more to revenues than to costs. Profits would rise by adding the 7th unit of input, as can be verified by the TR-TC column in the table. However, if we add the 8th unit of input, it costs 10, but only yields 9 in terms of additional revenues. Thus, it would *not* be profitable to add to the 8th unit of input. The theoretical limit, then, is that inputs are added to the point where MRC or MIC= MRP.

Now consider what would happen if the price of the input would rise to 14. Obviously, the firm would incur more additional costs (14) than additional revenues (12) if it continued to employ the 7th unit. However the 6th unit adds additional revenue of 15, so that level would still be profitable.

But the level of input used is declining as its price rises. We can continue this process to see that as the price of the input continue to rise, less is employed.

Recognizing that the theoretical limit is to employ inputs to the point where MRC, or the price of the resource, under pure competition in the input market, is equal to MP, we can plot the amount of inputs used with respect to alternative prices, as in Figure 69. We are, in essence, plotting the MRP cure. We now have a series of relationships between price of the input and quantity used, or demanded. Thus, we have a demand curve for the input. In fact, the student has now just witnessed why the MRP curve is the demand curve for that input in the one-variable input case.

Marginal
Revenue Product
(MRP)

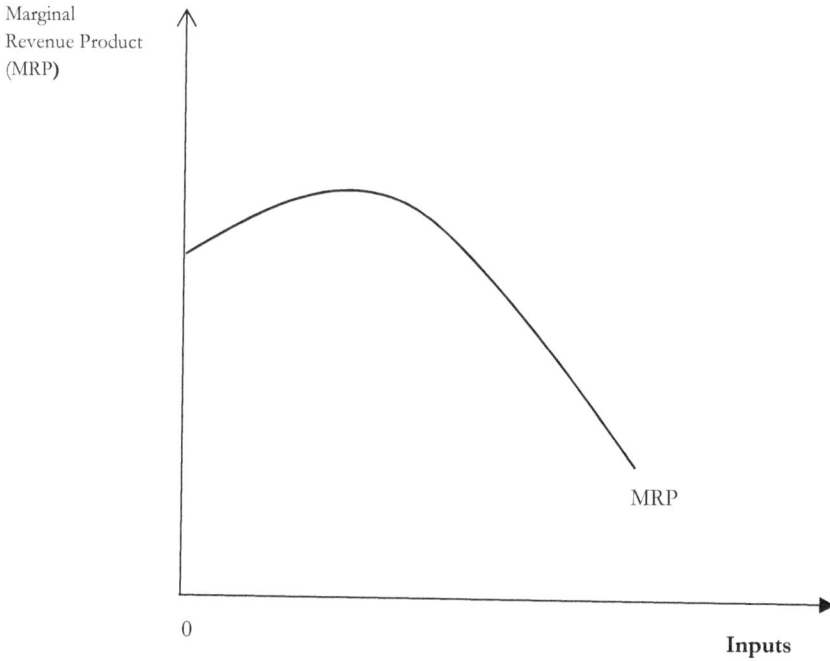

0

Inputs

Figure 69: The MRP curve of the firm (*The MRP curve is the firm's derived demand for the input in the single-input case*).

Again, note that the reason for the declining MRP has nothing to do with any change in the price of the product, as we are under pure competition in the product markets, and a constant price prevails as we produce and sell more. The declining MRP is solely a result of the declining marginal physical productivity of the input.

Also recall the supply shifters, studied in Chapter Five, one of which is the price of the input. What happens to product supply for the total market if all producers respond to declining input prices by employing more, and increasing their output? Obviously, the supply of the product would shift to the right.

What happens if consumers demand more of the product so that its price rises (still assuming pure competition – constant price of output at all levels, but at higher price)? It should be clear that this would increase the MRP at *all* levels of input, thereby amounting to an increase in demand for the factor of production. This shows once again that demand for the factor is *derived* from the demand for the final product for which it is used in production. An increase in demand for tea leads to an increase in demand for hired labour for picking it as well as for fertilizer and pesticides for improved husbandry. A decline in the demand for tea would have the opposite effect on the demand for these inputs.

Equilibrium Wage Rates for Labour

We have seen that the marginal revenue product curve represents the individual firm's demand for labour. The demand for labour may be increased as a result of an increased price of the product for which labour is used. In addition, an increase in the productivity of labour suggests an increase in MRP and, hence, an increase in labour demand by the firm.

The market demand curve for labour is *approximated* by the summation of the individual firm's MRP curves. No individual firm, acting individually, can affect the price of labour under the assumption of pure competition in the labour market. However, should all firms expand production in response to a reduced price of labour, the combined expansion of output results in a decreased product price, and shifts the MRP for labour to the left. The market demand curve shows the effect of changes in input price on the quantity of the input demanded when all firms in the industry respond at the same time.

Let us review the *market supply* curve of labour once again. Under pure competition in the labour market, the price, or wage, for labour is determined by the interaction of supply and demand, and the firm can hire as much or as little labour as desired. The labour supply curve appears as a horizontal line, or perfectly elastic to the firm, because the firm hires such a small proportion of the total labour that it has no effect on price. If the market demand for labour rises, the wage rate increases, as shown in Figure 70.

You should be aware of a peculiar phenomenon known as the 'backward-bending' supply of labour. Some economists assert that in some labour markets, above a certain wage, a higher wage will result in *fewer* rather than more units of labour offered in the market. How can this be?

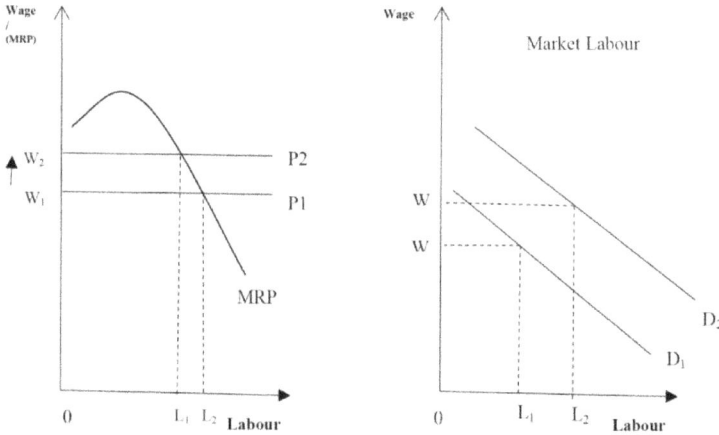

Figure 70: The market demand and supply of labour *(as it affects the supply of labour to the firm under the assumption of pure competition in the labour market)*

Bear in mind that labour is not produced, as such, but is offered by individuals at the expense of their leisure time. As wage rates rise, all else being equal, so do incomes. As incomes rises, people sometimes desire to take more of their time on leisure activities. There are two conflicting incentives as wage rates rise. As the wage rises, the opportunity cost of labour will rise and n will bend backwards as shown in Figure 71. The relative strength of these conflicting effects will depend on the nature of the labour market, the level of income and, obviously, the options and preferences of individuals for work, income and leisure.

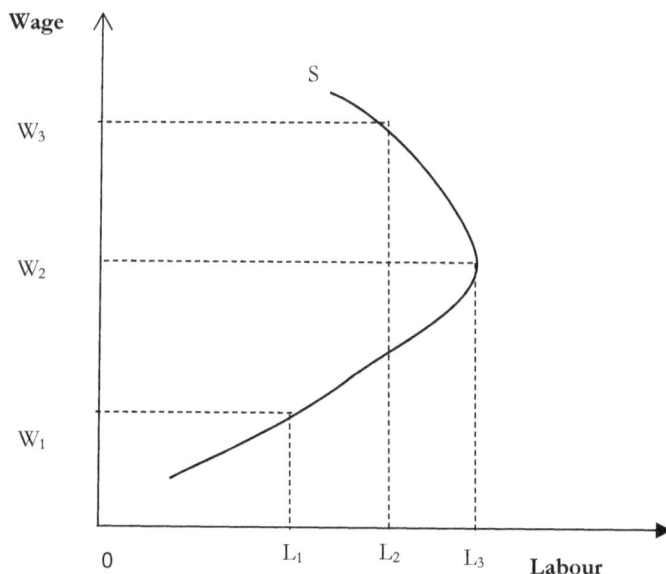

Figure 71: The backward-bending supply of labour

A Note on Multiple Inputs

We treat only briefly here some complexities introduced when several variable inputs are used. Suppose that input X is one of several variable inputs, with a MRP_1 curve as shown in Figure 72. At wage of W_1, labour is used to point A. If the wage rate falls and more labour is used, this would be expected to shift the MRP curves for the other inputs as well. Use of more of these other inputs in turn increases the productivity of labour and the MRP curve for labour shifts to MRP_2. Thus, as the price of labour declines, the use of labour moves form point A to point B, and not to point C as would be expected in a one-input case. The point is that, with more than one variable input, the degree to which one input is used will affect the productivity of the others. For example, if more capital is added, the productivity of labour will normally be increased.

Finally, we should note that when several inputs are used, the most efficient combination of resources use for any level of output is such that the marginal physical product per shilling spent on each input are equated. For example in the two input case,

$$\frac{MPP_1}{P_1} = \frac{MPP_2}{P_2}$$

In other words, the ratios of marginal physical product of each input to its price are equal. If, for example, the additional product from input X_1 was greater per shilling expended on it than for input X_1, the firm would wish to use more X_1. Thus, costs for a given level of output are minimized where the ratios of MPP to price are equal for all inputs.

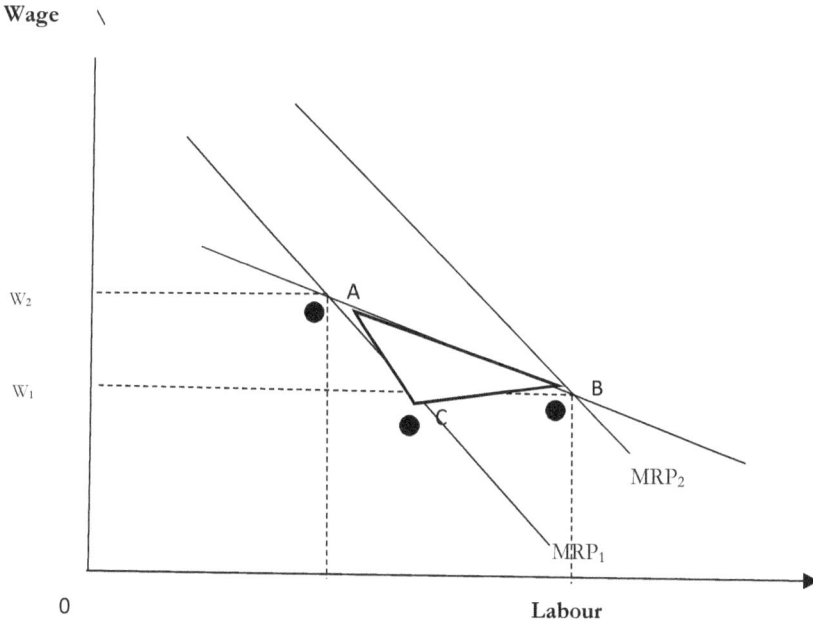

Figure 72: The demand for a resource in the input case

We should bear in mind that P_x/MPP_x is equal to the MC of the product.

As $P/(\Delta Y/\Delta X) = P_x(\Delta X/\Delta Y)$, this says that the price of the input multiplied by the amount used will give us the cost of producing another unit of output. Thus, for any level of output, costs are minimized by using inputs in such combination that:

$$\frac{P_1}{MPP_1} = \frac{P_2}{MPP_2} = MC$$

And, as we have learned before, since production is carried to the point where MC = MR, production should be carried to the point where

$$\frac{P_1}{MPP_1} = \frac{P_2}{MPP_2} = MC = MR$$

A Note on Labour Markets

The marginal productivity theory of labour gives some insights regarding incentives and behaviour in these markets. However, you must be aware of realities which affect labour markets. In many economies, there are legislated minimum wages for certain types of labour. If the market for unskilled labour, for example, approximates that in Figure 73, then w_1 would be the equilibrium rate with Q_1 being hired at that wage. If, however, a minimum wage of w_2 is legislated, then, clearly, a smaller quantity of labour will be demanded than will be supplied, and some involuntary unemployment will exist, as shown in the diagram. Is the minimum wage then 'good' or 'bad'? As with so many issues of public policy, there is no clear-cut answer. Certainly, some people will be better off because they will be earning a higher wage. However, others, who might be willing to work for that wage, will be unable to find work. Out of desperation, such potential workers may accept working for lower wages off the record. This, however, implies that they forego the supplementary benefits, workman's compensation etc., because they are not legally employed. In Tanzania, such practices are not uncommon for domestic, construction and farm workers.

Many economies combine a minimum wage for unskilled labour with other programmes, such as monetary and fiscal policies, to stimulate the economy to greater employment. You will study these policies in macro-economics.

In most economies, labour unions have some influence on labour markets. Labour unions might use several different strategies to raise wages for their members. First, they might try to increase the demand for labour. Some unions do this by participating with their employees in trying to increase the demand for the products, thereby increasing the demand for labour used in producing these products. One way of increasing demand for products is to attempt to keep out competing foreign products. For example, car workers in the USA have attempted to restrict imports of foreign cars in an effort to increase the demand for American-made cars. As you will learn in macroeconomics, however, restricting foreign trade often leads to inefficiency.

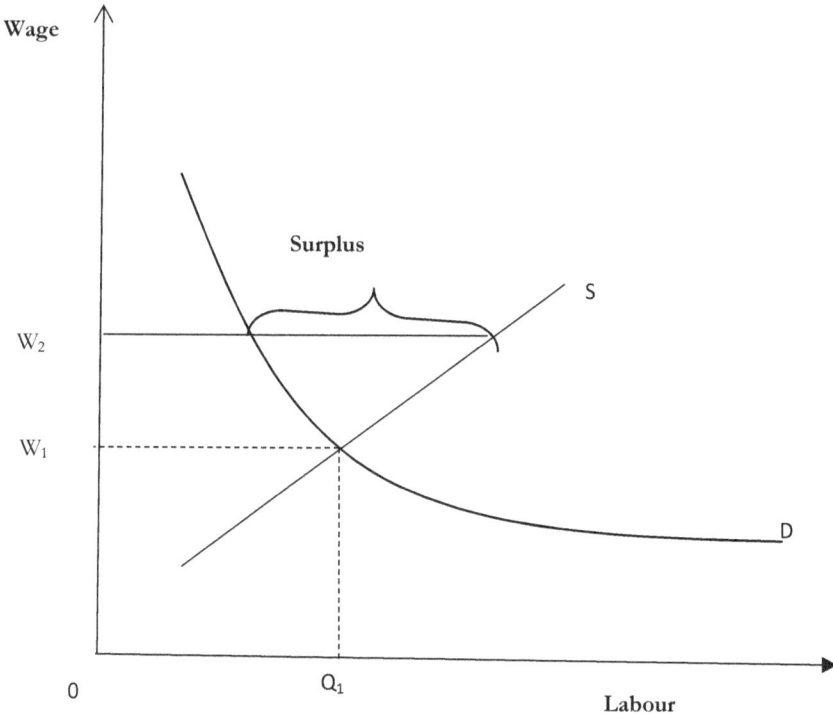

Figure 73: The effects of a 'maximum wage' set above the equilibrium wage rate

A second strategy is to restrict the supply of labour. This tactic is often used in industrial countries to restrict entry into skilled jobs such as carpentry, plumbing and electrical work. This is often done by restricting the numbers entering training programmes and by imposing lengthy apprenticeships. While this restricts supply, and possibly raises wages, it also restricts the numbers of entrants, some of whom would likely be willing to work at a lower wage. We must also remember the matter of incentives. As the price or wage of certain skills and craft rises, employers have the incentive to substitute capital and other labour-saving methods in production.

Finally, as is well known, unions may, through collective bargaining, attempt to impose an above-equilibrium wage rate. In most economies, there are well defined rules, legislated and enforced through government, on strikes and collective bargaining between employers and labour unions. The intent is to foster some degree of equity between employers and employees, and to provide an environment in which bargaining can occur in good faith.

It should be emphasized that most labour unions throughout the world are interested in more than wage rates. Labour unions have often been instrumental in improving working conditions, safety in the workplace, and in contributing to practices regarding hiring, firing and grievance procedures. Thus, the economics of the labour market must go beyond simply an understanding of the marginal productivity theory of labour. Yet, an understanding of that theory can give helpful insights into real-world problems.

Returns to Capital and Land

Thus far, we have studied returns to factors of production largely in the context of returns to labour. We now turn to some aspects of returns to capital and land, i.e. interest and rent. While the theory of capital and land (or natural resources) can be very complex in advanced analysis, there are many elementary aspects of the theory which you are now able to grasp, and which will be quite useful in understanding many economic situations in the real world.

The concept of capital

Capital goods are used in the production of other goods. The economist considers capital to be *real assets,* things such as tools, machinery, buildings and equipment. These goods are not desired as ends in themselves but are useful in producing other goods. Tools and machinery are used to produce other machinery, which may in turn be used to produce yet other tools and machines which are finally used to produce consumer goods. You can probably think of many examples, such as the manufacture of machines to process steel, which is used to manufacture still more machines, and so on. This is sometimes referred to as 'round about' production.

The essence of capital goods is deferred consumption. Since resources used for capital cannot be used for producing consumer goods, current consumption must be reduced if capital goods are to be produced. The sacrifice of consumption for the present allows for increased consumption in the future. Obviously, if one is to be induced to forego consumption today, one must expect higher consumption in the future as a 'reward'. This is the essence of 'return on capital' expressed as a rate.

Specifically, the rate of return on capital is the net return received per year. For example, if a person owns a building costing Sterling Pounds 10,000 and receives Sterling Pounds 500 per year return, the rate of return is 0.05, or 5%.

Real capital and financial assets

It is useful to distinguish between real capital assets and financial assets. The economist normally considers capital to refer to real or tangible assets such as tools, buildings and machinery. However, to the individual, money in savings accounts, stocks and bonds is considered as capital. In the economist's language these are financial assets, having in and of themselves no productive potential. However, such financial assets owned by the individual can be turned into real assets. Thus, the economist is concerned with financial markets for their effect in fostering the formation of real assets. The savings in terms of financial assets allows others to borrow for the purpose of investing in real assets.

To induce people to save, they are paid interest. When you put money say Sterling Pounds 1,000, into a savings account, if you are paid an interest rate of 10%, you receive Sterling Pound 100 per year. Thus, interest is also what the borrower pays for the borrowed money. The borrowing rate depends on whether the money is borrowed for long-term or short-term investment, on the degree of risk involved, and on other factors. If you lent money to a risky venture, you would insist on a higher rate of interest to compensate for the possibility of loss, relative to the interest rate you might ask if the ventures were seen to be safe. Interest rates also vary according to the supply and demand for loanable funds which, in turn, varies according to economic conditions.

Such factors as rates of return on investments are important in decisions which affect economic activity. Because the decision to invest money implies returns in the future, these future returns must be compared with money invested today. Let us look at this in greater detail.

Present value of assets

Decision to invest in assets, whether real of financial, depend on the expected return on investment. For money to be invested today, a return sufficient to reward the investor must be expected in the future. To put it differently, a given amount of money now is more valuable than the same amount of money sometime in the future. Thus, to be equivalent to a given amount of money now, future amounts must be greater. And the further in the future, the greater the amount needed to be equivalent to a given amount today. Thus, amounts of money in different periods of time must be compared at a given point in time. This is why the concept of *present value* is used to compare amounts of money in different times periods at a common point in time.

Let us use a simple example. If someone was to give you Sterling Pound 100 now, what is the value one year from today? Another way of asking the question is "What amount today is equivalent to Sterling Pound 100 one year from now? Of course, it depends on the interest rate. At an interest rate of 10%, 100 today would be equal to Sterling Pound 110 one year from now, because Sterling Pound 100 plus Sterling Pound 100(1.10) = Sterling Pound 110.

You are, doubtless, aware that an amount F, one year in the future, is equal to the principal, P, plus the principal times the interest rate. That is,

$$F = P + Poi, \text{ or } P(1 + I).$$

An amount two years from now, F2, is thus equal to

$$(P + Pi) + (P + Pi)i$$

which factors out to $P(1 + i) (1 + i)^2$, and generally $F_n = P(1 + i)^n$
In an investment decision, for purposes of analysis, we wish to bring future amounts back to the present.

If $F = P(1 + i)$, then to estimate the present value, P of $F_i = F_i/(1 + i)$ and P of $F_2 = F_2/(1 + i)^2$, and, generally, $P = P_n/(1 + i)^n$.

Thus, if we are considering an investment of a given amount which will yield returns for five years, we wish to know the *present value* of future returns. The formula would be:

$$P = \frac{F_1}{(1+i)} + \frac{F_2}{(1+1)^2} + \frac{F_3}{(1+1)^3} + \frac{F_4}{(1+1)^4} + \frac{F_5}{(1+i)^5}$$

Note, first of all, how the size of the interest rate would affect present value. As the interest rate increases, the denominators increase, thus making the respective present value smaller. Thus, to yield a given present value, the future returns must be greater with a higher interest rate. That is, the higher the interest rate, the more the present value of future returns are penalized, and the less attractive the investment appears.

Note, secondly, how the value of F declines as we get further in the future, as the exponent of (1 + i) increases. This means that the further in the future is a given amount the smaller the given present value.

Let us use an example of business deciding whether to invest in a machine costing Sterling Pounds 2,000. Let us assume the amount expected to be generated by the machine in years 1 through 5 are Pound 200, Pound 600, Pound 800, Pound 1,200 and Pound 1,200. If we can't tell whether the investment is wise or not. Thus, we must compare them at a common point in time. Further we must designate an interest rate. If the firm decides that a 10% rate of return is desired, the calculations to determine present value are as follows:

$$P = \frac{200}{(1+.1)} + \frac{600}{(1+.1)^2} + \frac{800}{(1+.1)^3} + \frac{1,200}{(1+.1)^4} + \frac{1,200}{(1+.1)^5}$$

If these values are computed either by calculator, or by hand for that matter, or looked up in interest tables, we find the amounts to be: Pound 181.80 + Pound 495.87 + Pound 601.05 + 819.62 + Pound 745.11 = Pound 2,843.45

Since the present value of the returns, Pound 2,843.45, is greater than the Pound 2,000, the investment appears to be justified.

Again, note what would happen if the interest rate would rise or fall. As the interest rate rises high enough, the present value of future returns would no longer be sufficient to warrant the investment. It is for that reason that interest rates are so important to investment decisions and affect the level of economic activity. Note also that a wrong choice of interest rate might lead to a wrong investment decision. The matter of interest rates and their effect on economic activity is an important topic in the study of macroeconomics.

The value of an income stream in perpetuity

When an investment yields a permanent stream of income of a given amount, the formula is $V = a/I$ where V is the value of the asset, a is the expected annual net return, and I is the interest rate. Thus, an assert expected to yield a net return of Sterling 100 per year, with a desired return of 5% would be valued at Sterling Pound 2,000. If instead, the desired return were 10%, the asset would be valued at Sterling Pound 1,000.

Economic Rent

The return to land and natural resources is referred to by economists as 'rent'. This is potentially confusing as rent is usually thought of as payment for the use of land, building or other property. However, in economic language, rent has a special meaning, namely, a 'residual' return to a factor of production which is fixed in supply.

An English economist, David Ricardo, was among the first to conceptualize 'rent' as a return to a fixed factor. He asserted that land, being fixed in supply, varied in quality and that land of superior quality received a residual return, or rent, which was attributable to that quality.

To illustrate this concept, consider three grades of land which can be used for growing maize; very productive land, less productive land, and marginally prodcutive land. We know from our earlier study that the variable costs of producing maize on productive land is less than the costs of producing on marginally prodcutive land. Thus, the respective costs, which exclude fixed costs attributable to l and, appear as in Figure 74.

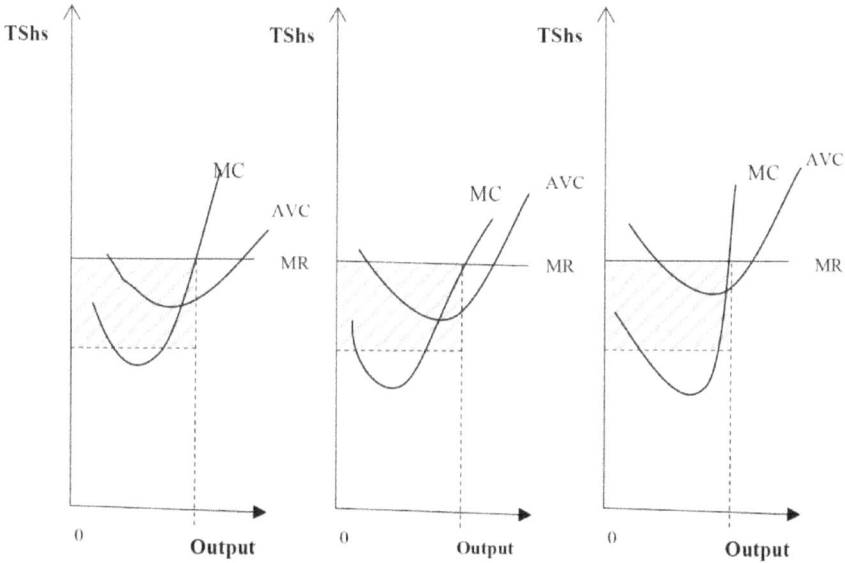

Figure 74: 'Residuals' attribute to quality of the fixed factor

Although the costs of production differ on the three grades of land, the *price* of maize dictated by the market is the same – whether the maize was produced on productive land or marginal land. Hence, the MR is the same over all three situations.

We can see that the difference is between the price and average cost and hence, in this case, the *residual* left over after other costs are paid, are as would be expected, greater for the productive land than for the other two classes of land. This *residual* is known as *economic rent*. Further, this residual attributable to the superior quality of the land which is fixed in supply.

What happens to this economic rent? From our study of asset valuation, we should be able to understand what happens. Because the high quality of land is responsible for a residual over and above other production costs, land becomes and asset capable of returning an annual net amount to the owner. This amount then becomes *capitalized* in to the value of the land. If the owner were to sell the land, the productive land would command a higher price than the less productive land because of its superior income-earning potential. Thus, while the productive potential of the land continues earning a residual to the new owner, the new owner must consider the fixed cost as part of the costs of production. The total cost curve appear as in Figure 75. The land continues to earn an economic rent, but this amount is capitalized into the costs to the owner.

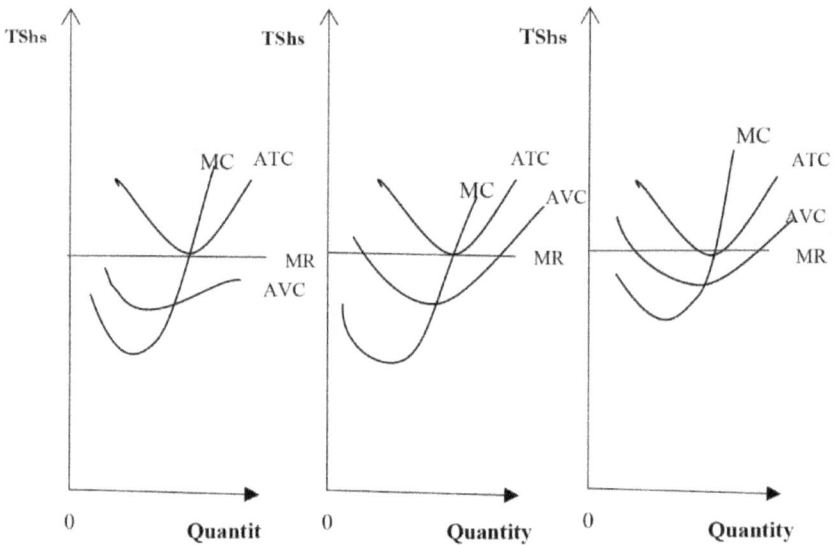

Figure 75: Total costs of production when 'rents' are capitalized into the value of the asset

You might ponder the following perplexing questions: "Is maize valuable because land is valuable" or, "Is land valuable because maize is valuable? It is helpful to distinguish between the viewpoint of the individual and a broader view from the standpoint of the economy as a whole.

The individual, who pays a high price for productive land, must treat land as a cost of production, that is, he must derive returns from his operations sufficient to cover his costs, lest he lose the land back to the bank or to the previous owner. Thus, to the individual, maize is costly to produce because its costs of production include land costs. Maize must yield returns at least as great as other uses to which the land can be put, or else something else will be produced.

But why did the land cost so much in the first place? Clearly, its value is derived from the productivity of the land for producing maize, or perhaps other crops. Thus, although the individual is forced to consider land costs as a cost of production, from the viewpoint of the economy as a whole it can be argued that land is valuable because maize, and other products produced from the land, have value.

Questions for Thought and Discussion

1. With the following production function data compute marginal revenue product if the price of the output is Sh 4 per unit.

Table 13: Production function data

Input	Output
0	0
1	5
2	11
3	16
4	20
5	23
6	25
7	26
8	26

Sketch the MRP curve and determine the level of input use and profits if the cost of the input is Sh 10 per unit. What happens if the price of output declines to Sh 2 per unit? What happens if the price of the output increases to Sh 5 per unit?

2. Explain how an increase in productivity of an input affects the demand for that input.

3. Explain carefully why the firm has the incentive to use inputs up to the point where MRC = MRP.

4. Explain why the MRP declines as more inputs are used.

5. Explain the concept of discounting future returns. What happens to the present value of future returns as the discount factor (interest rate) is increased?

6. Why does high-quality land cost more than low-quality land? On which class of land are the variable costs of production for a given crop lowest? What would be expected to happen to fixed costs of production on high-quality land? Explain

7. What would you suggest are the factors causing wage differences between Tanzania's agricultural workers and those working in the manufacturing sector?

8. Give several arguments for and against government regulation of the maize industry in Tanzania regarding consequences of return to

labour and land used in maize production.

9. A farmer intends to go into zero grazing which has the following cash flow annually:

	TShs
1990 present	--20,000
1991	+7,000
1992	+ 8,000
1993	+ 4,000
1994	+ 4,00

If the interest rate is 6% per year, should the farmer invest in zero grazing? How about if the interest rate is 18%

10. A taxi driver's income depends purely on his productivity and the demand for transport. Show whether this is true or false.

CHAPTER TEN

The Price System and the Economic Role of Government

Introduction

We have come a long way since our initial introduction to economics and the study of the price and market system. We have seen that market prices perform specific and necessary functions, such as rationing and guiding resource allocation. We have seen that, in a price and market system, many decisions are made automatically, with a minimum of central guidance. This is the essence of Adam Smith's 'invisible hand', as described in 1776 in his book *The Wealth of Nations*. This was the first major attempt to describe the functioning of a decentralized price and market system. Smith asserted that in such a system each individual, acting in his own self-interest, automatically furthered the welfare of society, as if guided by an invisible hand.

How accurate is the concept of the invisible hand? Some followers of Adam Smith have taken him literally, and by logical extension, have asserted that with pure capitalism, as self-interest automatically furthers the welfare of society. This allows for only a minimal role of government. If all happens automatically, and in the best interests of society, why does government need to intervene in the economy? Yet, clearly, all economic systems depend in some measure on the role of government in the economy, and for good reason.

The 'proper' role of government in the economy is a lively topic of debate in many nations, and one which is never totally resolved. But what most people can agree on is that ideology, be it capitalism, socialism, or some combination, is not an end but is only a means to a broader end – that of answering the basic economic questions and of serving economic goals, such as full employment, economic growth, and such other goals as we discussed in previous chapters.

Let us stand back from our previous, rather detailed analysis, and take a bird's eye view of the price and market system and discuss its strengths, as well as observe some points where it might require assistance from the helping hand of government to serve the broad objectives of society and the economic system.

Two Cheers for the Price System

As we have seen, a most impressive feature of a price and market system is that so many incentives are provided for efficient resource use and so many decisions are made automatically with a minimum of central direction. Price serves as a rationing device, and as a guide to the allocation of resources. When pries of product are high, this serves as an incentive to produce and for consumers to seek substitutes. When prices are low, consumers are encouraged to substitute that product for those which are more expensive. When resources are costly, their use is discouraged, and less costly resources tend to be used in production. The incentives of producers to produce those items which appear profitable, and by means which minimize costs, ensure that the questions of what and how to produce are answered with some measure of economic efficiency. And again, that this occurs with no central direction or guidance is of some considerable advantage.

In addition to a considerable degree of economic efficiency, the price and market system affords participants a large measure of economic freedom. Producers are free to produce, within broad limits, products which they perceive to be profitable, and in a way as to minimize costs. Consumers are free to purchase goods according to the pattern, which maximizes their utility.

So far so good. One can broadly commend the performance of prices and markets for promoting economic efficiency and economic freedom. Some people have extended this to promote a minimum of government 'interference' with an economic system. This is sometimes referred to as 'laissez-faire' capitalism, where the economic role of government is limited to the establishment of a monetary system and a legal framework within which prices and markets can operate. Such a framework provides a monetary system, provides for a system of weights and measures, provides for enforcement of contracts, and enables commercial activities to be carried out. Yet, the economic role of government is greater than this in virtually all the world's economic systems, including those of the United States, Canada, Western Europe and developing nations such as Tanzania. Let us see why this is so.

Private and Public Goods

Most goods and services which we have used as examples in our study are called 'private goods'. Private goods such as food, clothing, furniture, appliances, and a whole host of other goods purchased in the market can be produced and sold in small, divisible units. Further, the nature of these goods is such that the benefits of consumption are limited to one or a few individuals. That is, consumption is 'exclusive'. The net result is that these goods can be produced and sold by individual producers. As the benefits of consumption are exclusive to the purchaser, the producer can produce these goods and exchange them for the purchase price.

By way of contrast, there are many useful goods and services which do not have these characteristics. They are generally produced in large or 'lumpy' units. Further, the benefits are not exclusive to a few individuals. That is, use of these goods by one person does not exclude their use by others. Examples are a public or national park, national defence, and such items as research on agriculture, disease prevention and control and environmental protection. These items must be provided in some standard amount if they are provided at all. In addition, the benefits of these goods and services are not exclusive. Your use and enjoyment of the national park or your enjoyment of the clean environment, does not preclude similar use by your friends and neighbors.

Some goods have attributes of public goods, although not classified as pure public goods. Public education, and streets and roads are examples. These goods have limited capacity and when the point of congestion is reached one person's use excludes or interferes with that of another. However, up to the point of congestion, they resemble public goods. These goods also are usually provided by, or through collective action.

Public goods, and goods having public-goods attributes, are more effectively produced in the desired amounts collectively, most often through government. Because the benefits are not exclusive (and therefore not able to be captured by the private producer) such goods and services are not provided in sufficient quantity by the private sector through the price and market system. This then, is an economic role played by government in virtually all the economies of the world.

External Costs and Benefits

The world would indeed be far simpler than it is if the cost, or consequences, of each economic decision were incident only on the person making that decision. If the market price of a resource is high, the person paying that price clearly bears the cost, and has the incentive to economize on the use of that resource. However, although some decisions have a high cost, a substantial part of that cost is not borne by the decision-maker but by someone else not responsible for that decision. These costs are called external costs. For example, a large factory releases its effluent, which finds its way into Ruvu river. The river's water is used for drinking by residents downstream in Coast Region and Dar es Salaam. The fish in the river may also be affected and people could ingest pollutants by eating fish. The student should also be aware of other external costs such as air pollution, especially in Nairobi's industrial area.

If a producer such as a tannery or textile manufacturer uses a stream or river in which to discharge waste from production process, there is a cost to society in terms of reduced water quality and poisoned fish. However, to the producer, it is less costly to dump the waste into the stream than to purchase equipment with which to treat the waste. Clearly, there is a cost of using the stream, but that cost is borne mainly by society in general rather than the producer making the decision. In the absence of rules to the contrary, the producer has no incentive to take the costs of pollution into account. A way of forcing the firm to take these costs into account would be by putting a tax on each unit of output produced by the polluting firm, thereby raising its marginal cost of production.

The net result of external costs is that those goods for which there are external costs, such as environmental degradation, are produced artificially cheap, and in greater abundance, as the use of the environment is not paid for by producers who produce products causing pollution. In addition, there is more pollution than society would desire. This again, is where there is a legitimate economic role for government.

The government might establish rules and laws against pollution or otherwise force the polluter to take the external costs into account.

For some decisions, there are external benefits. An example is a public health campaign. If people are vaccinated against measles, for example, it benefits not only them but others as well, through reduced incidence of the disease. Thus, the government may see fit to subsidize such programmes as the benefits clearly go beyond the immediate beneficiaries.

Maintaining Competition

Early in our study we observed that competition was the force that reduced the opportunity for one economic player to exploit another. In the extreme, pure competition prevented anyone from setting a price by acting alone. Later, we observed that an increase in market concentration, or market power, afforded a greater measure of control over price. We have also assumed that each individual acts in his own self-interest.

You may have noted a potential conflict, which may arise against the public interest. If individuals act in their own self-interest, and competition is a restraining force, there is an incentive for firms to combine and form combinations to reduce competition and thus exercise market power. This is one of the explanations for mergers and combinations which enable firms to become bigger and more dominant in the market.

The most difficult task for government is to maintain some degree of competition while allowing a degree of economic freedom and the capacity of firms to utilize economies of scale in production. Obviously, this is not only a difficult, but a controversial role of government and the dilemma is never totally resolved. The task is perhaps even more difficult in a smaller economy with smaller markets which are more easily dominated by large firms. Uneven market power may rise on the purchasing side as well where, for example, farmers only face a single buyer or perhaps only a small number of buyers. In such instances, government sometimes steps in to provide an alternative or directly intervenes to ensure equitable prices to sellers.

Distribution of Income

The 'proper' distribution of income in an economy is an ethical question or, to use our more formal terminology, a *normative* matter. A price and market system will usually result in a distribution of income skewed toward those with the most resources.

There is nothing necessarily 'moral' about this distribution. Some people will certainly be very poor. Governments may take measures such as 'progressive taxation of income, i.e., taxing the rich more heavily than the poor or programmes of transfers to assist the needy. The solutions are as much political as economic. Suffice it to say that in so far as a reasonable distribution of income (however that might be defined), is an economic goal, many governments form programmes to ameliorate the most blatant hardship situations.

Recall in our study of elasticity that the prices of some commodities vary a great deal because of inelasticity of supply and demand. In such cases, governments sometimes form marketing boards to stabilize price and thus insulate producers against the devastating effects of severe price decreases. This is another example of how government action in the economy might influence the distribution of income as well as compensate for the lack of bargaining power of the producer.

Maintaining Employment

As you will learn when studying macroeconomics, there is nothing inherent in a price and market system to ensure that a high level of employment will automatically occur and be maintained. It is a primary function of government to attempt, through fiscal and monetary policy and other means, to bring about a high level of employment and stable price. Further attention to these problems is deferred until you study macroeconomics.

A Concluding Note

In summary, systems of prices and markets have proved to be powerful mechanisms for fostering production and economic growth throughout the world. The efficiencies and economic freedom afforded by such systems have been demonstrated time and again. Yet, a cautionary note is in order. The challenge of government and society is to encourage, maintain and take advantage for the common good and public interest the strengths of a price and market system, while at the same time addressing some of the problems we have just discussed. Possible roles of government in an economic system are to maintain some desirable level of competition, provide needed public goods, correct for external costs, encourage a good distribution of income and attempt to maintain a high level of employment with stable prices.

The challenge which each nation and society must meet is to find the appropriate combination of prices and markets and government policies for that particular economy. This is, no doubt, a formidable task and a most challenging one. But it is difficult to think of a task more worthy of effort, particularly for the developing nations which are striving for a better life for all their citizens.

Questions for Thought and Discussion

1. Explain in your own words the function of prices in a market economy. What incentive do price give us, and in what way are they useful in answering the basic economic questions?
2. Explain the concept of external costs and benefits. What tends to happen under a price and market system to the price and quantity produced of;

   (a) Products Having External Costs?
   (b) Of Products Having External Benefits

3. The eradication of coffee berry disease in Central Province is not a public service since it does not have cost and benefit implications for producers and consumers in Coast Province. Is the statement true or false?
4. An oil refinery producing Q barrels of output per week pollutes the neighbouring land. If the costs are given as C, from the point of view of the government what are entailed in these costs? How about from the point of view of the owners of the refinery? How would the owners of the nearby agricultural land be compensated? What effect would the compensation have on the output of the refinery?
5. In a developing economy, there are many tasks which the government needs to accomplish. In your judgment, what are the most appropriate economic functions of government? In what ways might the government rely on the price system to made economic decisions? In what way might the government need to intervene to accomplish certain economic goals?
6. What is the distinguishing feature of public goods? Why are public goods produced in insufficient amounts by the private sector?
7. Why are wildlife reserves considered to be public good? In what sense do the benefits of wildlife accrue to private individuals, and in what sense do such benefits accrue to the broader public of Tanzania? In the absence of government protection, do you believe that wildlife would be protected in sufficient degree to provide the

existing level of benefits? Use economic logic to support you position.

Bibliography

Abreu, R. and A. Sen (1990), "Subgame Perfect Implementation: A Necessary and Almost Sufficient Condition," *Journal of Economic Theory* 50, 285-299.

Abreu, R. and A. Sen (1991), "Virtual Implementation in Nash Equilibrium," *Econometrica*, 59, 997-1021.

Arrow, K. J. (1963). *Social Choice and Individual Values*. 2nd edition. New York Wiley.

Arrow, K. J. (1970). *Essays in the Theory of Risk Bearing*. Chicago: Markham.

Arrow, K., and F. Hahn (1971). *General Competitive Analysis*. San Francisco: Holden-Day. Association of America.

Bade, R. and M. Parkin (2001). *Foundations of Microeconomics*. 1st Edition. Addison Wesley. USA

Bernoulli, D. (1954). "Exposition of a new theory on the measurement of risk." *Econometrica* 22, 23–36. ·

Blomqvist, A., P. Wonnacott, and R. Wonnacott, (1987). *An Introduction to Microeconomics*. McGrawhill Limited. New York.

Bolton, P. and M. Dewatripont (2005), *Contract Theory*, MIT Press. USA.

Bowles, S. (2003). *Microeconomics: Behavior, Institutions, and Evolution*. Princeton University Press. USA.

Brown, S. S. (1995). *Principles of Economics*. West Publishing Company. San Francisco, USA

Calsarniglia, X. (1977), "Decentralized Resource Allocation and Increasing Returns," *Journal of Economic Theory* 14, 263-283.

Corch´on, L. C., (1996). *Theory of Implementation of Socially Optimal Decisions in Economics*, Macmilian Press, Ltd., New York.

Cowell, F. A. (2005). *Microeconomics: Principles and Analysis*. Oxford University Press. UK.

Daintith, J. and R. Maile. (Eds) (1983). *Dictionary of Economics*. Arnold-Heinemann. London.

Danilov, V. (1992), "Implementation via Nash Equilibrium," *Econometrica*, 60, 43-56.

Dasgupta, P, P. Hammond and E. Maskin (1979), "The Implementation of Social Choice Rules: Some General Results on Incentive Compatibility" *Review of Economic Studies* 46, 185-216.

Debreu, G. (1959). *Theory of Value*. Wiley. New York.

Debreu, G. (1960). *Mathematical Methods in the Social Sciences.* Stanford University Press. USA.

Dixit, A and J. Stiglitz. (1977). "Monopolistic Competition and Optimum Product Diversity" *American Economic Review,* vol. 67, 297-308.

Dunne, T, J. Bradford, and J. Mark. (2009). *Producer Dynamics: New Evidence from Micro Data.* University of Chicago Press. USA.

Dutta, B., M. O. Jackson, and M. Le Breton (2001). "Strategic candidacy and voting procedures." *Econometrica* 69, 1013–1037.

Maskin, E. (1999), "Nash Equilibrium and Welfare Optimality" *Review of Economic Studies* 66, 23-38.

Flaschel, P. (2010*). Topics in Classical Micro and Macroeconomics-Elements of critique of Neoricardian Theory.* Springer. New York.

Fogiel, M. (1995). *The Economics Problem Solver.* Research and Education Association. New Jesey. USA.

Frank, R. H. (1991). *Microeconomics and Behaviour.* McGrawhill. New York.

Gilboa, I., and D. Schmeidler (1995). "Case-based decision theory" *The Quarterly Journal of Economics* 110, 605–639.

Groves, T. and J. Ledyard. (1977). "Optimal Allocation of Public Goods; A Solution to the Free Rider Problem," *Econometrica* 45(4), 783-811.

Groves, T. and M. Loeb, Incentives and public inputs, *Journal of Public Economics* 4 (1975), 211-226.

Hart, O. (1985), "Monopolistic Competition in the Spirit of Chamberlin: A General Model," *Review of Economic Studies,* 52, 529-546.

Hicks, J. R. (1939). *Value and Capital.* Oxford University Press. London.

Hicks, J. R. (1939). *Value and Capital: An Inquiry into Some Fundamental Principles of Economic Theory.* Oxford: Oxford University Press.

Hicks, J. R. (1946). *Value and Capital.* Oxford: Clarendon Press.

Hicks, J. R. (1956). *A Revision of Demand Theory.* Oxford: Clarendon Press.

Houthakker, H. S. (1950). "Revealed preference and the utility function." *Economica* 17, 159–174.

Huber, J., J. Payne, and C. Puto. (1982). "Adding asymmetrically dominated alternatives: Violations of regularity and the similarity hypothesis." *Journal of Consumer Research.* 9, 90–98.

Hurwicz, L. (1979b), "On Allocations Attainable Through Nash Equilibria" *Journal of Economic Theory.* 21(1), 140-165.

Hurwicz, L. (1979d), "Socialism and Incentives: Developing a Framework," *Journal of Comparative Economics* 3, 207-216.

Hurwicz, L. (1999), "Revisiting Externalities," *Journal of Public Economic Theory*, 1, 225-246.

J. Roberts and H. Sonnenschein, (1976), "On the Existence of Cournot Equilibrium without Concave Profit Functions," *Journal of Economic Theory*, vol. 13, 112-117

J. Roberts and H. Sonnenschein, (1977), "On the Foundations of the Theory of Monopolistic Competition," *Econometrica*, vol. 75, 101-113,

Jackson, M. O. (1991), "Bayesian Implementation," *Econometrica* 59, 461-477.

Jehle, G. and P. Reny. (2003) *Advanced Microeconomic Theory* (2nd ed). Pearson. UK.

Jehle, G., and P. Reny (1997). *Advanced Microeconomic Theory*. Boston: Addison-Wesley.

Kahneman, D., and A. Tversky (1979). "Prospect theory: An analysis of decision under risk." *Econometrica* 47: 263–292.

Kahneman, D., and A. Tversky (2000). *Choices, Values, and Frames*. Cambridge University Press. UK.

Kalai, G., A. Rubinstein, and R. Spiegler (2002). "Comments on rationalizing choice functions which violate rationality." *Econometrica* 70, 2481– 2488.

Kannai, Y., and B. Peleg (1984). "A note on the extension of an order on a set to the power set." *Journal of Economic Theory* 32, 172–175.

Kasher, A., and A. Rubinstein (1997). "On the question Who is a J?": A social choice approach." *LogiqueetAnalyse* 160, 385–395.

Kelly, J. S. (1988). *Social Choice Theory: An Introduction*. Springer. New York.

Kreps, D. (1988). *Notes on the Theory of Choice*. Westview Press. Boulder, Colo.

Kreps, D. (1990). *A Course in Microeconomic Theory*. Princeton University Press. Princeton, N.J.

Laffont, J. J. and D. Martimort. (2002). *The Theory of Incentives: The Principal-Agent Model*, Princeton University Press. New York.

Li, Q., S. Nakmura and G. Tian, (1995), "Nash Implementation of the Lindahl Correspondence with Decreasing Returns to Scale Technology," *International Economic Review* 36, 34-50.

Liu, L., and G. Tian (1999), "A Characterization of Optimal Dominant Strategy Mechanisms," *Review of Economic Design* 4, 205-218.517.

Luce, D. R., and H. Raiffa. (1957). *Games and Decisions*. Wiley. New York

Luce, Duncan R. (1956). "Semiorders and a theory of utility discrimination." *Econometrica* 24, 178–191.

Spence, M. (1976), "Product Differentiation and Welfare," *American Economic Review, Papers and Proceedings,* 66(2), 407-414.

Spence, M. (1976), "Product Selection, Fixed Costs and Monopolistic Competition," *Review of Economic Studies,* 43, 217-236,

Machina, M. (1987). "Choice under uncertainty: Problems solved and unsolved." *Journal of Economic Perspectives* 1, 121–154.

Mankiw N. G. (1997). *Principles of Microeconomics.* South-Western College. USA.

Mansfield, E. (1991). Microeconomic Problems: Case Studies and Exercise for Reviews (7th Ed). W. W. Norton and Company. New York.

Markowitz, H. (1959). *Portfolio Selection: Efficient Diversification of Investments.* Wiley. New York.

Mas-Colell, A., M. D. Whinston, and J. R. Green (1995). *Microeconomic Theory.* Oxford University Press. Oxford.

Matsushima, H. (1988), "A New Approach to the Implementation Problem," *Journal of Economic Theory* 45, 128-144.

Matsushima, H. (1993), "Bayesian Monotonicity with Side Payments," *Journal of Ecomatical Economics,* 45, 113-123.

May, O. (1952). "A set of independent necessary and sufficient conditions for simple majority decision." *Econometrica* 20, 680–684.

McKelvey, R. (1989), "Game Forms for Nash Implementation of General Social Correspondence," *Social Choice and Welfare,* 6, 139-156.

McKenzie, L. (1957). "Demand theory without a utility index." *Review of Economic Studies 24,* 185–189.

Moore, J. and R. Repullo (1990), "Nash Implementation: A Full Characterization,"*Econometrica* 56, 1083-1099.

Mount, K., and S. Reiter (1974), "Informational Size of Message Spaces," *Journal of Economic Theory* 8, 161-191.

Muller, E., and M. A. Satterthwaite (1977). "The equivalence of strong positive association and strategy proofness." *Journal of Economic Theory* 14, 412–418.

Nicholson, W. (2001). *Microeconomic Theory: Basic Principles and Extensions.* South-Western College. Eco*nomic Theory* 59, 107-121.

O"Sullivan, A., S. Sheffrin, and S. Perez. (2009). *Microeconomics: Principles, Applications, and Tools.* (6th Ed). Pearson. New York.

Palfrey, T. and S. Srivastava (1987), "On Bayesian Implementable Allocations," *Review of Economic Studies* 54, 193-208.

Palfrey, T. and S. Srivastava (1989), "Mechanism Design with Incomplete Information: A Solution to the Implementation Problem," *Journal of Political Economy* 97, 668-691.

Palfrey, T. and S. Srivastava (1991), "Nash Implementation Using Undominated Strategy," *Econometrica* 59, 479-502.

Perloff, J. (2007). *Microeconomics: Theory and Applications with Calculus.* Pearson. Upper Saddle.

Pindyck, R. S and D. L. Rubinfeld. (1999). *Microeconomics* (5ᵗʰ Ed) Prentice Hall. UK.

Postlewaite, A. and D. Wettstein (1989), "Continuous and Feasible Implementation,"*Review of Economic Studies* 56, 603-611.

Pratt, J. (1964). "Risk aversion in the small and in the large." *Econometrica* 32: 122–136.

Rabin, M. (1998). "Psychology and economics." *Journal of Economic Literature* 36, 11–46.

Radner, R. (1993). "The organization of decentralized information processing." *Econometrica* 61, 1109–1146.

Reny, P. J. (2001). "Arrow's theorem and the Gibbard-Satterthwaite theorem: A unified approach." *Economic Letters* 70, 99–105.

Repullo, R.(1987), "A Simple Proof of Maskin's Theorem on Nash Implementation,"*Social Choice and Welfare*, 4, 39-42.

Richter, M. K. (1966). "Revealed preference theory." *Econometrica* 34: 635– 645.

Rothschild, M., and J. Stiglitz (1970). "Increasing risk *I*: A definition." *Journal of Economic Theory* 2, 225–243.

Rubinstein, A. (1988). "Similarity and decision-making under risk." *Journal of Economic Theory* 46: 145–153.

Rubinstein, A. (1998). *Modeling Bounded Rationality*. MIT Press. Boston

Rubinstein, A. (2002). "Irrational diversification in multiple decision problems." *European Economic Review* 46, 1369–1378.

Saleemi, N. A. (2007). *Economics Simplified*. Saleemi Publications. Nairobi.

Salvatore, D. (2000). *International Economics. Macmillan* Publishing Co. New York.

Samuelson, P. A. (1948). "Consumption theory in terms of revealed preference."*Economica* 15: 243–253.

Sawelson, P. A. and Nordhaus (2001). *Economics*. McGraw-Hill Book Company. New York.

Schmeidler, D. (1980), "Walrasian Analysis via Strategic Outcome Functions," *Econometrica* 48, 1585-1593.

Sen, A. (1970). *Individual Choice and Social Welfare.* Holden- Day, San Fransisco.

Sen, A. (1993). "Internal consistency of choice." *Econometrica* 61, 495–521.

Simon, H. (1955). "A Behavioral Model a Rational Choice." *Quarterly Journal of Economics,* 69, 99–118.

Slovic, P., A. Tversky and D. Kahneman (1990). "The causes of preference reversal." *American Economic Review* 80, 204–217.

Slovic, P. and S. Lichtenstein (1968). "Relative importance of probabilities and payoffs in risk taking." *Journal of Experimental Psychology Monograph* 78, 1–18.

Svend, R. (2010). Production Economics: The Basic Theory of Production Optimization. Springer. Illus.

T. Bergstrom and H. Varian, (1985), "Two Remarks on Cournot Equilibrium," *Economics Letters,* 19, 5-8.

Tian, G. (2000a), "Double Implementation of Lindahl Allocations by a Continuous and Feasible Mechanism," *Social Choice and Welfare,* 17 (2000), 125-141.

Tian, G. (2000b), "Incentive Mechanism Design for Production Economies with BothPrivate and Public Ownership," *Games and Economic Behavior,*33 (2000), 294-320.

Tian, G. (2006), "The Unique Informational Efficiency of the Competitive Mechanismin Economies with Production," *Social Choice and Welfare,* 26, 155-182.

Tonu, P. (2010). *Oligopoly: Old Ends-New Means.* Springer. New York.

Tversky, A., and E. Shafir (1992). "Choice under conflict: The dynamics of deferred decision." *Psychological Science* 3, 358–361.

Tweeten, L (1992). *Agricultural Trade: Principles and Policies.* Westview Press. Boulder. Uniquely," *Journal of Economic Theory,* 28, 1-18.

Varian, H. R. (1993). *Intermediate Microeconomics:* A Modern Approach, (6th Ed). Norton. W. W. New York.

Varian, H. (1981), "A Model of Sales" *American Economic Review,* 70(4), 651-659.

Varian, H. R. (1992), *Microeconomic Analysis,* (3rd ed). W.W. Norton and Company, USA.

Walker, M. (1978), "A Note on the Characterization of Mechanisms for the Revelation of Preferences," *Econometrica* 46, 147-152.

Walker, M. (1980), "On the Nonexistence of a Dominant Strategy Mechanism for Making Optimal Public Decisions," *Econometrica* 48, 1521-1540.

Walker, M. (1981), "A Simple Incentive Compatible Scheme for Attaining Lindahl Allocations,"*Econometrica* 49, 65 -71.

Wolfstetter, E. (1999). *Topics in Microeconomics - Industrial Organization, Auctions, and Incentives,* Cambridge Press. UK.

Yaari, M. E. (1987). "The dual theory of choice under risk." *Econometrica* 55, 95–115.

Glossary

Consumer Theory

Axioms of preference

In CONSUMER DEMAND THEORY, individuals are assumed to obey axioms of RATIONALITY and other axioms of behaviour which, combined, form a testable theory of consumer behaviour. Although terminology varies, some six axioms are usually cited as being required for consumer theory based on INDIFFERENCE CURVE analysis. These are:

1. The axiom of completeness which simply states that the consumer can order all available combinations of goods according to his PREFERENCES.
2. The axiom of transitivity which states that if some combination of goods A is preferred to another combination B, and B is preferred to C then (by transitivity) A is preferred to C. Transitivity also applies to indifference relationships. Violation of the transitivity axiom is widely construed as an indication of irrationality.
3. The axiom of selection which simply states that the consumer aims for his most preferred state. Axioms 1 to 3 are usually regarded as axioms of rationality. The remaining axioms are really assumptions about behaviour they are:
4. The axiom of dominance. This states that consumers will prefer more of all goods to less. Also known as the axiom of 'greed', non-satiation (see SATIATION) or monotonicity.
5. The axiom of continuity. Effectively, this states that there is a set of points which form a boundary (an indifference curve) dividing those combinations of goods in COMMODITY SPACE which are preferred from those that are non-preferred. More easily thought of as an axiom which ensures that the indifference curve is a curve or line rather than a 'smudge'.
6. The axiom of convexity (of preferences). The assumption that the indifference curve is CONVEX to the origin. Similar axioms are needed for REVEALED PREFERENCE.

Budget line

A line in COMMONDITY SPACE indicating what combinations of goods the consumer can buy with a given income. The slope and location of the line are determined by the prices of the goods in question. Thus, if all income, Y, is spent on two goods X and Z with prices p_x and p_z, then

$$Y = p_x X + Pz$$

which on rearrangement becomes

$$Z = \frac{Y}{P_z} - \frac{P_x}{P_z} \cdot X$$

so that the slope of the budget line is the ratio of the two prices. The budget line is also known as the income line, consumer possibility line budget constraint, wealth constraint and even price line. (See CONSUMER EQUILIBRIUM).

Cardinal Utility

Cardinal utility approach to the consumer choice problem whereby it is assumed that the satisfaction provided by any bundle of goods can be assigned a numerical or cardinal, value by a utility function of the form
U=U(X,Y)
Based on this cardinal utility assumption, consumers will be able to not only rank the preference (ORDINAL UTILITY) but can make such statement as "X is 5.36 times as good as Y. (SEE ORDINAL UTILITY)

Consumer

Any economic agent responsible for the act of consuming final goods and services. Typically, the consumer is thought of as an individual but in practice consumers will consist of institutions, individuals, and groups of individuals. In the last respect, it is noteworthy that the consuming agent for many decisions in the household and not the individual. This matters in so far as households may well take 'group' decisions based on some compromise of individual wants within the household, or, even more likely, on paternalistic judgments by older members of the household. Consumer demand may therefore be partly considered in the context of group decisions reflecting some SOCIAL WELFARE FUNCTION which covers all members of the household.

Consumer equilibrium

The situation in which the consumer maximizes UTILITY subject to a given BUDGET COSNTRAINT. In terms of an INDIFFERENCE MAP this situation is achieved when the consumer reaches the highest possible INDIFFERENCE CURVE given the limitations imposed by this BUDGET LINE. This will be a situation where the indifference curve is tangential to the budget line (i.e., their slopes are equal). Formally, the MARGINAL RATE OF SUBSTITUTION is equal to the price ratio of the two goods, that is,

$$MRS_{xy} = -\frac{\Delta Y}{\Delta X}$$

for two goods X and Y.

Consumer demand theory

That area of economics which defines testable theories of how consumers behave in response to changes in variables such as price, other prices, income changes and so on. The two main schools of thought are those based on INDIFFERENCE CURVE analysis and REVEALED PREFERENCE THEORY, but considerable attention has also been given to the theories based on the CHARACTERISTICS of goods.

Consumer goods and services

Tangible and intangible COMMODITIES which are consumed for their own sake to satisfy current wants.

Complements

A good which tends to be purchased when another good is purchased since it 'complements' the first good. Favourite examples are cups and saucers, cars and petrol etc. Complementary goods have a negative CROSS ELASTICITY OF DEMAND. The INDEFERRENCE CURVE for perfect complements is shown in the diagram.

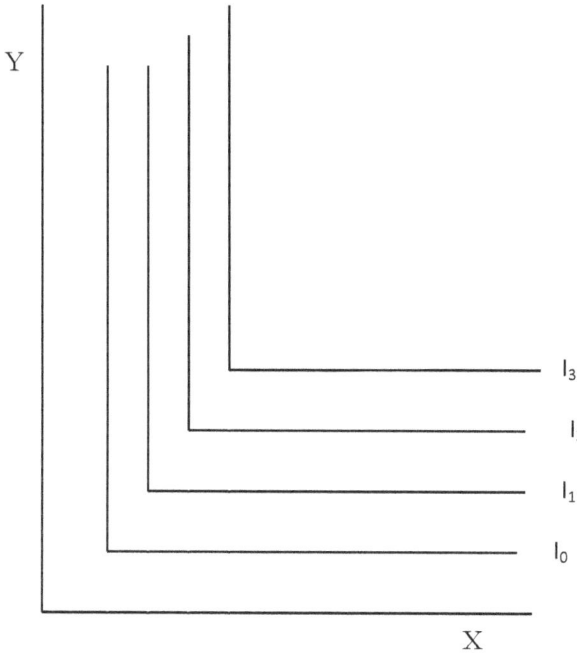

Figure 76: Perfect complement

Cross elasticity of demand

The responsiveness of quantity demanded of one good to a change in the price of another good. To avoid the measure being sensitive to the units being used, the measure is expressed as:

Cross Elasticity of Demand =

$$\left(\frac{\Delta Q_i}{Q_i} * 100\right) \div \left(\frac{\Delta P_j}{P_j} * 100\right) = \frac{\Delta Q_i P_j}{\Delta P_j Q_u}$$

Where Q_i is the quantity of good i, and Pj is the price of another good j.

The symbol Δ refers to a change in the variable in question where, goods i and j are SUBSTITUTES the cross elasticity will be positive (i.e. a fall in the price of good j will result in fall in the demand for good i as j is substituted for i). If the goods are COMPLEMENTS the cross elasticity will be negative, if good are substitute the cross-price elasticity will be positive and if good have no relationship their cross price elasticity will be zero.

Demand

The quantity of a good or service which an individual or group desires at the ruling price. The total demand in an economy is referred to as aggregate demand. Aggregate demand backed by actual payment may be described as EFFECTIVE DEMAND. (See DEMAND CURVE, NATIONAL DEMAND).

Demand curve

A graphical illustration of a DEMAND SCHEDULE OR DEMAND FUNCTION but, given that diagrams can only be drawn in two or three dimensions, showing the relationship between demand and only one or two variables affecting demand, the others being held constant. Most typically, the demand curve is shown as a curve relating quantity demanded to the price of the good in question (the 'own price'). It is also usually shown as sloping downwards from left to right. Slightly confusingly, the demand curve is almost always shown with price (the INDEPENDENT VARIABLE) on the vertical axis and quantity (the DEPENDENT VARIABLE) on the horizontal axis, contrary to mathematical convention.

Demand function

An algebraic expression of the DEMAND SECHEDULE expressed either in general terms or with specific numerical valued expressed for the various PARAMETERS, and usually including all factors affecting demand. Thus, a general form might be:

$$Q_i = f\ (P_i,\ P_j, \ldots P_n,\ Y,\ t)$$

Where Q_i is the quantity demanded of good i,
P_i is the price of good i (the 'own price'),
$P_j...P_n$ are the price of other goods j to n,

Y is income, and t is some measure of tastes.

The general algebraic form may be made more specific by postulating a particular from of the equation, for example:

$$Q_i = a * P_i^b * P_j^c . Y^e . e^k$$

where a, b, c, d and k are constants. This particular form is known as the 'constant elasticity demand function' since, on manipulation, b is found to be the (own) price ELASTCITY OF DEMAND, c is the CROSS ELASTICITY OF DEMAND, and d is the INCOME ELASTICITY OF DEMAND. The expression e^k is often construed in such a way that e is the value of the natural (Napierian) logarithm and e^k therefore represents some trend factor for taste.

The numerically specified form would then give actual values for a, b, c, d and k in the previous equation. These values would be obtained from statistical analysis, most usually REGRESSION analysis.

Demand schedule

A table showing the level of demand for a particular GOOD at various levels of price of the good in question. The schedule relates to a specific period of time (e.g., per month, per year etc) and is drawn up on the basis that other factors affecting the level of demand – income, tastes, the price of other goods – are held constant.

Income consumption curve

The tangency of the consumer's INDIFFERENCE CURVE and his BUDGET LINE defines the CONSUMER'S EQUILIBRIUM. If income is varied such that the budget line moves outwards in a parallel fashion, new equilibria will be established. The locus of all such equilibria is the income consumption curve. If the curve slopes upwards in COMMODITY SPACE it indicates that both goods (measured on the axes) are NORMAL GOODS. If it slopes backwards or downwards one of the goods is an INFERIOR GOOD. (See diagram). The income consumption curve is widely referred to as an ENGEL CURVE, although some writers distinguish the two.

Diagram

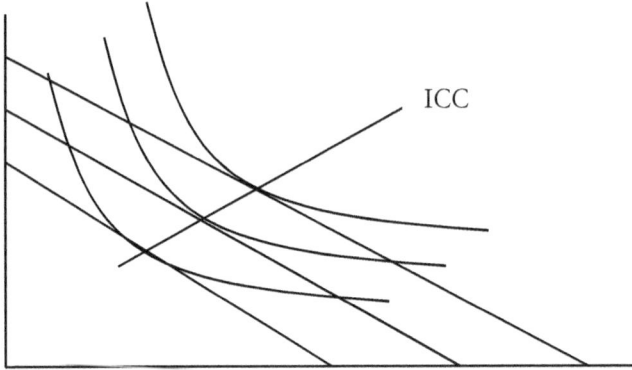

ICC

Income effect

A change in the price of a good will reduce or increase the consumer's real income. In response to this change in real income we can expect the consumer to buy less (or more) of all goods including the one which has changed in price. This is the income effect of a price change. (See SUBSTITUTION EFFECT, PRICE EFFECT).

Income elasticity of demand

A measure of the responsiveness of the quantity demanded of any GOOD to a change in the level of income of the person demanding the good. The avoid the measure being sensitive to the units used, the measure is expressed as:

Income elasticity of demand

$$= \left(\frac{\Delta Q_I}{Q_I} \right) = \left(\frac{QY}{Y} \right) = \frac{\Delta Q_i * Y}{\Delta Y * Q_I}$$

where Q_i is the quantity demanded of good i, Y is income and the symbol Δ refers to a change in the variable in question. (See ENGEL CURVE).

Indifference curve

A curve showing the locus of combinations of the amounts of two GOODS, say X and Y, such that the individual is indifferent between any combination on that curve. An indifference curve is usually assumed to be CONVEX (See diagram). (See INDIFFERENCE MAP)

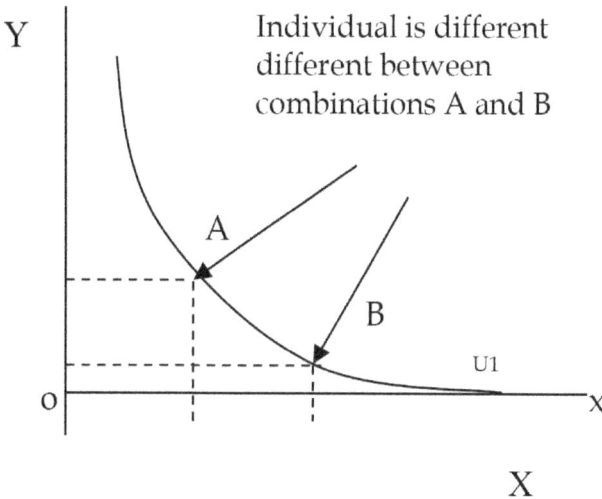

Y | Individual is different
different between
combinations A and B

A

B

U1

O

X

X

Indifference map

A set of INDIFFERENCE CURVES with each successive curve lying outside the previous one and in a north-east direction. 'Higher' indifference curve indicates higher levels of UTILITY.

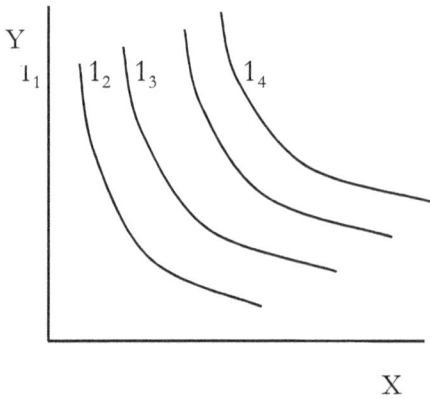

X

Indifference curves cannot cross each other if they do they violate the axiom of TRANSITIVITY OF PREFERENCES. They can touch the axes (see diagram) but are usually drawn such that this is not the case. Note that the distance between indifference curves does not indicate absolute differences in utility since indifference curve theory is based on ORDINARY UTILITY.

Market demand curve

The aggregation of a set of individual DEMAND CURVES for a good. Thus, if at price p, individual 1 would buy 10 units of goods X, individual 2 would buy 15 units, and individual 3 would buy 4 units, the market demand curve would show that $10 + 15 + 4 = 29$ units would be bought at price p_x. This kind of aggregation is generally valid for PRIVATE GOODS, but not if there is some form of interdependence (see SNOB EFFECT, VEBLEN EFFECT). Nor is this form of aggregation applicable to PUBLIC GOODS since, by definition, the provision of a given quantity of a public good to any one individual entails that quantity being simultaneously given to all other individuals.

Marginal utility

The extra utility obtained from an extra unit of any GOOD. Mathematically expressed as

$$MU = \frac{\Delta U}{\Delta X}$$

where U is utility, X is the amount of a good, and 'Δ' is a 'small change in'.

Marginal rate of substitution (MRS)

In CONSUMER DEMAND THEORY the marginal rate of substitution refers to the amount of one good, say Y, that is required to compensate the consumer for giving up an amount of another good, say X, such that the consumer thas the same level of welfare (UTILITY) as before. In INDIFFERENCE CURVE analysis it is in fact the slope of the indifference curve which, in turn, is equal to two goods in question, i.e.

$$MRS_{xy} = \frac{MU_x}{MU_y}$$

the term derives from J.R. HICKS' *Value and Capital* (Oxford University Press, 1939). Other writers prefer different terminology and the MRS is sometimes referred to as the personal rate of substitution, or the rate of commodity substitution.

Necessity

Not a widely used term in modern economics, but, if used, is taken to refer to a good with an INCOME ELEASTICITY OF DEMAND of less than unity but positive. That is, a smaller and smaller proportion of income is spent on the good as income rises.

Normal good

A good whose demand is reduced as income falls. For normal goods a price fall gives rise to an increase in real income such that the INCOME EFFECT always has the same sigh (with respect to the price change) as the SUBSTITUTION EFFECT, both are negative. Where income and substitution effects have different signs the reaction to a price change is determined by the relative absolute size of the two effects such that the good may be an INFERIOR GOOD, in which case demand will still rise as price falls but the rise will be smaller than in the case of a normal good.

If, however, the income effect is very powerful, demand may fall as price falls – the condition for a GIFFEN GOOD. Normal goods are also known as 'superior' goods.

Ordinal utility

In any ORDERING of goods etc., that with the highest UTILITY is ranked above the good with the next highest utility and so on. This ranking or ordering is ordinal if it is not possible to say by how much utility differs between the first and second ranked good and, say, the second and third ranked good. Ordinal utility is the cornerstone of neo-classical CONSUMER DEMAND THEORY. (SEE CARDINAL UTILITY.)

Optimum

The 'best' situation or state of affair. To achieve an optimum is to 'optimize' and a situation which is an optimum is said to be 'optimal'. Much of economics is concerned with analysing how groups or individuals may achieve 'optimal' arrangements. For example, the choices made by consumers are analysed in terms of attempts to obtain the optimal pattern of consumption. Definition of what is optimal does, of course, involve judgments concerning what is or should be desirable. Generally, it is assumed that the satisfaction of individual desires is the objective of the economic system. In attempting to attain an optimum we are usually constrained by the fundamental scarcity of goods and resources – individuals are constrained by their income – thus we speak of 'constrained optimum', the best that can be achieved in view of existing limits. Where we are faced with more than one objective, we sometimes speak of an 'optimum' – the best of the best situations. This simply means that a number of arrangements may be judged equal desirable in terms of one criterion (say efficiency) while the application of a second criterion (say a 'just' distribution of income) indicates the best overall arrangement. (See PARETO OPTIMUM).

Price elasticity of demand

The responsiveness of the quantity demanded of a good to its own price. To avoid the measure of ELASTICITY being sensitive to the units in which quantities and prices are measured, the elasticity of demand is expressed as the percentage change in demand that occurs in response to a percentage change in price. That is:

Price Elasticity of Demand =

$$\eta = \frac{\dfrac{\Delta Q}{Q} * 100}{\left(\dfrac{\Delta P}{P} * 100\right)}$$

$$\eta = \frac{\Delta Q_i}{Q_i} * \frac{P_i}{\Delta P_i}$$

where, a symbol Δ for 'change in', P and Q are the price and quantity of a good, respectively If is very small the resulting measure is known as the point elasticity of demand. If is significantly large the measure obtained is one of the responsiveness of demand to this change in price and is generally known as the elasticity of demand. Note that if the LAW OF DEMAND operates, a fall in price will result in a rise in demand, so that change in P would be negative and change in Q would be positive. The elasticity estimate would then have a minus in front of it (i.e., negative sign). In the economic literature this minus sign is often omitted and care should be taken if elasticity is used in any mathematical manipulation to remember this. Note also that the ratio. $\dfrac{\Delta Q}{\Delta P}$ is the

inverse of the slope of the DEMAND CURVE. The fact that the formula for elasticity has an additional expression indicates that the slope of the demand curve and the elasticity are not the same thing.

Price consumption curve

(Also known as an OFFER CURVE). The tangency of the consumer's INDIFFERENCE CURVE and the BUDGET LINE determines the CONSUMER'S EQUILIBRIUM. As the price of one good change so that budget line 'pivots' outwards in COMMODITY SPACE. New equilibria are established. The locus of such equilibria is the price consumption curve. Typically, the price consumption curve will show the demand for the cheaper good rising as its price falls. If, however, demand falls because of the price fall, the price consumption curve will curve back on itself (see diagram). Such a situation will arise if the cheaper goods is a GIFFEN GOOD.

Substitute

A good which can be substituted for another good, or an input that can be substituted for another input. In NEO-CLASSICAL theory substitution possibilities are generally assumed to exits, accounting for the 'smoothness' of INDIFFERENCE CURVES and ISO-PRODUCT CURVES. Where substitution is limited, this smoothness disappears and will be replaced by 'piecewise linear' curves. (See diagram). For substitutes the CROSS ELASTICITY OF DEMAND will be positive.

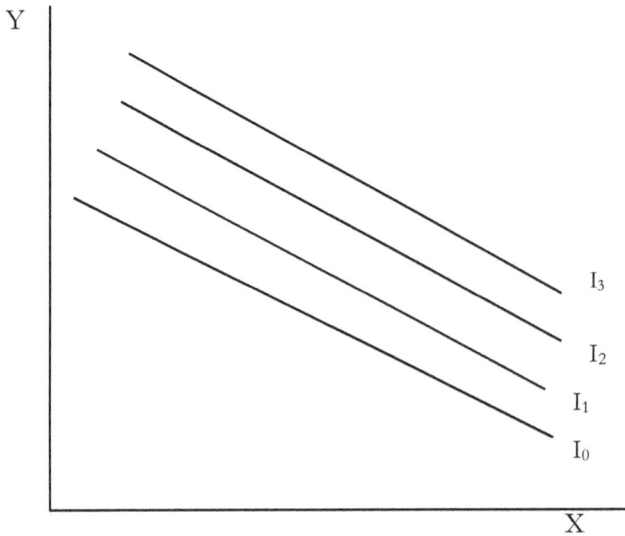

Substitution and Income effects

The effect on the demand for a good of a change in price of that good, assuming real income is held constant.

Chicken

AD= Income Effect
DC= Substitution effect
AC= Total Effect

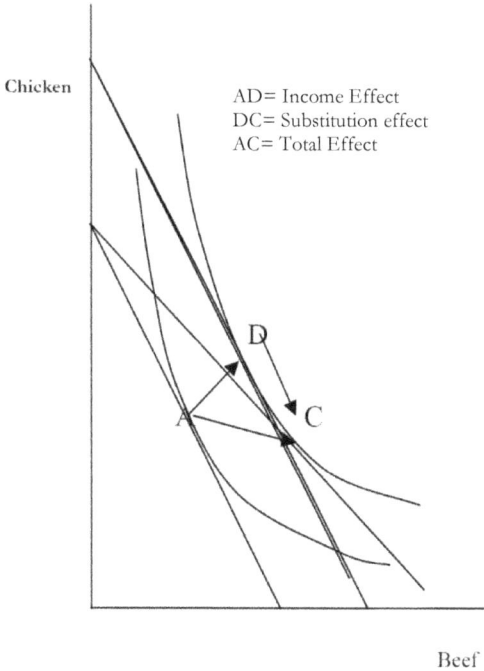

Income effect is reflected
as increase in purchasing
power of a consumer
equivalent to increase in
income thus a parallel shift
of the budget line

Substitution effect occurs
when consumer substitute
high prices item for cheaper
priced items. E.g., in this
figure consumer substitute
chicken for beef

D

A   C

Beef

Utility

Widely construed in economics to be synonymous with 'welfare',
ECONOMIC WELFARE, satisfaction, and, occasionally, happiness.
More strictly, however, to say that someone derives utility from a good
or event is to say that they prefer the good to exist rather than not to
exist. To say that they derive more utility from good X than good Y is
simply to say that X is preferred to Y. For an argument that utility is a
circular concept see J. Robinson, Economic Philosophy (Penguin,
Harmondsworth, 1964, p. 48).

Utility function

A function stating that an individual's UTILITY is dependent upon the
goods he consumes and their amounts. More formally written as:

$$U = U(X, Y, Z.....)$$

Where X, and Z are the amounts of the goods in question.

Production Theory

Iso-cost curve

A curve or line showing the combinations of any two INPUTS that can be bought with a fixed sum of money. It is analogous with the consumer's BUDGET LINE but relates to the firm's purchase of inputs. The tangency of the iso-cost curve with the ISO-PRODUCT CURVE defines the least-cost combination of inputs to produce a given level of output. The iso-cost curve is also known as the iso-outlay line (curve) (See COST MINIMIZATION).

Iso-profit curves

The locus of combinations of two or more INDEPENDENT VARIABLES of the PROFIT FUNCTION, which yield an equal profit. This is a commonly used concept in OLIGOPOLY theory.

Isoquant (Iso-product curve)

(Also known as producers' indifference curve, or isoquant). An iso-product curve traces out the combinations of any two or more INPUTS which give rise to the same level of OUTPUT. These combinations must be the most efficient ones (i.e., any point on an iso-product curve shows the minimum quantities of the inputs needed to produce the given output). Iso-product curves are typically drawn as being convex to the origin because of the assumed substitutability of inputs (curve 2 in the diagram). Where inputs are complementary the iso-product curve will be a perfect 'L' shape (curve 1). Where they are perfect substitutes the iso-product curves will be straight lines. (See PROCESS, ELASTICITY OF INPUT SUBSTITUTION).

Iso-revenue line (curve)

The locus of combinations of OUTPUT and marketing outlays which yield a given level of TOTAL REVENUE. Thus, for instance, the general functional form of an iso-revenue curve comprising output and ADVERTISING outlay combinations will be

(1) $\overline{TR} = f\,(Q,\,a)$

WHERE $\overline{TR}$ is the given level of total revenue, Q is output and a is units of advertising. This function will then trace out those combinations of a and Q which yield $\overline{TR}$. Totally differentiating (1) gives

$$(2)\;\; \overline{dTR} = \frac{\partial TR}{\partial X}dx + \frac{\partial TR.}{\partial a}da = 0$$

and manipulating to solve for

$$\frac{da}{dx}$$

yields:

∂TR

$$(3)\quad \frac{da}{dx} = -\,\frac{\dfrac{\partial x}{\partial TR}}{\dfrac{}{\partial a}}$$

(3) states that the slope of an iso-revenue curve, that is, the rate at which output can be substituted for units for advertising to maintain $TR = TR$, is given by the ratio of the MARGINAL REVENUE PRODUCT of output to the marginal revenue product of advertising.

Capital

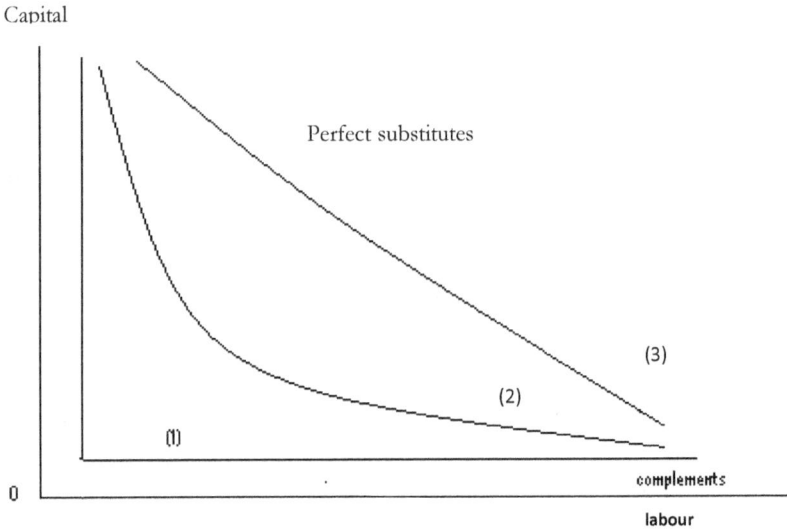

Perfect substitutes

(3)

(2)

(1)

complements

0

labour

Marginal product

The extra OUTPUT obtained by employing one extra unit of a given INPUT (FACTOR OF PRODUCTION). Thus, the term should be qualified with respect to which input is in question (e.g. The marginal product of labour, the marginal product of capital etc.). (See LAW OF DIMINISHING RETURNS).

Marginal physical product

The addition to total OUTPUT resulting from the employment of an additional unit of LABOUR, and may be derived from the PRODUCTION FUNCTION, holding other factors fixed. The marginal physical product schedule may be regarded as the demand CURVE for labour. Labour is employed up to the point at which the payment to the last unit is equal to the output produced by the last unit. It is more conventional, by means of a simple change in scale, to convert marginal physical product, by multiplying the former by product price (see MARGINAL REVENUE PRODUCT). If there is a rise or fall in the wage, then the number of units of labour employed will fall or rise according to the slope of the marginal physical product/value of marginal physical product schedule. In the long run, labour demand will still be determined by labour's marginal physical product, although in a more complex fashion. A wage rise, for example, will have a negative

SUBSTITUTION EFFECT as the firm substitutes cheaper CAPITAL for the more expensive labour, thereby reducing the quantity of labour demanded. There will also be a negative scale effect as a wage increase leads to a higher MARGINAL COST of production which in turn reduces the firm's optimal output and hence DERIVED DEMAND for labour.

The two effects reinforce each other to lead to an unambiguously inverse relationship between wages and the firm's demand for labour. This demand curve is more elastic than the short run demand.

Marginal rate of Technical substitution

The marginal rate of technical substitution of two inputs, for example, of LABOUR for CAPITAL, is the difference in the amount for capital that needs to be substituted for a very small reduction in the amount of labour employed to maintain the level of output. Its value is equal to the ratio of the MARGINAL PRODUCT of labour to the marginal product of capital and is equal to the slope of the production ISOQUANT.

Marginal rate of transformation

The numerical value of the slope of the PRODUCTION POSSIBILITY FRONTIER. The marginal rate of transforming good A into good B is the fall in the rate of output of good A which permits an additional unit of good B to be produced. It is equal to the ratio of the MARGINAL COST of good B to the marginal cost of good A.

Marginal revenue

The change in total revenue arising from the sale of an additional unit of output. In PERFECT COMPETITION, marginal revenue will equal price because the IRM faces an infinitely elastic DEMAND CURVE (i.e., it can sell any amount of output at the prevailing market price). Within market structures such as IMPERFECT COMPETITION, the firm faces a downward sloping demand curve and thus, to sell an additional unit of output, it must reduce the price on all the output it sells. Marginal revenue will then be equal to the new price minus the fall in revenue on those units which would otherwise have sold at the higher price. Marginal revenue is an important concept in the analysis of the firm. A necessary condition of profit maximizing EQUILIBRIUM is that marginal revenue be equal to MARGINAL COST.

Marginal revenue product

The MARGINAL PHYSICAL PRODUCT multiplied by the MARGINAL REVENUE from the sale of the extra unit of output resulting from the employment of the extra unit of input. Under PERFECT COMPETITION price equals marginal revenue, so that we can write

$$MRP = MPP * .P$$

where MPP is marginal physical product and P is price. Under IMPERFECT COMPETITION, however, price does not equal marginal revenue and it is necessary to modify the equation to:

$$MRP = MPP * .MR$$

where MR is the marginal revenue associated with the sale of the extra units of output.

Production function

The relationship between the OUPT of a good and the inputs (FACTORS OF PRODUCTION) required to make that good. In formal notation the production function has the genera form:

$$Q = f (L, K, t, etc.)$$

where Q is output, L is labour, K is capital, t is 'technical progress' and where the 'etc.' indicates that other inputs may also be relevant (raw materials, for example). While typically used in the context of the theory of the FIRM, it is possible to speak of a nation's output being dependent upon the various resources used to produce that output. Such a production function is termed an AGGREGATE PRODUCTION FUNCTION, and has the same general form as that indicated above save that Q would now be the GORSS NATIONAL (or domestic) PRODUCT and K, L etc. would refer to the whole capital stock of the nation, the entire workforce etc. Whether aggregate production functions are meaningful depends on the view taken on whether it is sensible or not to speak of a measured stock of capital.

Production functions may take many specific algebraic forms. Typically, economists work with homogeneous production functions. A production function is homogeneous of degree n if when inputs are multiplied by some constant, say, k, the resulting output is a multiple of k" times the original output. That is, for a production function:

$$Q = f (L, K)$$

then if and only if

$$Q = f (kL, kK) = k^n f (L,K)$$

is the function homogenous. The exponent, n, denotes the DEGREE OF HOMOGENEITY. If n = 1 the production function is said to be homogeneous of degree one or linearly homogenous (note that this does not mean the equation is linearly; it may or may not be). A linearly 'homogeneous production function' is of interest in that it exhibits constant RETURNS TO SCALE. This is easily seen since the expression $k_i^n f(L,K)$ when n = 1 reduced to $k^n f(L,K)$ so that multiplying inputs by a constant k k simply increases output by the same production.

Examples of linearly homogeneous production functions are the COBB-GOUGLAS PRODUCTION FUNCTION and the CONSTANT ELASTICITY OF SUBSTITUTION (CES) PRODUCTIONN FUNCTION. If n is greater than 1 the production function exhibits increasing RETURNS TO SCALE. If n is lower than 1 decreasing RETURNS TO SCALE prevail. (See ISO-PRODUCT CURVE).

Production

The act of transforming the FACTORS OF PRODUCTION into the goods and services that are desired for CONSUMPTION and INVESTMENT.

Production frontier

(Also known as production possibility curve or transformation function). This curve shows the possibilities open for increasing the output of one goody by reducing the output of another. In the diagram, resources are assumed to be limited so that if they are all devoted to the production of Y an amount Y_{max} could be produced. If they are all devoted to X an amount X_{max} could be produced. Alternatively, by 'mixing' the allocation of resources to X and Y points such as A and B could be secured. Note that point D and any other point 'outside' the frontier are unobtainable. A point like C, 'inside' the frontier, could well be achieved. It would not represent an efficient use of resources, however, since the resources available can reach a point like A at which there is more of both X and Y. In short, C could only be achieved by either not using all resources (i.e., there would be unemployment) or by using the available resources inefficiently.

The frontier is shown as being concave to the origin. The rationale is that the removal of resources from producing X will mean their allocation to producing Y and as more and more of Y is produced there will be DIMINISHING RETURNS. In fact, since it is all resources that are being transferred from one commodity to the other the returns in question are RETURNS TO SCALE. Since there is no specific reason for returns to scale to be decreasing, the frontier could equally well be a straight line (constant returns to scale in both X and Y) or curve inwards (increasing returns to scale).

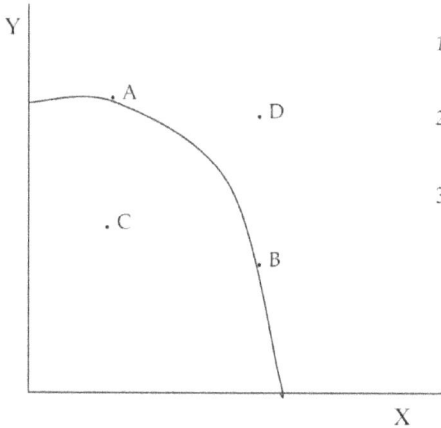

1. Point A and B are on the frontier using all resources
2. Point C is below the frontier, not using all the resources
3. Point D is above the frontier using more resources than what is available (unattainable)

Profit maximization

The hypothesis is that firms aim to maximize PROFITS. In the diagram profit is defined as the difference between the TOTAL REVENU received by the firm and the TOTAL COSTS it incurs. The point of maximum difference is seen to correspond to output level X^* which is thus the profit maximizing output. At this point the slopes of the two curves are equal. The slope of the total revenue curve is MARGINAL REVENUE (MR) and the slope of the total cost curve is MARGINAL COST (MC). Thus, profit maximization requires that

$$MC = MR.$$

To see why this is so, consider what would happen if $MC > MR$. In this case the costs of producing extra output are greater than the revenue obtained and hence profits are lower than need. Be. If $MR \succ MC$ opportunities exist for increasing profits by expanding output. Profit maximization may not, however, describe the motives of many firms. (See SALES MAXIMIZATION HYPOTHESIS, MANAGERIAL TH EOR-IES OF THE FIRM).

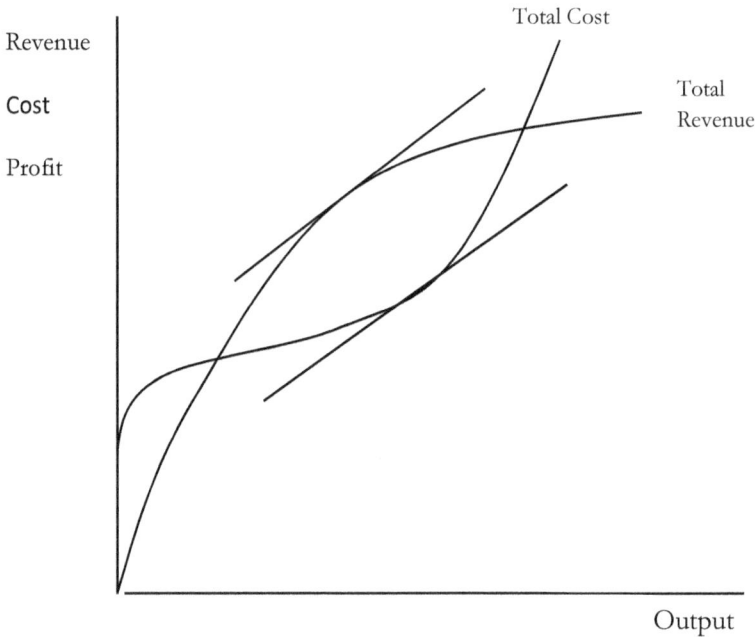

Profit Maximization

Profits

The difference between the revenue generated from the sale of output and the full OPPORTUNITY COSTS of the factors used in the production of that output. Included within costs are the premium charged for which costs are the premium charged for risk taking and the costs of using the owner's CAPITAL. These are not included as costs in the accountant's measure of profit which therefore does not correspond to this economic definition of profits. (See NORMAL PROFIT, SUPERNORMAL PROFIT).

Short run

The time period in the production process during which the fixed FACTORS OF PRODUCTON cannot be changed, but the level of utilization of variable factors can be altered. The concept was introduced by Alfred MARSHALL.

Supply curve

A graphical representation of the relationship between the supply of a commodity and its price (usually with price on the vertical axis, and quantity supplied measured along the horizontal axis). The positive relationship between these two variables is reflected by the fact that the supply curve slopes upwards from left to right.

Theory of Markets

Competitive markets

A market in which a very large number of small buyers and sellers trade independently, and as such no one trade can significantly influence price (See PERFECT COMPETTION).

Market economy

An economic system in which decisions about the allocation of resources and production are made on the basis of prices generated by voluntary exchanges between producers, consumers, workers and owners of FACTORS OF PRODUCTION. Decision-making in such an economy is decentralized (i.e. decisions are made independently by groups and individuals in the economy rather than by central planners). Market economies usually also involve a system of private ownership of the means of production (i.e. they are 'capitalist' or 'free enterprise' economies). However market economies can function, to some extent, under social ownership. (See PLANNED ECONOMY, MARKET SOCIALISM).

Market forces

Pressure produced by the free play of market supply and demand, which induce adjustment in price and/or quantities traded.

Monopoly

In the strictest sense of the term, a firm is a monopoly if it is the only supplier of a HOMOGENOUS product, for which there is no substitutes and many buyers. Such conditions are sometimes termed absolute monopoly and the DEMAND CURVE for the firm's OUTPUT is the MARKET DEMAND CURVE for the PRODUCT. As with PERFECT COMPETITION, absolute monopoly does not occur in real life and actual market structures vary between the two extremes of nearly perfect competition and near monopoly.

The simple economic analysis of monopoly relaxes the assumption of no SUBSTITUTES butassumes that the monopolist faces a relatively stable and predictable downward-sloping market DEMAND CURVE and that perfect competition exists in the markets in which the firm buys its INPUTS. Under such conditions a profit maximizing monopolist will set MARGINAL COST equal to MARGINAL REVENUE and sell a lower output and charge a higher PRICE than would pertain under perfect competition (see diagram). Further, lack of competition may lead to X-INEFFICIENCY AND PRODUCTION COSTS AT EACH OUTPUT LEVEL HIGHER THAN THEY WOULD OTHERWISE BE UNDER PERFECT COMPETITION. (See BILATERAL MONOPOLY, MONOPSONY, MONOPOLISTIC COMPETITION, MONOPOLY, OUPUT, MONOPLOY POWER).

Monopsony

In the strict sense a monopolist is the sole buyer of a FACTOR OF PRODUCTION; the classic example is provided by the one company town. More generally, monopsony refers to situation of reduced alternative in the LABOUR MARKET. This may result from the limited job search of workers and not simply from limited numbers of potential employers. Whatever the cause, the buyer confronts an upward sloping aggregate labour SUPPLY CURVE. In consequence, his decision to purchase more labour has some effect on the wage level. The monopsonistic employer realizes that the MARGINAL COST and the average cost (i.e., the wage) of an addition worker differ and because of this disparity he hires less labour and pays this labour a lower wage than would occur in competitive circumstances.

Perfect competition

A MARKET STRUCTURE is perfectly competitive if the following conditions hold; there is a large number of firms each with an insubstantial share of the MARKET. These firms produce a HOMOGENEOUS PRODUCT using identical production PROCESSES and possess

PERFECT INFORMATION. It is also the case that there is FREE ENTRY to the industry, that is, new firms can and will enter the industry if they observe that greater than NORMAL PROFITS are being earned. The effect of this free entry is to push the DEMAND CURVE facing each firm downwards until each firm earns only normal profits, at which point there is no further incentive for new entrants to come into the industry. Moreover, since each firm produces a homogenous product, it cannot raise its price without losing all its market to its competitors. Thus, the demand curve facing each firm in the LONG RUN will be horizontal and tangential to the minimum point of the LONG-RUN AVERAGE COST curve of the firm, as shown in the diagram.

Such conditions imply that both MARGINAL REVENUE and AVERAGE REVENUE are equal to price. Thus, firms are PRICE TAKERS and can sell as much as they are capable of producing at the prevailing MARKET PRICE. Given U-SHAPED COST CURVES a unique SHORT-RUN profit maximizing level of output exists where MARGINAL COST equals marginal revenue with marginal costs increasing at this point. Since the demand curve facing each firm is horizontal this condition implies that marginal cost equals price.

In the short run the profit maximizing condition can be satisfied at an output level such that AVERAGE COST lies above, equal to, or below average revenue, so that losses, NORMAL PROFITS OF SUPER-NORMAL PROFITS can be achieved. Free entry and exit ensure that the long-run EQUILIBRIUM output level is such that each surviving firm earns normal profits, with price equal to the minimum average cost of production. (See PROFIT MAXIMIZATION).

Oligopolistic behaviour

Conduct by firms, which is characterized by perceived interdependence in decision-making about major policy areas such as pricing, advertising and investment. (See OLIGOPOLY).

Oligopoly

A market structure within which firms are aware of the mutual interdependence of sales, production, and investment and advertising plans. Hence manipulation by any firm of variables under its control is likely to evoke retaliation from competing firms. These features are commonly ascribed to markets in which the number of sellers is few. There are several models of oligopoly in economic theory. These range from theories in which each oligopolist acts independently and bases decision-making upon some assumption regarding rivals' reaction, to those in which rivalry is overcome by means of co-operation and COLLUSION. (See KINKED DEMAND CURVE, PRICE LEADER SHIP, COURNOT MODEL, JOINT PROFIT MAXIMIZATION, CARTELS).

Oligopsony

A market in which few buyers face a very large number of sellers. This type of market is comparable to that of OLIGOPOLY

Index

www.ingramcontent.com/pod-product-compliance
Lightning Source LLC
Chambersburg PA
CBHW021941220326

41599CB00013BA/1475